REDECISION THERAPY
A Brief, Action-Oriented Approach

Contributors

Barbara Ann Allen, M.S.W., Ph.D.
Private practice and consultation, Tulsa, Oklahoma.

James R. Allen, M.D.
Professor, The University of Oklahoma, Health Sciences Center, Department of Psychiatry and Behavioral Sciences, Oklahoma City, Oklahoma.

Michael Andronico, Ph.D.
Clinical Professor of Psychiatry, Robert Wood Johnson Medical School, UMDJN, Piscataway, New Jersey. Private practice, Somerset, New Jersey.

Gail Ardman, M.S.S.W.
Permanente Medical Association of Texas, Dallas, Texas.

Caroline Avery-Dahl, M.S.
Private practice and training program, Dallas, Texas.

Julia Lacy Baird, Ph.D.
Private practice and training program, Dallas, Texas.

Linda Carmicle, Ph.D.
Adjunct faculty, Amber University, Garland, Texas. Private practice and training program, Plano, Texas.

Barbara Dazzo, M.S.W., Ph.D.
Clinical faculty, Department of Psychiatry, Robert Wood Johnson Medical School, UMDNJ, Piscataway, New Jersey. Private practice, Somerset, New Jersey.

John Gladfelter, Ph.D.
Faculty, The Fielding Institute, Santa Barbara, California. Private practice and training program, Dallas, Texas.

Mary McClure Goulding, M.S.W.
Retired, San Francisco, California. Former co-director, Western Institute for Group and Family Therapy.

Michael F. Hoyt, Ph.D.
Director of Adult Psychiatric Services, Kaiser Permanente Medical Center, Hayward, California. Clinical faculty, University of California School of Medicine, San Francisco, California.

Dean S. Janoff, Ph.D.
Co-director, Anxiety and Panic Disorder Clinic of Santa Barbara, California. Adjunct faculty, The Fielding Institute, Santa Barbara, California. Adjunct Faculty, Antioch University and Pacifica Graduate Institute, Santa Barbara, California.

Vann S. Joines, Ph.D.
President, Southeast Institute for Group and Family Therapy, Chapel Hill, North Carolina.

Eugene M. Kerfoot, Ph.D.
Faculty, The Fielding Institute, Santa Barbara, California. Private practice and training program, Carmel Valley, California. Management Consultant, Forum 2000.

Moon Kerson, Ph.D.
Adjunct faculty, Phillips Graduate Institute, Encino, and Ryokan

REDECISION THERAPY
A Brief, Action-Oriented Approach

Edited by
Carolyn E. Lennox, M.S.W., Ed.D.

JASON ARONSON INC.
Northvale, New Jersey
London

The editor gratefully acknowledges permission to reprint the following material: In Chapter 6, an untitled poem from "How to Survive the Loss of a Love," by M. Colgrove, H.H. Bloomfield, and P. McWilliams, 1976, Bantam Books. Portions of Chapter 12 are reprinted from the *Transactional Analysis Journal*, Volume 25, Number 4, 1996, pages 356–360, "The Treatment of Post-Traumatic Stress Disorder Using Redecision Therapy," © International Transactional Analysis Association; all rights reserved.

Director of Editorial Production: Robert D. Hack

This book was set in 11 pt. Granjon by Alabama Book Composition of Deatsville, Alabama, and printed and bound by Book-mart Press of North Bergen, New Jersey.

Copyright © 1997 by Jason Aronson Inc.

10 9 8 7 6 5 4 3 2 1

Library of Congress Cataloging-in-Publication Data

Redecision therapy : a brief, action-oriented approach / edited by
    Carolyn E. Lennox.
        p. cm.
    Includes bibliographical references and index.
    ISBN 0-7657-0043-3 (alk. paper)
    1. Psychotherapy.   2. Transactional analysis.   I. Lennox,
    Carolyn.
    RC480.5.R37   1997
    616.89'14—dc20   96-41624

Printed in the United States of America on acid-free paper. For information and catalog write to Jason Aronson Inc., 230 Livingston Street, Northvale, New Jersey 07647-1731. Or visit our website: http://www.aronson.com

College, Venice, California. Private practice and training program, Brentwood, California.

Marti B. Kranzberg, Ph.D.
Private practice and training program, Dallas, Texas.

Carolyn E. Lennox, M.S.W., Ed.D.
Private practice and training program, Richardson, Texas.

Vern Massé, M.A.
Director, Stanislaus County Drug and Alcohol Abuse Outpatient Treatment Program. Private practice and Vietnam veterans' support group, Modesto, California.

Nancy Porter-Steele, Ph.D.
Private practice and training program, Halifax, Nova Scotia, Canada.

Denton L. Roberts, M.Div.
Private therapy and consultation practice, Los Angeles, California.

James K. Speer, M.S.S.W.
Hill Country Crisis Council, Kerrville, Texas. Faculty, Austin Community College. Private practice, Fredericksburg, Texas.

Curtis A. Steele, M.D.
Queen Elizabeth II Hospital. Faculty, Dalhousie University School of Medicine, Halifax, Nova Scotia, Canada. Private practice and training, Halifax, Nova Scotia.

Charles F. Vorkoper, M.S.S.W.
Consultant to Texas Council on Problem and Compulsive Gambling. Co-director, Gambler Counseling and Education Center, Dallas, Texas. Private practice, Dallas, Texas.

To our clients

who are are not found on these pages.
Those described herein are composite and fictional characters.
Those in our offices have honored us in the sharing of their
sorrows, struggles, and triumphs, and in the process, have
taught us about the power inherent in a redecision.

Contents

Foreword

When I first heard Bob Goulding he was presenting some of his ideas about redecision therapy at the Evolution of Psychotherapy Conference at Phoenix in 1985. It was immediately clear that this man had something to say worth hearing: he was clear, incisive, practical, human, funny, and effective. After his lecture I went up and introduced myself and asked about possibilities for training in redecision therapy. He briefly told me about the training programs he and his wife, Mary Goulding, were then conducting at the Western Institute for Group and Family Therapy (WIGFT) on Mt. Madonna near Watsonville, California. I asked a few perfunctory questions, and then inquired: "What will happen and what will I experience if I come to a training?" With a twinkle in his eye, Bob laughed and answered, "Well, that will depend on what you choose to do!"

I was intrigued and knew something valuable was available. Rather than thinking about it, missing the opportunity and then kicking myself, I went home and a day or two later sent in my registration. In a few weeks I was at the Western Institute, participating in the first of several training programs. In addition to facilitating my own much-needed personal growth and making some friendships that endure to this day, I learned a very powerful model of therapy based on the principles of highlighting client autonomy and competency in the direction of achieving the client's realistically defined treatment goals. Bob and Mary had woven together some of the ideas and methods of Eric Berne and Fritz Perls, along with their own myriad innovations, to create a teachable theory and technology that rightly earned them world-wide recognition as master contributors. To borrow the titles of two of their books, they emphasized that when we recognize that *The Power is in the Patient* (1978) people can engage in *Changing Lives through Redecision Therapy* (1979).[1]

The Gouldings' redecision therapy model is based on a thinking structure that includes the following features (after Goulding 1989, Goulding and Goulding 1978, 1986):

1. *Contact*: forming an alliance with the client
2. *Contract*: co-constructing with the client the focus or goal of treatment in a way that can be specified and achieved
3. *Con*: emphasizing clients' power and responsibility by confronting their efforts to disown autonomy through various ways they attempt to fool ("con") themselves and therapists into believing that others control their thoughts, feelings, and behavior or with disingenuous claims of "trying" to make changes
4. *Chief bad feelings, thinkings, behaviors, and psychosomatics*: identifying the painful or problematic counterproductive symptoms
5. *Chronic games, belief systems, and fantasies*: clarifying the interpersonal and intrapsychic ways symptoms are maintained

---

1. Their other books include the co-authored *Not to Worry* (1989), Mary's *Who's Been Living in Your Head?* (1985), her poignant memoir of Bob, *Sweet Love Remembered* (1992), and her recent extraordinary account of grieving and going forward since Bob's death in 1992, *A Time to Say Good-bye: Moving Beyond Loss* (1996).

6. *Childhood early decisions*: bringing to vivid awareness a reexperience of childhood feelings via the imaginal reliving of an early pathogenic scene, including recognition of the chief parental messages (injunctions and counterinjunctions), childhood script formation, and stroking (reinforcement) patterns

7. *Impasse resolution*: including redecisions, ego state decontamination and reconstruction (involving the strengthening of distinctions between Parent, Adult, and Child functions), re-parenting, and other techniques. Two-chair Gestalt work is often used to help the client "extroject" a pathogenic parental introject and then, in powerful dialogue, reclaim a sense of autonomy and self-determination.

8. *Maintaining the victory*: including anchoring the client's new and healthier ways of responding, making changes in stroking patterns, and forming plans for how to use the redecision in the future.

The essence of the Gouldings' approach is distilled in the brilliant sentence that they (and other redecision therapists) would often use to begin a session: *What are you willing to change today?* Spelled out, almost like a haiku for therapeutic effectiveness, we can see all the key elements of brief (efficient or time-sensitive) therapy:

What (specificity, goal, target, focus)

are (active verb, present tense)

you (self as agent, personal functioning)

willing (choice, responsibility, initiative)

to change (alter, not just "work on," "try," or "explore")

today, (now, in the moment)

? (inquiry, open field, therapist respectfully receptive but not insistent).

Redecision therapy developed from the impetus to be effective and efficient, to help clients to use their strengths and resources to get unstuck and to make their desired changes. While the clinical and humanistic thrust of redecision therapy toward effectiveness, efficiency, and accountability long predated current pressures toward cost containment, managed care, and brief therapy, it is easy to see how relevant and applicable this model is in today's current health care environment. As I have discussed at length in *Brief Therapy and Managed Care: Readings for Contemporary Practice* (Hoyt 1995), psychotherapy under managed behavioral health care has certain key characteristics:

1. Specific problem solving
2. Rapid response and early intervention
3. Clear definition of client and therapist responsibilities, with an emphasis on client competencies, resources, and strengths
4. Flexible and creative use of time
5. Interdisciplinary cooperation, including concomitant use of allied health professionals and appropriate psychopharmacology
6. Multiple formats and modalities, including the use of individual, group, marital/conjoint therapy, and various community resources
7. Intermittent treatment or a "family practitioner" model
8. Results orientation and accountability, with an emphasis on achievement of specific goals and client satisfaction.

I am glad to acknowledge how much the Gouldings have influenced me, and I am delighted to see the timely publication of this book. The editor, Carolyn Lennox, has done a fine job bringing together different authors and presenting their views in a logical, coherent sequence. The writing is personal and practical, each chapter offering "from the trenches" illustrations that suggest applications each reader can use in her or his own practice. Students of comparative psychotherapies will see various points of contact between redecision therapy and other approaches, and practitioners of different theoretical orientations should find productive ways to integrate redecision ideas into their clinical repertoire. Psychodynamically minded therapists will appreciate the role of "insight," the redecision process involving the making conscious of something previously out of awareness (yielding a "cognitive restructuring" or "schema change," a cognitive behaviorist might say). The primary mechanism is not interpretation of a transference, however, but is having a new experience ("redecision") via a re-enactment of an early scene guided by the therapist who serves—to use Eugene Kerfoot's metaphor in Chapter 8—as a travel agent expert at facilitating routes to destinations (therapeutic goals) selected by client-travelers. There is an orientation toward new action. Explanation may lead to recognition, but experience leads to change. The client is seen as competent to resolve her or his own problem with skillful facilitation, rather than having to rely upon an outside expert to make sense of or reveal "the truth." "The power is in the patient," as the Gouldings say.

Readers acquainted with narrative therapy (White 1995, White and Epston 1990) may see the Gestalt two-chair part of the redecision process as an externalization of the problem with enhancement of the client's sense of personal autonomy, and may find it helpful to think of injunctions as narrative themes and of redecision as a form of re-authoring of the stories that shape and constitute lives. Solution-focused therapists such as de Shazer (1985, 1988) may appreciate the redecision therapist stroking the Natural Child (as discussed by Vann Joines in Chapter 7) as the evocation and amplification of exceptions to the problem pattern, and may see the use of anchoring, changes in the stroke economy, and Adult planning as ways to further structure and support the emergence of a pro-solution worldview and storyline. I would place all of this under the rubric of constructive therapies (Hoyt 1994, 1996), ones that draw from the social constructionist idea that reality is known through the knower and that we actively construct our notions of what is real within an interpersonal matrix. From this perspective, therapy can be conceptualized as the social construction of preferred realities (Freedman and Combs 1996, McNamee and Gergen 1992), with careful attention being paid to both intrapsychic and interpersonal-systemic factors and their real effects on the person.

Long ago St. Augustine noted that there is only *now* and that the present includes our memories (past) and our expectations (future).

We can't really go back. While it is interesting to consider different psychotherapy theories, I agree with Mary Goulding's comment in Chapter 5 that the therapeutic task is not to judge the validity of each childhood scene and to ferret out an objective truth but, rather, "what is important is that the client recover from the past, real and imagined, and go on to a fulfilling life."

Redecision Therapy: A Brief, Action-Oriented Approach contains many ideas that should be useful to therapists and their clients. The focus on client empowerment and the achievement of clear treatment goals makes it especially pertinent today. I am pleased to recommend it.

—Michael F. Hoyt, Ph.D.

References

de Shazer, S. (1985). *Keys to Solution in Brief Therapy*. New York: Norton.

——— (1988). *Clues: Investigating Solutions in Brief Therapy*. New York: Norton.

Freedman, J., and Combs, G. (1996). *Narrative Therapy: The Social Construction of Preferred Realities*. New York: Norton.

Goulding, M. M. (1985). *Who's Been Living in Your Head?* Watsonville, CA: WIGFT Press.

——— (1992). *Sweet Love Remembered*. San Francisco: TA Press.

——— (1996). *A Time to Say Good-Bye: Moving Beyond Loss*. Watsonville, CA: Papier-Mache Press.

Goulding, M. M., and Goulding, R. L. (1979). *Changing Lives through Redecision Therapy*. New York: Brunner/Mazel.

——— (1989). *Not to Worry!* New York: William Morrow.

Goulding, R. L. (1987). Group therapy: Mainline or sideline? In *The Evolution of Psychotherapy*, ed. J. K. Zeig. New York: Brunner/Mazel.

——— (1989). Teaching transactional analysis and redecision therapy. *Journal of Independent Social Work* 3:71–86.

Goulding, R. L., and Goulding, M. M. (1978). *The Power is in the Patient*. San Francisco: TA Press.

———— (1986). *Redecision Therapy*. (Videotape.) San Francisco: International Transactional Analysis Association.

Hoyt, M. F. (1995). *Brief Therapy and Managed Care: Readings for Contemporary Practice*. San Francisco: Jossey-Bass.

———— (1994). *Constructive Therapies*. New York: Guilford.

Hoyt, M. F., ed. (1996). *Constructive Therapies, vol. 2*. New York: Guilford.

McNamee, S., and Gergen, K. J., eds. (1992). *Therapy as Social Construction*. Newbury Park, CA: Sage.

White, M. (1995). *Re-Authoring Lives: Interviews and Essays*. Adelaide: Dulwich Centre Publications.

White, M., and Epston, D. (1990). *Narrative Means to Therapeutic Ends*. New York: Norton.

Acknowledgments

I am deeply indebted to two people, without whose help this book would not have been possible. Mary Goulding who, along with her husband, Robert Goulding, developed redecision therapy, has been most supportive of this project since its inception. She has read the early drafts of many chapters, and provided invaluable suggestions and encouragement throughout the process of writing and publication. John Gladfelter provided my own training in redecision therapy and encouraged me to put together this book. John provided introductions to other experienced redecision therapists and was consistently available to answer questions, listen, and comment on my ideas.

I have also been fortunate to receive encouragement and helpful suggestions from other therapists. Thank you, Leita Blair, John Cade, Leonard Campos, Ginny Conlon, Bill Falzett, Melody Fortenberry, Betty Gouge, Sara Harper, Cynthia Ann Harris, Shari Porter Jung, Jim Keedy, Paul McCormick, Marilyn O'Hara, Suzanne Rapley, Mary Robb, Silvio Silvestri, Emory Sobiesk, and Genie Weitzman.

My greatest thanks go to my husband, Bill, and daughters, Kristin and Kimberly. Bill and Kristin were unfailingly patient and supportive throughout the many months involved in this effort. Kimberly, who arrived midway through the process, was not at all patient, but gave me renewed appreciation for the energy and exuberance of the Natural Child.

Finally, I thank Michael Moskowitz, publisher, and the staff at Jason Aronson, particularly Bob Hack, Director of Editorial Production, and Norma Pomerantz, Director of Author Relations, for their help in creating a cohesive, polished final product out of 19 different computer disks.

1

Introduction: Redecision Therapy, A Brief Therapy Model

Carolyn E. Lennox, M.S.W., Ed.D.

The impetus for writing this book came from observing Mary Goulding as she demonstrated redecision therapy during the Erickson Brief Therapy Conference in Orlando, Florida, in December 1993. From the audience, I observed a cheerful white-haired woman of some sixty years who established an immediate and easy rapport with her clients on stage and with the therapists observing her work. As she demonstrated various aspects of redecision therapy, I was struck most by all the laughter. Mary would chuckle, her clients on stage would laugh, and the audience would laugh along with Mary and the clients. People would express their tears and anger as well, and Mary would be very respectful of these emotions, but she clearly rejoiced more in their humor and imagination. I sensed that the people who worked with Mary for that one hour had made important shifts in how they would view themselves and the world in days to come.

To the psychiatric establishment of the sixties, when Bob and Mary Goulding first developed redecision therapy, their claim to be able to cure longstanding emotional problems in a few hours or sometimes even in minutes appeared highly suspect. The Gouldings' work, to those unfamiliar with it, appeared magical. Still magical, it is teachable and learnable magic. This book is written to introduce a new generation of therapists to the Gouldings and the magic of redecision therapy.

Redecision therapy claims a unique ancestry among popular brief therapies. Alone among current brief therapy practices, it has its roots in transactional analysis, as originated by Eric Berne, and gestalt therapy, as developed by Fritz and Laura Perls.

Like many other therapists of the early sixties, Bob and Mary Goulding were dissatisfied with the length of treatment and the poor results of traditional psychoanalytic psychotherapy. Together they searched for ways to make psychotherapy briefer and more effective. Bob Goulding studied transactional analysis with Eric Berne and actively participated in his San Francisco seminars. Both Bob and Mary worked closely with Fritz Perls and other gestalt therapists of Big Sur, California. Together the Gouldings incorporated many of the techniques of gestalt therapy into their own unique interpretation of transactional analysis to form what is now known as redecision therapy (Goulding and Goulding 1978, 1979).

Although developed by the Gouldings apart from the influence of other schools of brief therapy, redecision therapy shares with them certain basic principles and techniques. Like other pioneers of brief therapy, the Gouldings believed that people could make important changes in a short period of time. They taught redecision therapists to begin each therapeutic encounter with the question, "What, specifically, would you like to change about yourself today?" The implication is that the client can and will make changes *now*, not in some unforeseeable future time. The statement also sends the message that the client is responsible for change, not the therapist.

As with other brief therapies, redecision work is based on a specific contract for change. Having an explicit change contract enables client and therapist to stay focused and allows both to know when the work of therapy is finished. Clients are asked early in each session what they want to change in terms of a concrete behavior or specific situation. In addition, they may be asked to describe what they will be doing differently in their life once they achieve their goals. Thus, in the initial stage of therapy, redecision therapists often use future-oriented questions similar to those used in solution oriented therapy (de Shazer 1985).

Like its cognitive therapy cousins (Ellis 1962), redecision therapy stresses the importance of both therapist and client employing the language of self-responsibility to bring about change. Any language that allows the client to avoid or put off change is confronted by the therapist. Phrases such as "I'll try" or "I would like to" are brought to the attention of the client and "I will" is suggested as a replacement. "I can't" is replaced by "I won't." Words that imply that outside forces are causing clients to feel certain feelings are replaced by words that encourage clients to take responsibility for their own thoughts and feelings. The therapist may suggest that the client try out "I scare myself about. . . ." as a replacement for "my fear." "I anger myself" takes the place of "he makes me so mad." In this way, clients are reminded that they are in charge of their own thoughts and feelings, the implication being that they alone have the power to change them.

Once a clear contract for self-change is agreed upon by client and therapist, it becomes the reference point for the rest of the therapy. During the remainder of the session, the therapist continues to play an active role in helping clients enact the desired change within the session itself. The therapist does this by structuring opportunities for clients to make new decisions about themselves within the session.

After change is achieved within the session, the therapist encourages clients to envisage various ways in which they will practice this change outside the session. Once again, clients are encouraged to come up with their own concrete, specific images of success.

These basic techniques of redecision therapy: contracting for change, insistence on a language of self-responsibility, enactment of change within the therapy session, and encouragement of action outside the session are shared with other forms of brief therapy (Budman and Gurman 1988, Wells and Phelps 1990). Redecision therapy is unique, however, in its theoretical basis in transactional analysis (TA) and in its reliance on the action-oriented techniques of gestalt therapy to bring about change within the therapy session (Hoyt 1993, 1995).

By now the reader may be wondering what a redecision therapy session looks like. In order to illustrate how a redecision therapist goes about combining cognitive work with gestalt technique in a brief therapy format, I will provide an example of an initial session from my own practice. After describing the work, I will discuss the theory and techniques involved. Later chapters in this book will describe how different therapists utilize redecision therapy to work with other types of problems commonly presented by clients.

Case Example

Kathryn has been referred to my office by an assessor from her managed health care company, who had also given her a referral to a psychiatrist for possible medication.

Kathryn is 35 years old, a large, heavyset woman who works as a secretary for a large local corporation. She lives alone with her 4-year-old daughter. She has been divorced since shortly after her daughter's birth and has little contact with her ex-husband, whom she describes as a drug addict.

Kathryn tells me that she has been battling with depression for several years. She has put off getting professional help, wanting to handle this by herself, but now her mood is affecting her performance at work and she fears losing her job. She has difficulty sleeping and has gained fifty pounds in the last two years. Kathryn is proud of taking good care of her daughter, whom she describes as looking like "a little princess," but says she neglects herself, often not bothering to care for her own clothes or do her own hair.

I ask Kathryn about her support system: Where is her family? Who are her friends? She tells me she has a mother and three younger siblings, whom she rarely sees because they reside in a distant state. Her parents divorced when she was 2. Her father lives in Tennessee. She describes their relationship as polite but distant;

she cannot bring herself to call him Dad. Kathryn's major source of emotional support is her church. She has attended regularly since moving to Dallas four years ago and has several good female friends through her church and at work. She does not date.

Making contact with Kathryn, getting her assessment of the situation, and finding out a little about her background has taken the first twenty minutes of our hour together. I praise her for coming to therapy and encourage her to keep her appointment with the psychiatrist for medication, saying these are both steps she has already taken toward taking better care of herself.

I ask Kathryn what she wants to change about herself today. Kathryn says she wants to treat herself better and she wants to feel better about herself.

What, I ask, would she be doing differently if she were treating herself better? Kathryn describes how she would take time to dress well and do her hair every day, and maybe buy herself some new clothes. I ask what feeling better about herself would feel like to her. How would she be feeling? What might she be saying to herself that would be different? Kathryn tells me she would feel "peaceful" inside.

I ask Kathryn how she is feeling and what she is saying to herself when she is not taking care of herself and not feeling good. Can she give me an example?

Kathryn describes driving down the street and wishing her car would crash, wishing she didn't have to be here anymore. She assures me she will not kill herself since she has to take care of her daughter and suicide is against her religious beliefs. Sometimes she just wishes she did not exist anymore. She feels sad and despairing during these episodes.

I ask Kathryn to think back over her life. Can she remember previous times when she felt sad and despairing and did not want to go on existing?

Kathryn pauses, then describes having these same thoughts and feelings when her stepfather, whom she loved dearly, told her he was leaving her mother. She was 6 years old at the time. Kathryn said she remembers very clearly thinking she did not want to live without him. As she describes the pain she felt at that moment, she adds, "I guess I must have felt the same when my father left when I was 2. I don't remember, but my mother tells me that I had always been a Daddy's girl and that I cried and cried when we moved to Minneapolis after the divorce."

I ask Kathryn if she wants to say goodbye to either of these men. Kathryn says no, she said goodbye to her stepfather many years later when he was dying. She thinks that perhaps she needs to say goodbye to her first boyfriend, Steve. They had gone steady for two years and were engaged to be married when he broke off the relationship. She was 19 at the time.

I draw up an extra chair and ask her what she would like to say to Steve. I add that while Steve might be in the chair, there might be other important men in her life standing behind him. Kathryn agrees that this is so.

I suggest she start by telling Steve what she has appreciated about the relationship. Kathryn turns toward the chair and thanks Steve for taking such good care of her, for listening to her, and for giving her hope that caring men existed in the world. I ask her if she has any regrets or resentments. Kathryn tells Steve she resents that he left without much explanation and without giving them a chance to work on the relationship. I ask Kathryn if she wants to tell Steve that she is choosing to live and go on with her life, or will she tell him that she will continue to be sad and mourn the relationship forever? Kathryn's voice becomes stronger as she tells Steve that she is going to go on with her life. She says goodbye to him and visualizes him driving away. She is quiet.

After a moment, I ask what she is experiencing. "Very peaceful," Kathryn replies with a grin. In the few minutes remaining in the session, I complimented her on the work she has done and I ask her how she might care for herself over the next few days. She says she will go home and do her hair.

The following week, Kathryn reports that she had a good week. She noticed she was feeling much happier and more at peace with herself. In addition, she had more energy and was more productive at work and at home. We discuss in detail all the positive changes she has made in her life. Kathryn continued in therapy, using basically the same process, and quickly made additional significant changes in her life.

Looking at this one session, the basic elements of redecision therapy are apparent. Kathryn describes what she wants to change, both in terms of how she would like to be and how she experiences herself in her most painful moments. Gestalt techniques are utilized to help Kathryn connect painful present affect with past experiences. The experiences are dramatized and Kathryn makes changes that carry over immediately to the present.

Redecision Therapy

In order to talk about how people change through this process, Mary and Bob Goulding utilized the concepts of transactional analysis, as developed by Eric Berne, with a few significant differences. Like Berne, Bob and Mary Goulding believed that a person can be described as consisting of different ego states: Parent, Adult, and Child. The Parent is the sum of all the beliefs, values, behaviors, and rules for living that are incorporated by a person during childhood from parents and other important figures (Berne 1962).

The Adult ego state consists of a person's capacities for problem solving and rational thinking. It is often likened to the central processing unit of a computer. Its capacities are present at birth, although it evolves throughout a person's life.

The third ego state, the Child, consists of physiological needs with accompanying emotions, as well as emotionally charged memories from early years (Berne 1962). The Child may be further divided into Free (or Natural) Child, and Adapted Child. The Adapted Child is the slightly older child who has found ways to adapt to the demands of his parents.

In their development of redecision therapy Bob and Mary Goulding utilize these basic concepts developed by Berne with significant modifications. Whereas Berne considered the contents of the Parent ego state to be incorporated indiscriminately by the young child, in much the same way as data on a disk is fed into a computer, the Gouldings taught that the child, from infancy, is an active participant in selecting and interpreting information from the world around him. The child constructs his own Parent based on available data and makes decisions about how best to respond to this Parent in order to survive. These early decisions regarding rules for living become the child's template for all future decisions. In this respect, redecision therapy reflects the current thinking of cognitive therapists regarding the creation of basic core beliefs about self and others that govern perception and decision making throughout life (Beck and Weishaar 1989, Dowd and Pace 1989, Edwards 1989).

The Gouldings (1979) call the most important of these early rules for living "injunctions" and "counterinjunctions." Both are created and accepted by the young child in response to perceived parental behavior and early life experiences. Counterinjunctions are perceived commands by the Parent. They include such statements as "be perfect," "try hard," "hurry up," "be strong," "be careful," and "please me." On the surface, they appear to be benevolent advice from parent to child, but when embraced rigidly by the Child they cause much unnecessary suffering.

Injunctions, on the other hand, when accepted by the Child, sound more like curses. They include such commands as "don't be," "don't be you," "don't succeed," "don't think," "don't feel," or "don't think what you think, think what I think," to name a few. These messages, whether spoken or implied, are delivered out of the distressed Child ego state of the person's parent. Children decide to accept these prohibitions based on early traumatic experiences and on their own observations of what appears to please their parents.

While obeying these injunctions and counterinjunctions may ensure the child's survival during childhood, these early decisions may not work as successfully for the child in later life. New situations require new responses, yet the person continues to repeat old behaviors and finds herself unhappy and unproductive but unable to find a way out of the impasse.

Fortunately, there is a way out of this dilemma. According to the Gouldings, people change when they make new decisions to think, feel, and behave differently in response to old injunctions and counterinjunctions. This decision (or redecision), to be meaningful, must involve the childlike portion of the self. Reason and logic are not sufficient. The creative, emotional part of the individual must be involved. The payoff for the person must involve a sense of fun, freedom, and other good feelings. The cognitive awareness of "doing the right thing" or a duty performed is seldom sufficient reward for permanent behavior change. In the language of TA, the redecision must come from the Child ego state, not the Adult.

In the example given earlier, it was necessary for Kathryn to experience the emotions involved in saying goodbye to her boyfriend in order for her to decide to go on with her life. Simply talking about her loss would not have had the same impact.

Redecision in Action

Redecision therapy is not alone in insisting that successful solutions to old difficulties must involve the creative, emotional side of the individual. Milton Erickson, grandfather of many brief therapies practiced today, was noted for his use of humor, laughter, and the absurd as important tools in bringing about behavior change (Rosen 1982). Albert Ellis, creator of rational-emotive therapy, encourages clients to develop a sense of the ridiculous with his jokes, exaggerations, and funny songs. Today many cognitive-behavioral therapists recognize the importance of assisting clients to experience their emotions during the recreation of a problematic situation in order to better identify dysfunctional beliefs and to bring about lasting change (Edwards 1989).

Given the importance of using the client's own creativity to find a solution to the problem, redecision therapists choose to reply predominantly on imagery and enactment techniques borrowed from gestalt therapy as the surest and swiftest method of accessing the client's creative Child. Within the session, the focus is on enactment of the problem and its solution.

The most frequently used techniques in redecision therapy are variations on gestalt empty chair work. The client is encouraged to enter into a scene, playing all the roles himself. The characters in the scene may include himself, other people, such as a parent or spouse, animals, objects in a dream, physical symptoms, or different aspects of herself. The setting may be the past, the present, the future, or a fragment of a dream. Redecision therapists often like to use early scenes, involving dialogue with a parent, since these frequently produce major changes in individuals. However, clients can and do make redecisions while working in all different types of scenes. What is important is that clients experience themselves as actively engaged in the dialogue, talking directly to the other figures and experiencing the emotions involved, not just talking about the situation to the therapist. Clients and therapists may think they know ahead of time what such a dialogue will reveal, but both are frequently surprised by the thoughts, feelings, and new decisions that emerge while actually doing the work.

The therapist's role in the drama is that of a director in an improvisational theatre. The therapist, based on the client's contract for change, helps the client choose the setting and characters, and keeps the actors talking to each other rather than to the therapist. The therapist listens and observes the client-created drama, notices and highlights possible injunctions and counterinjunctions, and encourages the client to confront and change negative messages to positive ones. As director, the therapist's task is to assist clients in rewriting scripts that begin as tragedies, with clients casting themselves as victims. The goal is to assist the client in changing the final scene of the drama so that the self is experienced as a triumphant protagonist.

After the client has made a redecision, the therapist's task is to assist the client in translating this new decision into concrete action that he or she can take in the present. Every movement by the client to implement the new decision is greeted with enthusiasm by the therapist. As with other brief therapies, noticing and complimenting positive change, no matter how small, is a big part of the therapist's job.

Of course, redecision therapists are not alone in using imagery and enactment techniques to bring about change. Therapy with children has traditionally relied on the playful use of drama and imagination to bring about change. In many respects, redecision therapy is a form of play therapy for adults.

Other therapies designed primarily for adults have recognized the value of drama and imagery as catalysts for change. Cognitive therapists sometimes use gestalt techniques to access and change early schemata and basic beliefs (Edwards 1989). Other brief therapists have written about the use of enactment and dialogue to enable clients to change their perceptions and find creative solutions to old problems (Mittelmeir and Friedman 1993). Redecision therapy is unique, however, in its use of redecision theory, including the constructs of ego states, injunctions, impasses, and redecisions, to provide the therapist with helpful clues to the effective use of dramatic dialogue and imagery techniques.

In the ongoing debate on the proper goal of therapy—character change or problem solution—redecision therapy chooses both. As people make new decisions regarding long-held beliefs and behaviors, they quickly discover new solutions to their immediate problems. Redecisions, although they may profoundly alter a person's view of himself and the world, do not automatically involve long-term psychotherapy. A small change, a redecision made in perhaps only a single session, can have a lasting impact on a person's life.

As one watches an experienced redecision therapist such as Mary Goulding at work, one may observe the client quickly decide what he or she wants to change, find a relevant scene to reenact, and without much delay, recognize and confront early dysfunctional injunctions and counterinjunctions, resulting in new and more rewarding behavior in the present. Naturally, the process is not as easy as a master therapist makes it look. Experienced redecision therapists have a sophisticated cognitive road map in their heads as well as many hours of experience in doing redecision therapy under supervision of more experienced clinicians.

Structure of Chapters

This book cannot hope to impart all that knowledge and experience to the reader. What it will do in the chapters ahead is provide more information on how therapists actually use the concepts and techniques of redecision therapy. For the past twenty years this information has been passed along from workshop leader to participant. This book seeks to give readers the benefit of that accumulated knowledge.

For purposes of clarity, the following chapters are divided into three parts: Theory, Practice, and Training. In the section on Theory, Julia Baird describes in detail the crucial task of negotiating a clear contract for change. Caroline Avery-Dahl continues with a description of impasses commonly encountered in therapy. She discusses the techniques used by redecision therapists to help clients move past their "stuck" places. In the next chapter on the treatment of lethal ideation, Denton Roberts discusses why a no-suicide contract is necessary and gives a detailed description of how to obtain a contract that will be honored by the client. In chapter 5, Mary Goulding elaborates on the ways in which redecision therapists work with childhood scenes. Charles Vorkoper describes goodbye work, another important therapeutic tool used by therapists to help clients who are in some respects "stuck" in their grief. Finally, Vann Joines concludes this section with a look at the key to redecision therapy: accessing the Natural Child. He illustrates this process with a piece of redecision work involving a snake phobia.

In the second section of this book, entitled Practice, other redecision therapists share their expertise in working with a variety of problems and in different modalities. Eugene Kerfoot describes the process of doing redecision therapy with groups and how redecision groups differ from other therapy groups. Other chapters in this section describe redecision work with clients who present various problems commonly seen by therapists: depression, panic disorder, bulimia, post-traumatic stress, and spouse abuse. The section concludes with chapters describing work with families and children and the use of redecision therapy within an HMO setting.

For those readers who are interested in learning more about this exciting form of brief therapy, the book concludes with chapters on supervision and training in redecision therapy. This form of therapy is best learned in an experiential setting. Michael Andronico and John Gladfelter describe the unique process developed by the Gouldings to train therapists in this modality. Finally, Moon Kerson and Marti Kranzberg conclude the book with a brief look at the core values underlying redecision therapy.

Redecision therapy is an exciting and powerful form of brief therapy. Although it has been used successfully by therapists around the world for over twenty years, it continues to provide exciting opportunities for growth to both therapist and client. It is my hope that interested readers will use this book as a starting point for their personal explorations of this efficient and effective psychotherapy.

References

Beck, A. T., and Weishaar, M. (1989). Cognitive therapy. In *Comprehensive Handbook of Cognitive Therapy*, ed. A. Freeman, K. M. Simon, L. E. Beutler, and H. Arkowitz, pp. 21–36. New York: Plenum.

Berne, E. (1961). *Transactional Analysis in Psychotherapy*. New York: Grove.

Budman, S., and Gurman, A. S. (1988). *Theory and Practice of Brief Therapy*. New York: Guilford.

de Shazer, S. (1985). *Keys to Solution in Brief Therapy*. New York: Norton.

Dowd, E. T., and Pace, T. M. (1989). The relativity of reality: second-order change in psychotherapy. In *Comprehensive Handbook of Cognitive Therapy*, ed. A. Freeman, K. M. Simon, L. E. Beutler, and H. Arkowitz, pp. 213–226. New York: Plenum.

Edwards, D. J. A. (1989). Cognitive restructuring through guided imagery: lessons from gestalt therapy. In *Comprehensive Handbook of Cognitive Therapy*, ed. A. Freeman, K. M. Simon, L. E. Beutler, and H. Arkowitz, pp. 283–298. New York: Plenum.

Ellis, A. (1962). *Reason and Emotion in Psychotherapy*. Secaucus, NJ: Lyle Stuart.

Goulding, M. M., and Goulding, R. L. (1979). *Changing Lives Through Redecision Therapy*. New York: Brunner/Mazel.

Goulding, R. L., and Goulding, M. M. (1978). *The Power is in the Patient*. San Francisco: TA Press.

Hoyt, M. F. (1990). On time in brief therapy. In *Handbook of the Brief Psychotherapies*, ed. R. A. Wells and P. A. Phelps, pp. 115–144. New York: Plenum.

——— (1995). *Brief Therapy and Managed Care*. San Francisco: Jossey-Bass.

Mittelmeier, C. M., and Friedman, S. (1993). Toward a mutual understanding: contructing solutions with families. In *The New Language of Change*, ed. S. Friedman, pp. 158–181. New York: Guilford.

Rosen, S. (1982). *My Voice Will Go with You*. New York: Norton.

Wells, R. A., and Phelps, P. A. (1990). The brief psychotherapies: a selective overview. In *Handbook of the Brief Psychotherapies*, ed. R. A. Wells and P. A. Phelps, pp. 3–26. New York: Plenum.

I

Theory

2

Contracting for Change

Julia Lacy Baird, Ph.D.

Through teaching redecision therapy, I came to realize the importance and significance of contracting with clients for change. I knew that the basic premise of redecision therapy involved contracting with the client what they want to change, but was not aware of how foreign this concept was to many other therapists who were good therapists but who were not familiar with the benefits of empowering their clients. In my training groups, the majority of the first day is spent understanding the concept of a good change contract. Watching trainees learn to make a good contract and to be a part of their excitement with the effectiveness of the contract in producing change is precisely what motivated the writing of this chapter. The essence of good therapy is a completed change contract.

Case Example

When I first began my career, one of my clients was a single mother who came into my office stating, "I can't handle my 12-year-old son."

I believed her. I did crisis intervention and spent several sessions with her teaching her to set limits and reasonable consequences, as well as contracting these expectations with her son. This process worked well and their relationship became tolerable, her stress level improved, and they left therapy to begin some semblance of normal life. They both felt good and were pleased with their treatment. Ten months later she returned in more turmoil than ever. By the time she returned, I had been introduced to redecision therapy and she found a different therapist. Previously, I had delved into problem solving. This time I pursued a change contract.

During our first meeting, my first contract was contact. We renewed our relationship and began building rapport. I listened to her presenting problem and let her know that I heard her dilemma. I focused on her language, demeanor, physical appearance, body language, feelings, and belief system as she related her conflict with her son. As she related her problem, she was slumped into her chair, tearful, and somewhat disheveled as she stated, "I don't know what to do. I've tried what you said but it's not working. He's running wild and I'm scared he's going to get hurt or arrested. It's too hard to deal with him, I've tried to get him to listen to me but it's not working."

At this point, I began to pursue a contract. I heard the words: I don't know, I've tried, it's too hard, it's not working, and I could have confronted those initially but I chose the following:

Therapist: What do you want to change about you that would further enhance your life?
Client: [looking puzzled] What do I want to change about me?
Therapist: Yes.
Client: What do you mean?
Therapist: [I repeat the question.]
Client: If he didn't give me so much trouble, I'd be O.K.
Therapist: And what do you want to change about you that will help you handle him?
Client: I do the best I can. [becomes teary]
Therapist: What are you feeling right now?

Client: Hopeless. [still teary]

Therapist: And what does hopeless feel like?

Client: Helpless.

Therapist: Hopeless and helpless are thoughts, so that's what you're thinking right now, and what is the feeling?

Client: Sad. [crying]

Therapist: Is this feeling sad a familiar feeling?

Client: Oh yes, I've felt sad all my life. [clue that this involves some early decision]

Therapist: Stay with that feeling. Are you aware of how you're making yourself sad right now?

Client: I'm thinking about how he doesn't listen to me and treats me as if I'm not there.

Therapist: Is there anything you want to change about you right now so that you'll feel better, right this minute?

Client: I don't know. I'd like to stop letting him take advantage of me so I don't feel so weak.

Therapist: And what will you change about you in order to do that?

Client: I'd have to feel important and stop being a pushover. Right now I don't feel very important.

Therapist: Do you want to change that? [Important is not a feeling but I decide to pursue it further.]

Client: Yes, but I don't know how.

Therapist: What do you want to feel instead?

Client: I want to feel important.

Therapist: And how will you know that you feel important?

Client: I won't let my son take advantage of me or talk me into doing something that I've already said he can't do.

Therapist: O.K. When you change and stick to your limits, how will you feel?

Client: Oh! [long pause] My first thought was scared!

Therapist: So why would you want to stick to your limits if you're going to scare yourself?

Client: [laugh] I wouldn't. I want to stick to my limits and not be scared and feel good.

Therapist: So what do you want to change about you so that you can not only stick to your limits, but feel good in the process?

Client: I'd have to not be scared when he's angry.

Therapist: O.K. That sounds like you scare yourself with other people's anger.

Client: Yeah, even when they're not angry at me, but more so when they're angry at me.

Therapist: So you want to change how you scare yourself with other people's anger.

Client: Yes.

Therapist: Good. How will you know when you've accomplished this change?

Client: I'll be able to stand up to my son even though he doesn't like me when I say no.

Therapist: And how will you feel?

Client: I won't like his anger but I'll feel good and strong about not being taken advantage of.

Therapist: Good. You want to stop scaring yourself and feel good about you when others are angry.

At this point, I have a good, solid change contract. Usually I go for an early scene around anger and fear in order to discover the origin of the early decision. When establishing a contract, there are several ways to proceed. When I invited the client to stay with her feeling and she switched to thinking, I followed the client and continued to negotiate. If she had stayed with the feeling, I could have pursued the early scene, and contracted for a redecision during the process. When pursuing a change contract, it's important to keep in mind that I must follow, not lead, the client.

Clients usually come to therapy because they are experiencing stress in some area of their lives. This stressor is usually the presenting problem, therefore during the initial contact I have access to the Child ego state. They describe their reason for seeking therapy with emotion (e.g., anger, sadness, frustration, or confusion) and all feelings are expressed from the Child ego state. As they discuss their problem, I observe the thinking, feeling, and behavior involved in an early decision. Decisions made as a child are not bad decisions at the time they are made, but the decision may not serve a useful purpose now. However, the client is behaving automatically, out of awareness, in an effort to abide by those early decisions. My task as a redecision therapist is to help the client become aware, and then to pursue a change contract with the client.

A client came in stating that her life was a mess and everything was going wrong. She feared that she was going to lose her job as well as her primary relationship. As she talked, she was tearful and fidgety, and her voice vacillated between sadness and anger. After listening a few minutes to her problem, I began to explore:

Therapist: As you're relating this dilemma, what are you feeling?
Client: What?
Therapist: What are you feeling, right now?
Client: Uh, bad.
Therapist: O.K. You feel bad. What does bad feel like?
Client: Just bad. [pause] I guess it's sad.
Therapist: You guess? [choosing to clarify "guess" as opposed to "it's."] If you don't guess and know, what's the feeling?
Client: Well, I'm crying all the time and worried, so I'm sad.
Therapist: So when you cry and worry yourself, you say to yourself that you're sad?
Client: Well, sometimes when I cry, I cry because I'm mad.
Therapist: O.K. Focus on what you're feeling right now.
Client: I'm feeling confused. You're confusing me.
Therapist: O.K. You're feeling confused. What does confused feel like? [One way to confront this statement is to point out her lack of autonomy, i. e., "you make me feel." However, I chose to stay with the goal of encouraging her to identify and claim her now feeling.]

> *Client:* Well. [Pause] I'm feeling sad, helpless, and—mad. I'm
> mad at you. [said with a stronger voice]
> *Therapist:* Good. So you're feeling sad, helpless, and mad right
> now?
> *Client:* Yes.
> *Therapist:* Is this feeling new or familiar?
> *Client:* New. [pause] No. It's quite familiar. I feel like this all the
> time. I feel like no one listens to me. [She becomes tearful,
> covers her face with her hands, and begins to sob.]

Through this procedure, it's evident that, although her sadness and anger may have been triggered from a current event, her response to the event involves an early decision. At this point, the client may be available to negotiate a change contract for a redecision.

Redecision therapy as developed by the Gouldings (1977, 1978, 1979) was designed to be utilized in groups. However, change contracts can be developed in individual, marital, and family therapy as well. The contracting procedure follows the same guidelines as in group process, and involves the three major components of redecision theory:

1. Contracting—obtaining a clear and concise contract about what the client wants to change
2. Impasse Clarification—identifying where the client is stuck in an early decision
3. Redecision—moving from the present impasse back to the origin of the decision, an early scene where the decision was made. From experiencing the early scene, the client *re-decides* to take care of herself in the early decision, thereby integrating cognitive information with feelings and effecting change.

Theory and Key Terms

Since the techniques and theories of redecision have their roots in TA (Barnes 1977, Berne 1961) and analyzing ego states, a basic knowledge of TA terminology is useful in formulating change contracts. Ego states, injunctions, counterinjunctions, and how they play a role in Levels I, II, and III impasses, cons, rackets, and contaminated ego states or decontaminations are a few of the terms. A detailed understanding of these concepts is not within the scope of this chapter, but a few simple definitions will help in understanding contracting.

First, the ego states represent the Parent, Adult, and Child ego parts of our personality. These ego states are readily observable based on how we present ourselves verbally, behaviorally, and emotionally. The Parent consists of tapes about how we should feel, behave, and think. We chose these tapes while we were growing up based on our perceptions of parental messages and have incorporated them into our own Parent. The Parent can be either nurturing or critical (Nurturing Parent or Critical Parent). The Adult ego state is the thinking part, like a computer, which simply stores and retrieves data, and is the decision maker, based on the facts. The Child ego state is where all feelings are expressed and experienced. One part of the Child ego state is the Free Child, or Natural Child, which is a fun-loving, free, happy part who only knows what he or she wants. The other part is the Adapted Child, or the intuitive part, which adapts and finds a way to please the parents of the world in order to survive. Redecision theory believes that change contracts must be of advantage to the Free Child, or the Adapted Child will sabotage the process. Since early decisions are made from the Child ego state for the purpose of survival, the redecision contract must involve the Child ego state.

Early decisions are choices children make in response to messages (injunctions and counterinjunctions) from parents or parental figures. While these decisions suffice at the time they are chosen, they no longer work in an adult world, and often appear in therapy as impasses. Decisions result from overt messages, or counterinjunctions. From these messages, the child decides how to "be" (be perfect, be successful, etc.), and incorporates these "be's" into his or her own Parent ego state. This type of decision involves a Type I impasse, where the client has developed a value system that supports the decision.

Other messages are more covert, and these are the injunctions. These result in choices about how *not* to be and involve the "don'ts," such as don't exist, or don't feel. Injunctions come from the Child ego state in the parent or parent figure, and usually materialize when the parent is experiencing extreme stress. Children become compliant and obey the injunctions. They make these decisions when they are defenseless and dependent on others for protection. These decisions result in automatic behavior and develop as Type II impasses.

Early decisions also involve attributes, or messages the child tells herself about herself, "I'm just that way," or "I'm just stupid." The belief is that this problem is innate, that they were born dumb, and clients use language like "always." These messages appear in therapy as Type III impasses, and the belief system is that she *is* dumb and the message comes from inside herself. Although the Free Child may openly object to the attribute, both the Adapted Child and the Free Child agree with the attribute. As in the other decisions, the intuitive Child ego state makes these decisions and subsequently figures out games and rackets to assist in supporting the decisions. These rackets become automatic and deny autonomy.

When negotiating change contracts, it's important for the therapist to be aware of rackets. Rackets are the way the Child ego state supports the early decision, and they serve as a way of receiving strokes or recognition. The rackets represent the perpetual bad feelings that are used to manipulate other people or to blackmail others into giving what they want. As children, they chose to obey the messages in order to survive psychologically (and sometimes physically) and the racket serves to maintain that survival.

For example, a client had negotiated a clear change contract to stop feeling confused when experiencing conflict with her husband. The work progressed:

Therapist: Remember a time growing up when you felt confused.
Client: [after searching her memory] There are many.

Therapist: O.K. Choose one. [pause] What's the scene?

Client: I remember one time when I came home from school and had forgotten to bring home my new sweater and my mother was furious with me.

Therapist: O.K. Good. Be in that scene right now. Be that little girl. How old are you?

Client: Seven. [From her facial expressions and posture, it is clear that she is in the scene]

Therapist: What are you feeling?

Client: Scared.

Therapist: There's your mother. [I move an empty chair in front of her.] What is she doing?

Client: She's furious. She's yelling at me.

Therapist: What's she saying?

Client: She's yelling, "You are so absent-minded you can't do anything right. I told you this morning that you had better bring that sweater home."

Therapist: Tell her how you feel as she is yelling.

Client: [speaks softly and through tears] Mom, I'm scared.

Therapist: And what is she doing?

Client: [smiles] She looks shocked.

Therapist: Tell her.

Client: Mom, you look shocked. [pause, and her smile fades] Now she looks even more shocked but is getting mad and yells, "How dare you talk back to me. You're not scared. I'll give you something to be scared about."

Therapist: Now what are you feeling?

Client: Scared and confused. I'm afraid she's going to hit me.

Therapist: Tell her.

Client: Mom, I'm scared you're gonna hit me.

Therapist: Now what is she doing?

Client: She's saying if I can't learn to do what she tells me, she just might show me what scared is.

Therapist: Does she know what you're talking about when you tell her you're scared?

Client: No. She has no idea. She just gets more angry.

Therapist: Tell her, "Mom, if you don't change, I'm going to feel. . . ." and fill that in.

Client: Mom, if you don't change, I'm going to feel confused when you're mad at me.

Therapist: Is she going to change?

Client: No, she won't ever change.

Therapist: [returning to the change contract] Do you want to change that decision and give up your confusion?

Client: Yes.

Therapist: Will you? [changing the child "want to" to an autonomous adult statement "I will"]

Client: Yes. Mother, I won't confuse myself when you're mad.

Therapist: Is that true?

Client: Yes. No matter how mad you get, Mother, I won't be scared and confused when you don't hear me.

Therapist: Good. Tell her how you are going to feel instead.

Client: Mother, when you get mad at me, I'm going to feel good. I'll feel calm and will be clear-headed.

Therapist: How do you feel right now?

Client: I feel like a ten-ton weight has been lifted off me. I feel calm. And powerful!

In this example, the client made an early decision to be confused and scared when her mother was angry. It was a good decision and kept her safe, as she would only increase her mother's anger if she attempted to intervene. Now, whenever anyone is angry at her, she automatically confuses herself to protect herself from being hurt.

Cons are ways clients protect themselves from disobeying the injunction or early decision. The con may manifest itself verbally ("I'll try"), emotionally (gallows laughter), or whatever the clients do in an attempt to get the therapist to do what they want, for example, an invitation to a game. Cons are usually related to some early decision and may represent a specific impasse. While the Free Child may want to change, the Adapted Child is fearful of the consequences, so the con serves as protection.

For example, the client comes in and states:

Client: I've tried and tried to quit smoking and I just can't. I just thought you could help me. [He makes this statement with a big grin on his face.]

Therapist: Do you want to try to quit smoking, or do you want to quit smoking?

Client: Well, sure I want to quit. That's why I'm here. I've tried and just can't seem to get it done.

Therapist: O.K. My question is, will you quit or not?

Client: I want to, I've just been unable to do it by myself.

Therapist: Are you saying that you can't quit smoking or that you won't?

Client: [with a big smile] I guess I'm saying I won't.

Therapist: Will you say I won't without guessing?

Client: I guess I won't.

Therapist: Be aware of your smile. How do you feel when you claim that you guess you won't stop smoking?

Client: I guess I've known that. It's just that everyone else thinks I should.

Therapist: You're still guessing. Will you claim that you won't stop smoking?

Client: Yes. I won't stop smoking.

The client was not interested in stopping smoking. His efforts had to do with pleasing someone else. Until he makes a grownup decision that he will stop smoking, no amount of trying will help. The Adapted Child does not want to experience withdrawal, give up something that he thinks is pleasurable, or to be told what to do.

A good change contract must have an advantage to the Free Child. In developing a change contract, the therapist must be cognizant of the early messages and decisions, rackets, cons, and the consequences for the client. Change has both behavioral and emotional consequences. While the Free Child may want to change, the Adapted Child may fear the consequences and sabotage any effort. When the Free Child wants to stop smoking, the Adapted Child will agree to "try." However, when the craving for a cigarette arises, wanting a cigarette takes precedence over trying and the decision is undermined.

A good contract involves identifying the message, injunction, and/or impasse, and redeciding to be who they are feeling good about themselves, rather than abiding by the early injunctions about who they thought they had to be in order to be loved and accepted. Contracting with clients about what they want to change is the primary focus. The therapist's task is to be a guide to assist clients in claiming their power, and minimizes the concept of the all-knowing therapist. In redecision therapy, the power is in the client to determine what he or she wants to change.

Contracting

Contracting with the client enables both the client and the therapist to specify the goals of therapy. Negotiating a clear change contract prevents psychological games, such as guessing what the client wants and enabling the client to assume the role of victim while the therapist attempts to rescue. Contracting places the responsibility for change in the client's hands. The client, not the therapist, decides what "needs" to change. This gives the power to the client, thereby avoiding dependency and eliminating caretaking. This protects both the client and the therapist. The goal is always to work within the context of the contract and to recognize that the only contract likely to lead to change is one for which the client assumes full responsibility. In redecision theory, contracting involves certain assumptions. The basic assumptions in contracting are:

1. Autonomy—the client isn't helpless.
2. Clients are aware, on some level, of what they want.

3. A belief of competency (both the client and the therapist).
4. Expectation—both the client and the therapist get and give clear, concise, and straight information.
5. Therapist's belief that the client *can* change and take charge of his or her life.

Therapists pursue a change contract based on these assumptions.

Contract Requirements

When working from the context of a change contract, there are essential requirements. The contract must be specific, reasonable, possible, and measurable. My task is to watch for clues and be aware of the ego states, rackets, cons, and impasses. "I want to feel better" is not a specific contract. I must assist her in becoming aware of what she is feeling at that moment and deciding what she wants to feel instead. When she states that she wants to feel calm rather than angry when her boss corrects her, then I can proceed. If the boss is abusive, then the contract isn't reasonable. However, if the bad feeling pertains to an early decision around accepting criticism, then the contract is reasonable. Whether or not a change contract is possible is contingent upon whether it is reasonable. The Adapted Child will always sabotage unreasonable contracts. The contract must also be measurable. She must be able to identify the change after it occurs by determining what will be different in her behavior, thinking, and feeling after she has re-decided.

In negotiating a workable contract, attention is given to who, when, where, what and how. *Who* involves an I—thou dialogue, without talking about anyone else. Talking about others implies wanting to change someone else rather than keeping the focus on the client. *When* and *where* refer to keeping the client in the here and now. Even when talking about the past, it's important to bring the feeling to the now, as if the event is happening right now. This involves keeping the language in the first person, present tense. *What* pertains to being precise and interesting. Rather than getting involved in long drawn-out stories that may or may not be interesting, it's important to get to the bottom line rather than "talking about." When relating a story, the client is in the there and then as opposed to the here and now. History cannot be changed, therefore the question is what do you want to change now, and how does the story relate to the now feeling? Finally, a good contract entails the client discovering how she will be different and how she wants to feel once she completes the contract.

To fulfill these requirements, the contract must be stated in the here and now, not then and there, and must be phrased in positive terms. A good contract is crisp and fun and capable of being expressed in one sentence in the first person with clearly specified behaviors. It must be in simple language that an 8-year-old can understand, since it must be made by the Adapted or Free Child. The contract has to have some advantage to the Child. In addition, the contract must have sufficient clarity so that both the therapist and the client fully understand the specific contract.

Finally, the contract must provide the three P's: permission, protection, and potency. The client must have *permission* to be who she is and to confront the parent messages. All permission requires protection, that is, adult autonomous protection and support. As a therapist I assist the client in affording herself that protection. This is necessary both internally and externally to provide protection from the Critical Parent, regardless of whether the parent in her head is real or imagined. John Gladfelter (1994) describes the Critical Parent as being similar to a cobra. The cobra is not mean and vicious, it just does what it does and what comes naturally. We don't need a regular fanging from a Parent, and I am not in the business of snake taming, so the client's choices are to change herself and claim her own power. When I relate this analogy to my clients, it serves to demonstrate potency. I claim my potency as a therapist by presenting myself in a direct way. I tell my clients, "If you're in therapy, you are in serious danger of changing; in fact, you will change." I suggest that they think long and hard, and if they don't want to change, they're in the wrong place.

Contract Benefits

Establishing a good change contract provides benefits for both the client and the therapist (Gladfelter 1985, Goulding and Goulding 1979). First, it provides a specific place from which to work, rather than sitting around for ten years processing. Second, the contract provides a point from which to measure success. Both the client and the therapist recognize the completion of the contract. Finally, a negotiated contract provides a point to stop the work (Goulding 1992). The points at which to stop are 1) at the contracted time or end of the appointment; 2) at the point of victory; 3) at a solid impasse, where the client is stuck and not willing to continue; and 4) after 30 minutes. My task as a therapist is to watch for clues and be willing to stop the work by saying, "Let's stop for now."

This is the step that my trainees find difficult, because it often leaves the client feeling bad. I understand their discomfort since this was also contrary to my initial training. However, I've found that not only is it acceptable to leave clients feeling bad, but also, more often than not, this assists them in getting beyond the impasse. By the next session, they are ready to move toward change. Stopping the work also provides permission, protection, and potency.

The final point to stop the work is after 30 minutes on one specific contract. Working any longer is futile. If the client hasn't moved toward redecision after 30 minutes, then they are not ready to proceed. My responsibility is to honor where the client is for that moment, again modeling protection and permission and remembering that the client isn't helpless and is responsible for herself.

Contract Goals

My goal as a therapist is to establish a workable contract with the client. For a contract to have a successful ending, it has to have a successful beginning. My intent is to assist clients in refining their contracts and to arrive at mutual change contracts that are clear, precise, measurable, possible, and that refer to real behaviors. Procedurally, a contract can be clarified by obtaining clear and specific answers to three basic questions:

1. What do you want to change about you that will enhance your life?
2. How will you and I know that you've accomplished this change (behaviorally)?
3. What will you feel or do differently and what will you put in its place?

These basic questions must be answered in order to establish a good, clear change contract that has advantages for the Free Child ego state. While clarifying answers to these questions, I look for the chronic bad feeling, thinking, and/or behavior and rackets, as well as how the client maintains the chronic bad feeling. I am also alert to the games involved, or any series of moves that maintain the bad feeling. In addition, I will monitor what the client's fantasy or belief system might be, so that I will know where to confront the client with her con and offer her an opportunity to further refine her change contract.

Other Contracts

Several different types of contracts can be established while working with clients. These contracts can be both short and long term. While the ultimate goal is to obtain a change or redecision contract, there are other contracts that are acceptable, and some that may provide important information to enable the client to determine a change contract. The three basic types of contracts are *administrative, therapeutic,* and *psychological*. The initial contract is one of contact, without which no other contract can occur. Usually this is by phone when the appointment is scheduled. During the initial session, the *administrative* contract is formed by discussing scheduling, time, money, limits, and the content of the sessions. Therefore, the first contract is clear and specific information about how I work and what I have to offer the client.

During this time, I will also get a contract from the client to close her escape hatches. Escape hatches are discussed at length elsewhere in this book but their relevance to contracting is of utmost importance. The Child ego state is not safe, and change contracts are not possible unless the escape hatches are closed. I will secure a commitment from the client to herself (not to me, since it's her responsibility to keep herself safe) that she will not harm herself, harm anyone else, or go crazy. Closing escape hatches is the initial therapeutic contract. *Therapeutic* contracts come in several different sizes and shapes. A *social* contract can be considered a therapeutic contract. This type of contract is simply one of case management. When this type of contract is made specific and clear by both me and the client, then I will accept this type of contract, knowing that this is not a change contract. When acquiring a social contract, I will seize any opportunity to offer the client the option of a change contract.

Another type of social contract is a *tourist* contract. This contract involves primarily "mucking around." Even though a tourist contract can occur anytime during the therapy process, it usually occurs during the initial session. Clients discuss what's not working in their lives. I respond by asking them what they want to do differently and what they want to change about themselves to achieve that change. The client learns what change is about and how I work and what I have to offer in terms of treatment. This contract is usually dealt with in the first session and often lasts for only one session. During this time, both the client and I will decide if we want to work together. This involves sizing up each other. While I evaluate what I hear the client wants from therapy, the client is hearing what I have to offer. I discuss this decision overtly and explain that I work from a change contract format. At the end of the session, the decision is made whether or not we will enter into a therapy contract. During the course of therapy, I may enter into another tourist contract, but unless it leads to a change contract I will limit it to 10 minutes.

An *information* contract can be utilized for specific groups such as divorce, single parenting, grief, and so on, or for nonspecific groups. These contracts provide a sharing of information and interaction between group members but are not change contracts. However, these contracts may lead to a change contract within the context of the group. Information contracts in nonspecific topic groups may also involve sharing of information and feedback. The group provides an advantage to the therapist since the feedback can be beneficial to group members as a whole, often providing clarification and support. This information validates the client and may help them to move toward a redecision contract. My responsibility is to be alert to the possibility of psychological games between group members. I critique the interaction, and intervene if I perceive the feedback to be detrimental to the client or if the one providing the feedback is engaged in projection. If so, I may ask the client, "Whose face are you putting on her?" or "What are you feeling as you say ———?" This type of intervention is essential in information contracts that involve group interaction and feedback. While information contracts may last longer in a group environment, I usually limit them to 10 minutes in individual therapy.

Another type of therapeutic contract is the *experiencing* contract. This has to do with parenting issues or injunctions such as "don't think" and "don't feel." This type of contract may be beneficial when clients say "I'm not angry" when they are red-faced, tense, with clenched jaws and fists, or clients who say that they are extremely depressed but laugh and giggle about their predicament. I will ask the client to remember a time when she was angry or sad when she was growing up. I then invite her to reexperience those old feelings in the present. I'll ask her to relax and allow herself to be aware of what is going on with her physically, at that moment. I allow her a few moments to experience this awareness. If she has difficulty becoming aware, I may ask her to go inside her body and become aware of any physical sensations and to report this experience. This process may or may not lead to a change contract. However, it does provide the client an opportunity to disobey the injunction or counterinjunction in a safe environment, and to access her Adult ego state to process the experience. My responsibility during this process is again to avoid games, monitor the client carefully, and stop the process if I see the client moving toward abreaction.

I also work utilizing a *homework* contract, although I now call it *practice*, since I find that clients seem to rebel against homework. A practice contract is just that. "Will you practice saying no or asking for what you want?" The practice is related to a specific behavior that the client wants to change. The practice can be accomplished within the context of a group, may be applied outside of the group, or both. The contract may be practiced in the session to assist the client in deciding on language and accessing the Adult ego state. This practice may also be utilized subsequent to a redecision in order to further integrate the change, or it may be assigned to assist in moving toward a change contract.

Another type of contract is an *exploratory* contract. The client doesn't know what she wants to change but wants an opportunity to talk and discover what may be getting in the way of feeling good. This is more of a fishing expedition. An exploratory contract differs from a tourist contract in that it has a direction. The client is aware that she plays a part in the problem and wants to explore what her part is. The goal is to lead to a change contract. During the discussion, I will invite the client to do double chair work and begin a dialogue with mother, father, or whoever seems to be relevant to the situation as she begins to explore. This may or may not lead to a change contract but usually helps her to clarify the issue or discover the message or impasse. During the experience of exploring, I can always re-contract for a redecision. For example:

Therapist: What do you want to change about you today?
Client: I'm not sure. I'm judgmental and opinionated and I don't want to be.

Therapist: What do you mean by judgmental and opinionated?

Client: I size people up, and once I make a decision I just won't be around them, I just write them off.

Therapist: Are you talking about strangers, acquaintances, friends?

Client: Both. If someone disappoints me or gets angry with me I just walk away and won't have any more to do with them.

Therapist: If you don't write them off, what will be different?

Client: I'd have to deal with conflict.

Therapist: Sounds like writing people off is a good way to avoid conflict.

Client: Yeah, I don't deal with conflict well at all.

Therapist: Do you want to change anything about you around how you deal with conflict?

Client: I'm not sure.

Therapist: What's the risk?

Client: I'm scared I'll get hurt.

Therapist: Where would you like to go from here?

Client: I want to think some more. I know I'm judgmental to avoid conflict and I'm scared of being hurt. I'm not sure I want to risk being hurt.

Therapist: Good information for you. When you want to explore another way of protecting yourself, I'll be available to work with you around that.

The essence of good therapy involves negotiating and completing a change or redecision contract. All of the contracts I've discussed are designed to lead to a change contract. They assist in developing a cognitive understanding of the restrictions imposed by adhering to early decisions. This understanding facilitates change. While working within the context of any of the therapeutic contracts, I look for the opportunity to negotiate a change contract. With a good, clear contract, the client will arrive at a specific change she wants, move to an early decision, and redecide. This leads to a change in behavior and feelings. This change may result in a dialogue with the parents in the client's head or in impasse resolution. The client will state in clear, precise, and positive language, "I'm giving up my scare, right now. I won't scare myself anymore and I will feel good about me." The contract has completed all of the goals of an effective change contract and the client claims her autonomy by redeciding whatever is restricting her today.

Futility Contracts

The third type of contracts, *psychological*, are contracts that get nowhere: futility contracts. My responsibility as a therapist is to cut through the psychological games or the underlying assumption, "I want to, but I can't." The games, cons, and rackets lead to a symbiotic relationship. Therefore, I must listen carefully and confront the games in order to prevent a psychological contract, that is, a contract that goes nowhere.

Effective change contracts are made by either the Adult ego state or the Child ego state and must benefit the Free Child. Futility contracts are offered by the Parent ego state. Often, a parent contract is covert. The client may say the right words, but if I watch her language and nonverbal behavior, she is telling me that she has no intention of changing. This is a result of the secret resolve of the child. If she changes, she will lose something that she is not ready to give up, that is, strokes. One example is a parent contract that is designed to please someone else. "I want to stop drinking" sounds like a clear contract. However, with further clarification, I usually find that "I should stop drinking" to make a parent or spouse happy, and the client has no intention of giving up alcohol. This contract will be one of futility. My task is to urge her to decide whether or not she will stop drinking for herself by accessing her Adult or Child ego state to participate in the decision. She will either move toward that decision or at least claim overtly, "I won't stop drinking."

A cousin to the parent contract is the covert social contract, which I perceive as different from the overt case management social contract. The client will say, "I want to be nicer, more loving, a better parent, and so on." I will attempt to identify the covert "should" message that may involve a "don't be" injunction, such as "don't be angry," or "don't be close." Injunctions are automatic and often out of awareness, and may be relevant in the client's assumption that she is not nice, loving, or a good parent. While the desired behavior, being a better parent, may be beneficial, this is not a change contract. Rather than dismiss her statement, I use it to pursue whether there is a change contract hidden in that statement. For example:

Client: I just want to be more loving.

Therapist: What does more loving mean?

Client: I don't know. My wife says I'm not very loving.

Therapist: That's what your wife says. What do you say?

Client: She's mad at me because I work so much and when I come home, I just want to go to bed.

Therapist: What does that have to do with loving?

Client: Well, I should want to spend more time with her.

Therapist: How come? [I don't ask why, as this is often perceived as a critical parent.]

Client: She says if I were more loving, I would spend more time with her.

Therapist: That's what she says. What do you say?

Client: I don't know.

Therapist: Will you claim, "I won't answer that question"?

Client: What question?

Therapist: Will you claim, "I won't even listen to the question"?

Client: [laughter] Yeah. My wife is the one that says I need to be more loving.

Therapist: I don't know where to go from here. What I know is that I won't help you be more loving for your wife. If you want to look at yourself and determine if you want to change something about yourself that will make your life better, I'm willing to work with you around that.

This man was not in therapy to change something about himself. He was there to please his wife. Had he been willing to look at what was getting in the way of feeling as close to his wife as he wanted, we might have moved toward a change contract. However, unless a contract is specific, reasonable, and measurable, there is no change contract. Psychological contracts involving shoulds or vague requests fulfill none of these requirements, so they get nowhere.

Some clues that will assist in recognizing futility contracts are language, copouts, sneaky child behavior or scare, and a belief system that they can't change. When a client states, "It happens, it feels, it happens" it's important to intervene and ask "What's 'it'?" When she says "I can't," request that she claim "I won't." Another statement that's exemplary of the sneaky child is "I'll try" or "I guess." Both these statements are copouts and I confront them immediately by explaining the difference between trying and doing, and between guessing and knowing. "Try" is a child's word that means, "God knows I tried." My clients soon learn this, and after several sessions the begin to correct themselves when they use the words "can't" or "try."

There are many clues to watch for when establishing change contracts. Nonverbal clues, body language, facial expressions, and gallows laughter are also important cons to confront. As a therapist, I know I won't be perfect and will miss clues, but I am constantly monitoring and refining myself. Contracting is an ongoing process during therapy. Clients will complete contracts and move toward another change. Sometimes, the client changes the contract during the course of therapy. My goal is to arrive at a mutual contract with my clients that is clear, precise, measurable, and possible, and that has to do with real behaviors for which the client assumes full responsibility.

Contracting for change is one of the advantages of redecision therapy. The most exciting factor is that it provides techniques to assist therapists in empowering their clients. Clients often come in for therapy with no awareness that they have the ability to change. Some merely come wanting a miracle cure. As a redecision therapist, my task is to help them formulate a change contract, that is, decide what they want to change.

When I began my career, I was committed to helping people. Through my training in redecision therapy I learned the advantages of being responsible *to* the client as opposed to being responsible *for* the client. Clients are responsible for themselves. Efforts to "help" result in colluding or supporting the client's lack of power. The basic premise of redecision therapy is to assist clients in claiming their autonomy. Contracting with the client to decide what she wants to change promotes autonomy and power over her own life. The therapist's role is to facilitate clients' discovery of early decisions that no longer suffice or serve as protection. The task is to discover the origin of early decisions and to find new ways of responding to archaic messages, that is, redeciding to claim their own power and respond in new ways. Redecisions result in lasting changes that improve the quality of life.

References

Barnes, G., ed. (1977). *Transactional Analysis After Eric Berne: Teachings and Practices of Three TA Schools*. New York: Harper & Row.

Berne, E. (1961). *Transactional Analysis in Psychotherapy*. New York: Grove.

Gladfelter, J. (1985). Dreamwork from a redecision approach. In *Redecision Therapy: Expanded Perspectives*, ed. L. Kadis, pp. 104–105. Watsonville, CA: Western Institute for Group and Family Therapy.

———— (1994). Personal communication.

Goulding, M. (1992). *Sweet Love Remembered*. San Francisco: TA Press.

Goulding, R. (1977). No magic at Mt. Madonna: redecisions in marathon therapy. In *Transactional Analysis After Eric Berne: Teachings and Practices of Three TA Schools*, ed. G. Barnes, pp. 77–98. New York: Harper & Row.

Goulding, R., and Goulding, M. (1978). *The Power is in the Patient*. San Francisco: TA Press.

———— (1979). *Changing Lives through Redecision Therapy*. New York: Brunner/Mazel.

3

Impasses: Accessing, Experiencing, and Resolving

Caroline Avery-Dahl, M.S.

Organizing is what you do before you do something, so that
when you do it, it's not all mixed up.
                                        —Christopher Robin

Resolution of impasses is crucial to the success of redecision therapy.
In this chapter I will be discussing the rationale for impasse work,
illustrating the different types of impasses commonly encountered in
therapy, and offering suggestions on how to facilitate clients in
accessing, experiencing, and resolving impasses.

To organize my thinking during a therapy session, I am interested
in determining the type of impasse with which my client is strug-
gling. Impasses are present-day situations in which clients feel stuck.
They experience themselves as being powerless to change. Impasses
are predicaments from which clients see no obvious escape, for which
they have no alternative solutions.

When stuck in an impasse, clients are frequently operating without awareness in obedience to their early childhood decisions. They
are unable to envision other options. They wind up in blind alleys,
limited by their chronic bad feelings, restricted thinking, and ineffective or inappropriate behaviors. Determining my client's impasses

allows me to have some ideas about what we will be doing during treatment and what strategies are likely to be most productive for successfully resolving the presenting impasses.

Therapeutic change is initiated in redecision therapy by facilitating clients in gaining a clear understanding of the relationship of their impasses to their archaic past. By having an awareness of how they have not completed early experiences, clients become aware of how they are still attempting to do so through avoiding, repressing, projecting, and other constricting relational behaviors (Goulding 1976).

Clients may change these adaptive responses that are no longer working for them by making redecisions. They can do this through re-experiencing distressing scenarios out of their past and confronting the memories that have led to their present-day impasses (Gladfelter 1992, 1995). Their new decisions about how they will feel, think, and act in similar situations in the present and future result in a resolution of their impasses. Clients may then become unstuck and empower themselves to function autonomously.

Successful resolution of impasses is the precursor for therapeutic change, the beginning of growth. Like taking away the rock that holds a boulder in place, resolving an impasse initiates the momentum for change to occur. Once one impasse is resolved, another may be uncovered, allowing clients to continue the process of change.

This chapter addresses what many redecision therapists describe as one of the more difficult concepts of redecision therapy to understand and integrate. Paradoxically, identifying clients' impasses is one of the most powerful tools for diagnosis and for planning therapeutic treatment interventions. I have discovered that the more I use redecision therapy in my practice, the easier it has become to recognize clients' impasses. As the process becomes clearer, the theory seems beautifully simple and most instructive.

The concept of *impasse*, initially used by Fritz Perls, was further developed by Bob and Mary Goulding (1978, 1979) to describe the internal conflict between the compulsion to act on the early decision and the longing to do something else instead. The Gouldings would look for clients' impasses by asking, "What is the stuck place?" They believed that achieving a rapid resolution of the impasse was critical for successfully empowering autonomy and change in brief therapy.

I view impasses as critical diagnostic divining rods that therapists may employ as powerful conceptual tools to access and bring into awareness the feelings, thoughts, and behaviors of early transactions. These divining rods point the direction to the fault line where clients may find the way out of their stuck place.

When stuck in an impasse, it is as if clients are actors in an early scene, locked into their Child ego state. The therapist, operating like a stage manager and director, moves very carefully, thoughtfully, and precisely to manage the transactions in the scenario, thereby enabling and supporting clients in empowering themselves to change. Achieving this level of therapeutic craftsmanship is possible by developing knowledge and skills about working with different types of impasses.

Since impasses are exceptionally valuable and useful keys for organizing my thinking about my clients' treatment, understanding and learning to recognize the three different types of impasses further enables me to clarify and focus specifically on the impasses they are presenting in today's sessions. I can then make timely therapeutic treatment decisions, such as what form of chair work or other experiment will be most effective in resolving the dilemma of today's presenting gestalt.

I determine the type of impasse my client is presenting by:

1. Identifying primary bad feelings
2. Identifying belief systems
3. Identifying contaminated thinking (assuming for fact data that is only a belief system or fantasy)
4. Identifying "parental messages" (injunctions, counter-injunctions, or attributes that have contributed in forming early childhood decisions)
5. Identifying early decisions.

The three distinctly different types of impasses are defined by overt and covert messages clients received from parents and other important figures in their lives. Impasses are categorized by these messages as follows (Goulding 1989):

Type One impasse: "drivers" (counterinjunctions);
Type Two impasse: "stoppers" (injunctions);
Type Three impasse: "attributes" (innate qualities or longstanding life patterns).

Type One Impasse

In a Type One impasse the messages are out in the open, overtly delivered from the Parent ego state of the client's authority figures or caretakers to the Child ego state of the client. These messages are called counterinjunctions or "drivers." Frequently heard counterinjunctions are: "Be strong," "Hurry up," "Be perfect," "Try hard," "Be careful," and "Please me (not yourself)."

I will hear clients telling themselves messages that sound like "shoulds," "oughts," "musts," or "have-tos." On first glance such parental messages appear to be socially or culturally appropriate, having to do with what one should, ought to, or must do or be. The impasse is created when the client, in obeying such messages, feels constrained or disabled from being autonomous. Most of the work we do in therapy is on Type One impasses.

Clues to Type One impasses include common physical symptoms such as headaches and stomachaches, which may signal psychosomatic complaints supporting the client's belief systems, games, or fantasies. I listen for nonautonomous language, such as "I can't," "I'll try," or "It makes me." I also listen for bad, nonsensical, or inadequate information, such as "I don't know why I feel this way, I just wanna feel better." When operating under counterinjunctions, clients believe other people are responsible for their feelings and that someone or something else "makes" them feel this way: "It scares me. . . . He makes me angry!"

Case Example:

A 45-year-old male client, Derrick, presenting with symptoms of depression, complains of being overworked, stating he has not taken a vacation in 14 years. "I know I should be more dedicated to my work, but I just can't take it anymore! I need to take time off, but I just can't justify it. I know I'm working myself to death, but you gotta eat!"

Inviting Derrick to check out what he learned from Mom and Dad about work and taking vacations, I direct him to address this issue to his father and/or mother by putting them in the empty chair. Then I invite Derrick to move over to the other chair and "be Dad/Mom" and respond.

Derrick, as his "dad," responds with, "Vacations are for rich people; we just can't afford the time and expense. You should worry about making money, not spending it." His "mom" reprimands with, "Besides, an idle mind is the devil's workshop."

Having Derrick return to his chair, I ask him to check out if these messages still fit him today. He says he wants to give up believing that he should work so hard that he dies standing up. In order to do this, Derrick will need to give up wishing and hoping for his dad to magically change in the past and give him permission not to work so hard. Derrick's been getting strokes from Dad all these years for working hard, so he will need to develop strategies for stroking himself for taking time off. Otherwise he is likely to remain adaptive, and sabotage himself by secretly rebelling against this decision, thus setting himself up to continue working harder while blaming others (Goulding 1989).

To finish this piece of work, it is important to counter the injunction, anchor the redecision, and make a plan for the future. Providing Derrick with reality information, I invite him to educate his Adult with new data about work, stress, productivity, mental and physical health, and the value of time off. The therapeutic task then is to capture the creative imagination of Derrick's Free Child by having him sit in the Parent chair and "reparent" himself by giving himself nurturing messages that it's O.K. to take time to play. By directing Derrick to make a plan for next week to include minivacations during his work day, I invite him to anchor his redecision by making future plans for taking healing vacations.

Case Example:

Travis, age 32, is having serious problems in his marriage of ten years. He believes he should be strong as the "man of the house" and is unable to be sensitive and understanding toward his wife. He thinks he ought to be tough when she is vulnerable and is unwilling to show nurturing behaviors toward her. When she is unhappy or crying, he reacts by becoming critical and intolerant, judging her for her weakness. In contracting for what he wants to change, Travis says he wants to learn to be more tolerant and understanding, to be more sensitive to his partner's needs, and to allow himself to feel and express his emotions.

Therapist: What do you want to change about yourself today in order to make this relationship better for you?

Travis: I want to pay attention to what I'm feeling. I'd like to be able to talk about what's going on with me so I don't shut out the people I'd like to be close to. Instead of telling my wife I'm feeling sad or angry about my problems with her, I just stuff it. She thinks I'm cold and hard-hearted.

Therapist: So you want to give up being a tough guy. What's in it for you to change that about yourself?

Travis: I want to stop feeling sad all the time and I want to save my marriage. I'd like to be more open and honest with my wife so we can talk about what's really going on. I'd like to at least have a chance to work out our stuff. I want her in on what's going on with me. I'd like to get closer to her.

Therapist: When you're a kid and you're feeling the way you are in this relationship, what's going on with you? How far back does it go?

Travis provides an early scene in which he is feeling sad and tells himself to be strong and not express his feelings. He relates the following:

Travis: When I was a kid. . . .

Therapist: Will you be in the scene and tell it as if it's happening right now?

Travis: When I'm a kid and my dog gets run over I'm crying. My dad tells me to stop crying. He says big boys don't cry.

Therapist: Will you let yourself be that kid whose dog just died? Will you put your dad in the chair and tell him what's going on with you?

Travis: I can't stand it, I am so upset! I am really sad! My dog was my best pal and I'll miss him so much.

Therapist: Will you move over to that chair and be Dad? What's Dad saying?

Travis (as Dad): Get over it—we can always get another dog! Good for you for not crying—you're my little man.

Therapist: Switch back to your chair. What do you experience when you hear Dad discount your feelings?

Travis: I feel really pissed! Yeah! He just went right on by—like dogs are a dime a dozen and there's nothing special about this one.

Therapist: What do you say to yourself in your head about Dad?

Travis: He's mean. He doesn't care about my dog or what I think.

Therapist: What do you say to yourself about yourself?

Travis: I need to be strong just like Dad. I'm not important. My feelings don't matter.

Therapist: What do you call yourself?

Travis: I'm nothing.

Therapist: What do you decide about your life?

Travis: You've gotta be tough! Don't get attached to anyone or anything.

Therapist: What do you want to change about that decision?

Travis: I want to be sensitive to people I care about. I don't want to push them away anymore.

Therapist: Tell Dad.

Travis: Dad, I'm not going to listen to you anymore. I have a right to care and I don't need to act strong for you anymore.

Therapist: Will you say, "I won't act strong for you?"

Travis: I am going to start caring, Dad, I won't act strong for you anymore.

Therapist: Will you tell Dad what you will do instead?

Travis: I'm gonna care about how I feel and about how others feel, and I know it's O.K. for me to be sensitive. I'll cry when I'm sad.

Therapist: Will you move over to the chair and be Dad? [Client moves to other chair.] As Dad will you respond.

Travis (as Dad): I'm disgusted and ashamed of you. You're never gonna grow up to be a real man like me.

Therapist: Move back to your chair and respond to Dad.

Travis: I've tried all my life to be the kind of man you were and I don't like myself. I don't like living like this and I don't like what I'm doing to my wife and my kids.

Therapist: Tell Dad, "Even if you stay angry and ashamed of me, I won't act tough all the time. I'll let myself feel my feelings."

Travis: Whether you like it or not, I'm gonna quit being a hard ass. I'll feel what I feel and cry when I'm sad.

Therapist: Will you move over and be Dad and respond.

Travis (as Dad): You'll be a wimp, and people will make fun of you. You'll never be able to command the troops. No one will ever respect you.

Therapist: Move back to your chair and respond.

Travis: I don't care what you think. I never felt close to you because you were like a brick wall, you never acted like you cared. I'm not gonna do it your way anymore. I want to give my wife more than you gave Mom or us. I'll respect myself for this even if you don't!

Therapist: [bringing client back to the present] And how will you be different with your wife today? Put her in the chair and tell her.

Travis: I'm giving up being the tough guy. I'll let you know when I'm feeling bad. I'll pay attention to your feelings and I'll be more gentle when you want comfort or support.

By having Travis move over into the other chair and "be Dad," he has an opportunity to think about that part of himself in his head that he uses to "parent" himself as a part that is separate from himself. This allows him to reparent himself, decontaminate his thinking, and become autonomous (Gladfelter 1977). He now has options for how to respond to other people's feelings and he has options for how to respond to his own feelings besides having to "be strong." As he continues his therapy, Travis may next choose to decide to give up some of his injunctions, such as don't be you, don't feel, or don't get close. These are Type Two impasses and are discussed in the next section.

A frequent concern I hear from therapists in my training or consultation groups is "How do I get my clients to do chair work?" By having trainees role-play their clients, I demonstrate different ways of working with therapists' own resistance. Usually it is the therapists' own discomfort or lack of experience in doing chair work that leads them to be faint-hearted or reluctant to try something new. If therapists claim their own resistance to doing chair work, they can free themselves to experiment with different techniques and just do it!

Rarely in my experience have my clients refused to do chair work. I am always very understanding with the novice client's awkwardness in talking to an empty chair or moving over and "being" someone else in the other chair. I use the client's words and respond with "I understand you feel awkward doing this exercise, and will you do it anyway?" It is very important to preface his request with "will you" (Gladfelter 1977). When the client declares "I feel stupid doing this!" I respond with "and will you let yourself feel good about how well you are doing it anyway?"

Type Two Impasse

In a Type Two impasse the message is covert, delivered out-of-awareness from the parent's Child ego state to the child's Child ego state. These messages are called *injunctions* or stoppers. Injunctions are derived from the parents' pain and suffering from their own childhood, reflecting their own fear or anger, which is then transmitted to their child in covert transactions. The impasse is created when clients are unaware of how they are stopping themselves from being autonomous by obeying these messages.

These injunctions, coming from the contaminated thinking of the Child ego state of the client's parent(s) and received in the Child ego state of the client, result in contaminated, ruminative, and obsessive thinking. The client, as a child, adapted to take care of the parent(s) by symbiotically compensating.

For instance, clients may have denied their autonomy by acting cheerful when Mother was depressed, by being quiet when Father was angry, or by joining in the feeling state of the parent(s) by being anxious when Mom was anxious, depressed so Dad would not be, or by escalating their parents' anger and chaos. When in this impasse, clients will frequently describe themselves as being depressed, feeling anxious most of the time, or just plain feeling bad and not knowing why. They are dealing with very powerful feelings and very powerful "parents."

Frequently implied injunctions are: don't be, don't be you, don't be the sex you are, don't be a child, don't grow, don't think, don't be important, don't have fun, don't feel, don't be successful, don't make it, don't be close, don't be sexual, don't belong, don't be well, don't be sane, don't do, don't want, don't trust, don't . . . (anxiety or phobias) (Goulding 1976, 1989).

As discussed in the chapter on contracts, it is critical to first address any lethal injunctions and close all "escape hatches" such as suicide, homicide, going crazy, becoming violent, or abusing substances such as alcohol, drugs, or food (Avery-Dahl 1985). Have your clients make the commitment to themselves that "No matter how bad I feel, no matter what happens, I will not hurt or harm myself or anyone else, accidentally or on purpose, and I will not make myself crazy."

To keep the work crisp, efficient, and potent, the Gouldings (1978) believed there were four points at which therapy was to be stopped:

1. At the contracted time
2. At the point of a victory, no matter how much time remains in the session
3. At a solidly stuck place in an inflexible impasse to allow clients to actively feel the impact of the impasse
4. Within thirty minutes in order to keep therapy crisp, fruitful, and fun.

One of the most delightful examples in my experience of doing Type Two Impasse work occurred during my month long training with the Gouldings at the Western Institute for Group and Family Therapy (WIGFT). I was working as "therapist" with a "client" who was stuck in his "don't be you" injunction. Suwat, a high ranking corporate executive in his late thirties living in an Asian metropolis, was feeling stuck in his cultural training, which required him to be formal and traditional in his interactions with others. He wanted to be more spontaneous and creative, to be able to express himself authentically.

During his work, Suwat told of his grandmother instructing him to behave always as if the Emperor was watching his every move. I was having him dialogue with the Emperor in the other chair when Suwat, misunderstanding my English, thought he heard me suggest he "show his ass to the Emperor," an extremely disrespectful act likely to receive severe punishment. Much to my surprise, Suwat jumped to his feet and spontaneously "mooned" the Emperor, giggling with delight as he did so.

Bob Goulding, who was supervising and videotaping our work, let out one of his robust guffaws at this rapid impasse resolution, which transcended language restrictions. The infectious laughter of the group as they shared in Suwat's victory supported his joy and delight in himself as he dared to defy convention and be spontaneous.

The validation and support offered by other group members strokes clients' sense of empowerment and autonomy, anchors their changes, and encourages them to put energy into practicing their redecisions. Coat-tailing off another client's work is part of the contagion of group (Gladfelter 1992). When clients see others experiencing the joy of an impasse resolution, they want some of that good stuff too.

Follow the client's feelings to lead into Type Two impasse work. I ask my client, "What are you feeling right now?" or "When you are 5 years old and your mother is talking to you, what are you feeling, what is the scene?" The client almost always feels like a *victim*.

I am interested in helping my clients create their own early scenes in vivid detail, as if they were there now, so they may experience an intense environment for facilitating their desired change. Identify which parent the injunction comes from by asking the client who is in the scene with them. If both parents are present, have the client dialogue with them one at a time to determine which parent they will be working with in this impasse.

Using an I–Thou dialogue, have clients put their parent in the chair. I might ask: "Will you confront Mother or Father over there?" The client's response may be, "I can't. I want to, but I can't." I respond, "Tell her or him 'I want to but I *won't*'." It is important to confront all nonautonomous statements to enable and empower the client's shift to autonomy.

If I get stuck in a power struggle, with the client tenaciously declaring "I can't . . . ," I end the session with, "Let's stop here, this is what you've chosen for now." I want to stay out of my own contaminated Parent ego state, so I avoid operating as a Not-OK Critical Parent or Adapted Child by not pushing the client to meet my agenda. It is most useful for me to stay curious rather than assuming I know what is going on or what my client needs to change today. The power after all is in the patient!

Case Example:

Allison is a 40-year-old attorney who has been working for the same large law firm for the last ten years with no indication of being made a partner. She feels frustrated about reaching her career goals, since no matter how successfully she handles her caseload she continues to be overlooked for advancement. For the past several weeks she has been unable to sleep soundly, waking with "anxiety attacks" about her upcoming review. She has come in to get a handle on her stress.

Allison: No matter how hard I try, I just don't ever seem to be able to satisfy my boss.

Therapist: And what are you feeling right now?

Allison: Scared and worried that I'm not going to get a good review.

Therapist: And what do you want to change about yourself today?

Allison: I want to stop scaring myself and stop worrying about things I can't control.

Therapist: How do you want to feel instead?

Allison: I want to feel comfortable and confident.

Therapist: When you are a kid and you're feeling scared and worried about being out of control, what's going on in your family?

Allison: Mom is yelling at me for messing in my panties and she tells me she's ashamed of me, that she can't take me with her, and that nobody will like me or play with me.

Therapist: And will you see yourself as an adult being there in that scene to protect and support you as a kid?

Allison: [to herself as a child] Yeah! Hey kid, you're gonna turn out O.K. and you're gonna learn how to take care of yourself and you're gonna have lots of friends.

Therapist: There's Mom. Will you tell her that Allison's just a kid, back off and give her a break.

Allison: [as her own ally in the scene] You care more about whether they think you're a perfect parent and you're blaming Allison

for being a kid. You're so worried and afraid of looking bad, so
you shame her. You're the one with the problem—all you're
gonna succeed in doing is having one constipated kid! Leave
her alone. I'm in charge now!!

Therapist: Will you tell your kid that you're gonna help her to not
be afraid to take her time learning how to do new stuff? Will
you tell her you won't worry or make her feel ashamed when
she makes mistakes while she's learning?

Allison: [to herself as a child] I'm right with you, kid! I will stop
scaring you and take my time learning and I will not worry or
shame you when I make mistakes. Actually I won't even call
them mistakes anymore, I'll call them stages of training. [She
laughs as she makes the connection with "potty training"!]

Another interesting option for uncovering the early messages is to
conduct a "parent interview" to get at the old tapes (Gladfelter 1992).
By conducting an interview of the parents or caretakers from the
client's family of origin, the therapist obtains history and elicits
information and advice regarding the client. Inviting the client to
move into the empty chair and "be your mom," the therapist begins
the interview by addressing "Mom" with her given name.

Inviting the introjected parent to speak provides a means to see
what is going on in the other chair with the parent introject that the
client is not aware of or does not want to know about. So seldom do
folks get an opportunity to speak with themselves from the vantage
point of the introject, they often discover it frees up a part of themselves that is within them that they haven't wanted to claim. I am
always amazed at the wealth of information that pours out of my
clients when they are being interviewed as their parent.

Type Three Impasse

The Type Three impasse is about attributes or seemingly inherent
characteristics. These are messages clients tell themselves about them-

selves. These attributes have been generated from their experiences of themselves with others, as well as whatever qualities others have attributed to them that they continue to believe to be true.

This impasse is identified in clients by an I—I dialogue. I will hear my client saying, "I was telling myself the other day . . ." or "Part of me thinks I should change careers and another part wants to stick to what I know." To uncover the attribute, I might ask, "What do you tell yourself about you?" Some commonly expressed attributes are: "I'm stupid," "I'll always be . . . ," "I was always the pretty one," "I'm shy," "I'm the fat one in my family," or "I'm a nerd and have no social skills."

The therapeutic importance of Type Three impasse work lies in getting resolution between the Free Child who is seeking freedom, life, and spontaneity, and the Adapted Child who adapted very early, often nonverbally, to parental injunctions, experiencing these attributions as a natural state of being (Goulding 1979). In this impasse, clients experience themselves as always having felt and thought this way about themselves and about the world and as having been this way since birth (Goulding 1976).

The client's Child is Adaptive when listening and responding to internal or external "parents." The client's Child is Free when not under parental influence. The Adapted Child masquerades so effectively it can sound convincingly like Adult or Parent dialogue. Transactions between the two will sound like a fourth-grader or bossy older sibling talking to a kindergartner or younger kid.

Using two additional chairs to represent these two parts, have the client move from one to the other as you help each part to verbalize the internal dialogue between them. It is not always necessary for the therapist to know right away which part is in which chair. This will become clearer through the process of dialogue.

Listen for incongruities between verbal language and body language, such as clients who say "I want to let go" while holding their arms tightly, indicating the part of themselves that does not want to let go. In this impasse, clients often are so disconnected from themselves that they deeply discount their feelings as well as their physical symptoms. Listen also for concrete thinking in this impasse as clients will be very dogmatic, seeing things as black or white, good or bad.

Case Example:

Brett has been an occupational therapist for five years, having changed careers from teaching high school. Now in her mid-forties, she is questioning her competence in general, doubting her ability to be effective in any profession. She describes evidence of her incompetence as her failure to be organized and keep all her patient records up to date. She experiences herself as hopeless and feels "paralyzed" when she stares at all the piles of stuff to be done. She wants to feel better about herself and be able to make a decision about staying in this line of work. She agrees to an exploration contract.

> *Therapist:* Will you see the "piles of stuff" in the other chair? What do you experience as you look at them?
>
> *Brett:* I'm furious! I hate to even look at them.
>
> *Therapist:* Tell that to the piles of stuff.
>
> *Brett:* [to the piles] I resent the hell out of you! I wish you'd just go away—I hate your mess. I feel like I can't do anything as long as you're there waiting for me. I can't even quit my job until I clean you up!
>
> *Therapist:* Will you move over and be the piles and respond to Brett over here?
>
> *Brett:* [as piles] You're worthless. You always say you'll take care of getting stuff done and then you just sit there like a bump on a log. I can't count on you. I wish you'd just go away and get someone else to do this job.
>
> *Therapist:* [indicating second chair] Will you move over here and be that part of you that feels paralyzed, and respond?
>
> *Brett:* I wanna run away. You're mean! I've been going over to my office on weekends to take care of you and then I just sit in the car and do nothing 'cause I can't stand to look at you.
>
> *Therapist:* Will you switch to the other chair?

Brett: [as piles] You are so repulsive. You even have piles of stuff at home you never get cleaned up! You'll never amount to anything until you grow up and take care of your responsibilities.

Therapist: Will you switch to the other chair?

Brett: You're right. I'm never gonna make it. I'll never get it together. I've always had a hard time getting stuff done.

Therapist: What are you experiencing?

Brett: I feel stuck.

Therapist: Will you stand up and come over here to consult with me about these two parts of you? How old is that kid sitting over there? [indicating the chair with piles of stuff]

Brett: Oh, I guess she's about 9 or 10.

Therapist: How old is that part of you in the other chair who feels so hopeless?

Brett: Really young, maybe 3.

Therapist: It sounds like they each want the other to go away.

Brett: Yeah! Actually, they act like they'd like to get rid of each other.

Therapist: As the adult in charge here will you keep them both alive and will you not allow them to die or kill each other off?

Brett: Absolutely. I will not let you kill each other or yourselves. There's got to be another way to work things out.

Therapist: Good for you!

Brett: [looking at therapist] But I haven't a clue what! I'm really feeling stupid and hopeless!

Therapist: You sound like you're speaking from that part of you that's 9 years old. Will you stay in your Adult, knowing that you can figure it out?

Brett: You're right. I sounded just like that part of me that beats up on myself. I don't have any answers, but I will take the time to figure it out.

Therapist: What do you think needs to happen for these two kids to work out this tug-of-war? My hunch is that each has something important to offer. How can you work things out so they both get taken care of?

Brett: I'm not sure. I think they each need something, but I don't know what.

Therapist: Will you do some thinking about these two parts of you during this next week? Listen to their dialogue, maybe do some writing, and figure out what you'll do to take care of each of them. It sounds like the 3-year-old never gets to have fun because the 9-year-old is always on her case about unfinished stuff.

Brett: [deep in thought] Yes, this should be interesting.

Treating a Type Three impasse is slower work because it involves an intrapsychic process and will most likely not come to a tidy conclusion in one session. The purpose of this I–I gestalt exercise is to develop awareness by externalizing the internal dialogue, so that clients can explore their early decisions and experience their stuck place. This opens opportunities for them to examine their belief systems, develop options, and make new decisions.

Since work on this impasse may continue over several sessions, it is important to stop when there is an obvious stuck place, such as when you hear that the power struggle between Adapted and Free Child is firmly entrenched. I will usually wrap up a two-chair dialogue by having the client stand with me for a consultation. Sometimes I will ask, "What will you do to resolve this tug-of-war?" or "How will you go about working out the differences between these two parts of you?" and then we discuss options adult to adult.

Standing up and walking around with clients helps to move them out of their "trance." This will assist in breaking their cathexis and move clients into their Adult ego state for data processing and feedback about what they have observed going on between these two parts of themselves. Concluding each piece of work on a Type Three impasse by having the client stand with me (or move back to their original chair) for a consultation to discuss what is going on facilitates their figuring out how they can help mediate and resolve their internal conflict. It is also a good way to help them decontaminate their thinking. Primarily this consultation allows the client to shift into the here-and-now Adult ego state and integrate the split. Again, be on the alert for the client slipping into Adapted Child or "Child masquerading as Parent" dialogue when they are supposed to be in clear Adult.

People get into really stuck feelings in this impasse. It is important therapeutically to let them stay there. As long as clients are into their pain, they are not available to work further. Frequently clients will continue to work on this dialogue between sessions and may return to the next session reporting they have resolved the impasse on their own. Working through this impasse will likely lead to other work on Type One or Type Two impasses.

The pain in a Type Three impasse is like a lifelong drug clients have been on that prevents them from moving. Having clients dialogue with their physical symptoms may be productive when dealing with complaints that are psychologically based; however, since their pain may have medical etiology, it is important to get a physician to check it out. I can't do therapy with someone who has a toothache. George Gershwin died in his second year of psychoanalysis of a previously undiagnosed brain tumor.

Suggestions For Consultation and Self-Supervision

Advance and retreat from any position you take.

—Carl Whitaker

Some basic guidelines for therapeutic craftsmanship in working with impasses involve utilizing the subtlety of tacit knowledge much like having a pen in hand that never touches paper. The therapist becomes a part of the world at large and consequently cannot not know, cannot not care, and cannot not have an opinion.

The following are some false beliefs held by therapists that serve to reinforce and maintain clients' impasses: grandiosity—therapists believe they are responsible for figuring out the problem and fixing the client; omnipotence—therapists tend to take on a mantle of power, operating on the premise that they must deliver or else; omniscience—therapists pressure themselves into believing they need to have an idea of how to proceed. These belief systems have evolved from the medical model, which presumes that the doctor has to fix something and the patient does not know what it is. As a consequence, therapists provide therapy as if dealing with a comatose patient, thereby discounting the power of the patient.

One creative solution I find useful in countering these beliefs is to practice being Martian (Berne 1972), operating as if I have just arrived on this planet and have no clue about how these aliens function. In giving up what I think I know about the client, I become open to being Martian, setting aside my preconceived notions and allowing myself to not know what the hell is going on. It can be most intrusive to stop acting as if I know what is going on with clients or what was in their past. The power then shifts to the clients to lead me where they need to go.

The danger in acting all-powerful is that I am encouraging and inviting transferential transactions. The intimate association between client and therapist creates the opportunity for transference (sometimes benignly referred to as symbiosis) or mutual dependence (Massey 1991). Operating in an out-of-awareness symbiotic dynamic, the therapist may unwittingly maintain and validate a client's stuck position by reinforcing dependency and discouraging autonomy (Joines 1991).

Redecision therapy is designed to discourage and minimize transference. For example, when clients confront redecision therapists with feelings of anger or disappointment toward them, the therapist directs the client to put the "therapist" in the other chair and dialogue. This gestalt provides an opportunity for therapeutic intervention and diffuses opportunities for transference or countertransference. The therapist is not "stuck" as the object and may freely direct transactions to uncover the early decisions.

A therapeutically beneficial symbiosis can be created by being conscientiously aware of this dynamic and being deliberately in charge of maintaining healthy boundaries. Therapeutic mastery in redecision therapy is attained through making contact, joining with and "dwelling in" the client (walking in their shoes) without becoming a partner in perpetuating the original crime. The therapeutic task therefore is to keep transactions with clients open and upfront, being aware of not inviting covert transactions that lead to an afflicted mutual dependence.

Redecision therapy has been called controlled group therapy. It is controlled in the sense that the therapist works one-on-one with clients, doing individual therapy within the group setting rather than encouraging process between group members. The therapist is responsible for maintaining these clear boundaries (Aveline 1993) and for deflecting transactions that come out of left field aimed at another group member. This is much like catching a fly ball before it hits its intended target and tossing it back to the initiator by asking, "And what is going on with you right now?" There are no innocent bystanders in groups. Other clients are present, are watching the work, are having their own internal experiences, and are making their own projections. By managing transactions, a safe protected environment for change is provided.

Mirroring the client by being deliberately symbiotic, attending to the client's injunctions and counterinjunctions, the therapist will have an idea what ego state to come from and be in attunement with whatever ego state is available in the client. In other words, utilize parallel transactions to create a deliberate symbiosis by matching feeling and content and using the same tone of voice and affect as the client. In this way the therapist can nurture rapport and communicate empathy without becoming enmeshed.

Another major responsibility of the redecision group leader is to create an atmosphere for clients to experience permission to be different and feel their potency. "It's pretty hard to feel very good when you're with somebody who's out of it. You are a special, unique, and autonomous individual." To avoid wasting time mucking about, clients are discouraged from telling their horror stories and are encouraged to enter into a change contract: "Yes, that happened to you and you feel bad about it, so what do you want to change about you?"

Therapists may also minimize transference by being assertive and clear in response to transactions inviting dependence. For example:

Client: Aren't you going to be here next week?

Therapist: No, I am not.

Client: I feel awful. I don't know how I'll manage without you.

Therapist: I understand that you are making yourself feel bad, and I know you will take care of yourself. Do you want this same appointment time in two weeks?

A powerful way to open access to the client's Adapted Child is for therapists to use humor out of their Adult ego state: very purposeful and very conscious, not put-downs, not sarcasm. Most Adapted Child humor is gallows humor, which means that clients will be laughing at transactions that have a lethal intent or will be making fun of serious content. "It was a riot. My girlfriend said I nearly wrecked my car driving home drunk as a skunk last night, ha ha." It is imperative to listen for and confront gallows humor over and over. Powerful validation and support for change, on the other hand, comes from stroking Free Child humor.

It is handy to use information about the client's impasses in making concise case notes. By briefly jotting down at end of each session or group what type of impasse clients were working through, noting the injunctions, counterinjunctions, and early decisions, the therapist has a quick reference for follow-up and a guide for clarifying the therapy contract.

Model O.K. Parent behavior by being clear, consistent, and in charge. Attend to the following:

1. Crispness: as therapists we often tend to muck about
2. Economy: of time and of words
3. Carefulness: avoid overstepping clients' boundaries by using

care in what we say and in what we do, and by not getting into what they do not want to or are not ready to

4. Specificity: contract for what they want and what is possible and doable
5. Options: be thinking of other threads to pull
6. Nonverbal: be aware of the body language of both therapist and client
7. Nonautonomous language: listen for "I can't," "it makes me," "I'll try," and other discounting or minimizing statements
8. Working with resistance: the resistance is usually in the therapist and not in the client.

There are no "casual" conversations in life. When we are in a therapeutic relationship with an individual we are in that role all the time no matter what or where. Consider following these three pearls of wisdom, attributed to Ram Dass, while you are working with clients: expect nothing, appreciate everything, and stay in the now.

Making a redecision is only a beginning point for clients, a marker to pick up on in the next session. Perhaps they will be celebrating the changes they have made, the successes they are enjoying in how they feel about themselves and in how they are handling their relationships. Perhaps they will be reporting on new insights or an awareness of how they keep themselves stuck and will be contracting for another change. Perhaps they will be continuing to work through an impasse from a previous session. Perhaps they will be reporting on ways they are practicing their new decisions and anchoring their changes.

I have discussed with you the crucial role impasses play as the core of redecision work. Gaining experience in knowing what type of impasse you are dealing with is like choosing the correct instrument for intricate surgery. Facilitating clients in discovering their stuck place, accessing their early scene, bringing it into the present experientially, and making changes to gain resolution are the fun and the magic. Redecision therapy creates an intensive environment for change. Once you have got it, you cannot not know anymore.

References

Aveline, M. O. (1993). Principles of leadership in brief training groups for mental health care professionals. *International Journal of Group Psychotherapy* 43(1): 107–129.

Avery-Dahl, C. (1985). Redecision and the criminal personality. In *Redecision Therapy: Expanded Perspectives*, ed. L. B. Kadis, pp. 205–213. Watsonville, CA: Western Institute for Group and Family Therapy.

Berne, E. (1972). *What Do You Say After You Say Hello?* New York: Grove.

Gladfelter, J. (1977). Enjoying every minute. In *Transactional Analysis After Eric Berne*, ed. G. Barnes, pp. 394–424. New York: Harper's College Press.

——— (1992). Redecision therapy. *International Journal of Group Psychotherapy* 42(3): 319–334.

——— (1995). Imagery in redecision therapy. *Transactional Analysis Journal* 25(4): 319–320.

Goulding, M. M., and Goulding, R. L. (1979). *Changing Lives through Redecision Therapy*. New York: Brunner/Mazel.

Goulding, R. L. (1976). Gestalt therapy and transactional analysis. In *Handbook of Gestalt Therapy*, ed. C. Hatcher and P. Himelstein, pp. 615–634. New York: Jason Aronson.

——— (1989). Teaching transactional analysis and redecision therapy. In *Variations on Teaching and Supervising Group Therapy*, pp. 71–86. New York: Haworth.

Goulding, R. L., and Goulding, M. M. (1978). *The Power is in the Patient*. San Francisco: Transactional Analysis Press.

Joines, V. (1991). Transference and transactions: some additional comments. *Transactional Analysis Journal* 21(3): 170–173.

Massey, R. F. (1991). The evolution of perspectives on transference in relation to transactional analysis. *Transactional Analysis Journal* 21(3): 155–169.

4

The Treatment
of Lethal Ideation

Denton L. Roberts, M.Div.

Introduction

My first encounter with redecision therapy occurred five years prior
to meeting Robert L. Goulding, M.D. A client of mine who was
going to Carmel, California, to sort herself out prior to initiating a
divorce asked me for the name of a therapist she might see in Carmel.
I gave her the name of Bob Goulding, whom I knew by reputation.
When she returned she reported that she had made an appointment
with Dr. Goulding. During that appointment he asked her to make a
no-suicide contract and she had refused. He in turn told her that he
would not let her out of his office if she was unwilling to give up
suicide as an option for solving her problems. She said that she was
resolute in her refusal and he was resolute in his demand. He explained to her that neither he nor her regular therapist could effectively treat someone under the threat of death. A decision to live was
critical to her therapy and future happiness. She acquiesced to his
judgment and made a no-suicide contract. She reported that the three
weeks since she made that decision had been the best of her life. She

was peaceful and decisive in a way that she had not been before. Her therapy with me progressed nicely over the next few months as she proceeded to rearrange her life.

Five years later when I met Bob I told him the story and expressed my thanks. "Yeah," he said, "you can't get any real work done in therapy until people decide they won't destroy themselves or others, or go crazy."

Bob explained to me that lethal injunctions (*"Don't be"* and *"Don't be sane"*) were "crazy" messages that people pick up at a very early age in highly disfunctional families. When a person has introjected such messages (injunctions), clinician and client must decommission them *before* proceeding with treatment of their presenting problems.

Although I was a fully trained and credentialed therapist at the time, my training had not provided me with a clear-cut protocol to effectively detect and eliminate the threat of lethal ideation. In the ensuing thirty years, working with a large number of clients in individual and group therapy, I have never had a client kill him- or herself, kill anyone else, or go insane. I attribute this not to good luck, but to learning how to effectively detect and decommission clients' lethal ideation.

Lethal Ideation

From transactional analysis we learn that there are two main lethal injunctions: *Don't be* and *Don't be sane* (Phillips 1975). Obeying a *don't be* injunction, the client ends up in the morgue. Obeying a *don't be sane* injunction, he ends up in the hospital. Because of their lethal nature, when either of these injunctions is the root cause of pathological behavior they must be eliminated before other issues can be addressed effectively. Simply stated, a person under the threat of death, self-destruction, or insanity is not free to devote his or her attention to running a life. With these injunctions left untreated, a client's behavior and ideation may be increasingly consumed by fending off these potentially lethal messages. Lethal pathological messages, unless decommissioned through corrective experience (therapy or other), can be likened to dormant volcanoes slowly accumulating power and ultimately erupting.

Therapeutic Assumptions

The therapeutic assumptions of redecision therapy for treatment of *don't be* and *don't be sane* injunctions are:

1. Lethal injunctions are passed on implicitly during the developing years. For example, the woman who has an unwanted pregnancy may fail to bond with the infant through her mothering and subtly and unintentionally pass on the information that she wished the child didn't exist (*don't be*). Or parents, through denial, may fail to validate the child's recognition of their conflict and anger and implicitly pass on the injunction *don't be sane.*
2. Lethal injunctions take precedence over all other injunctions and must be decommissioned before effective therapy can be achieved.
3. Pathology is decisional, and irrational and destructive decisions from the past can be undone and replaced by healthy ones.

These three assumptions underlie the remainder of this chapter. In order to clarify the redecision treatment process I will write specifically about treating the *don't be* injunctions. However, this information applies equally to the *don't be sane* injunction.

No-Suicide, No-Homicide, and No-Insanity Contracts

I state with some level of pride and some level of humility that I have never failed to negotiate a no-suicide, no-homicide, or no-insanity contract. Pride because it reflects well on my work, humility because dealing in such potentially dangerous coin is risky. However, I credit my success to sound theory and effective techniques. Let me say a word about redecision theory and technique.

Redecision is both a theory and a technique. In theory and practice it combines the deepest insights of the dynamics of transactional analytic, psychoanalytic, and gestalt theories into an intervention process (technique) based on the assumption that human beings at core are healthy and psychological cure is possible. If a therapist does not personally hold these assumptions, success in the treatment of lethal injunctions will be increasingly chancy. This is due to the commonly accepted fact that the client in treatment is empathically attached to the therapist (transference), and if the therapist has ambivalence about the client the client will intuit this ambivalence.

Indicators of a Lethal Injunction

All well-founded intake procedures explore the question of whether or not the client is or has been suicidal, homicidal, insane or in fear of any of these conditions.

Not all clients are completely forthright in intake interviews, therefore the therapist may not get reliable answers to these questions. If during the intake process the therapist intuits a lack of forthrightness on the part of the client, she or he will need to explore these issues until she or he is confident that the client is not in danger. For example, the question, "Are you now or have you ever been suicidal?" if answered "No, that's not an option I have considered" is straightforward and matter-of-fact, and if the therapist perceives it as an honest and congruent statement then no further investigation is necessary. If, however, the "no" is hedged ("No, I don't think so *now*"), more investigation is indicated. Or if the "no" is not congruent with the rest of the client's presentation—the client reflects physical discomfort by squirming or twitching, looking away, or some other distortion of contact—then the therapist will need to investigate further. "I noticed you looked away when you said 'No.' Were you aware of that? How do you account for that?" In other words, the clinician should confront and explore any incongruity until she or he is comfortable before proceeding to another topic. How to do this will be illustrated in the case material to follow.

Another critical and often overlooked indicator of lethal injunctions is nonproductivity during the treatment process. If a client in treatment appears to understand information well but does not apply it to life outside of the consulting room, then this *may* be an indication that a primary injunction has not been dealt with. Frequently, I have found that raising questions relating to the lethal injunctions during the course of treatment leads to undisclosed lethal ideation. As a general rule, when therapy is not proceeding satisfactorily, the clinician has to make sure there are no lethal injunctions lurking in or out of the client's awareness. As the therapeutic alliance is increasingly strengthened, it is not unusual for forgotten material from the past to come into awareness.

Yet another indicator of the existence of a lethal injunction is the therapist's intuition. If questions of suicide, homicide, and insanity arise in *your* thoughts as you work with a client, seemingly from nowhere, or between sessions with the client, then you as therapist need to explore these issues. Thoughts such as these come from intuition. As intuition is *incredible* information, it is fair to assume that you may be receiving such information from the client. When such intuitive speculations occur to you as a therapist you must resolve them. How this is accomplished will be dealt with in the following case examples.

The four primary indicators of the existence of lethal injunctions are:

1. Explicit statements
2. Incongruities between words and affect
3. Treatment not progressing satisfactorily
4. The therapist's intuition.

Any time one of these four indicators of lethal injunctions comes to the therapist's attention indicates the need for thorough investigation. This is a strong statement and it is intended to be—any time means *any time!* Lethal injunctions lead to lethal actions and may not under any circumstances be left untreated.

Obeying Lethal Injunctions

There are four possible ways that a person can obey a lethal injunction.

1. Kill himself or herself
2. Kill someone else
3. Provoke someone to homicide
4. Go insane.

Any activity a client is involved in inside or outside of the consulting room that advances his or her life in the direction of these potentially lethal actions is indicative of a lethal injunction lurking in the person's psyche. (It may appear that killing someone or provoking homicide does not fit here. However, I remind you that taking another's life is self-destructive, for example, post-traumatic stress disorder. In addition, provoking homicide, while studied very little, is a common phenomenon among criminal or character disorder clients.)

Redecision and Lethal Injunctions

When a previously suicidal or homicidal client has made a decision to live she or he will state with ease, enthusiasm, and congruence, "I will not kill myself, anyone else, or go crazy no matter what. I will not provoke anyone to kill me or others, or go crazy, no matter what." When the client in treatment freely makes this statement and, having made it, reports positive feelings and a sense of well-being the redecision is made. (To validate this I invite you to make the following statement out loud and be aware of *your* internal experience: "I will not kill myself or anyone else, or go crazy, not matter what. I will live." Hearing yourself make this statement always feels good.)

In the clinical setting, redecision experiences are often quite dramatic, and everyone present feels affectual relief. With the client who has worked through suicidal or homicidal injunctions, it is good practice for the therapist to reinforce this decision periodically during the process of treatment. This is done by having the person repeat the above statement or by the therapist saying matter-of-factly, "Are you still clear that you will not kill yourself or anyone else, or go crazy?" If the client answers yes to this question and reports and/or demonstrates heightened positive affect, it is all right to proceed with the issue at hand. However, if there is hesitation, uncertainty, or lack of positive affect, then it is important to have the client reinforce the decision to live until affectual relief is evident and the therapist is comfortable that the client is in no danger.

Lethal injunctions more often than not arise from early unconscious decisions and are held in both cognitive and eidetic memory—mind and body. When a redecision is made the nonverbal and verbal expression of relief is the prime indicator of effectively decommissioning a lethal injunction. Just as we feel relief when saved from a life-threatening danger, affectual relief in the clinical setting demonstrates that the person is now experiencing the newfound psychic safety. In other words, as therapists we want to see and hear clear information that the client is not in imminent danger.

The Redecision Process and Lethal Injunctions

Redecision therapists vary in the application of technique according to their unique *style*. However, they do not vary in *process*.

Here is how this process works:

The client and the clinician have a contract for change. (Contracts
   are covered in Chapter 2.)

The therapist and/or client become aware of one of the above-
   mentioned indicators of a lethal injunction.

The therapist initiates the redecision process proceeding from the
   present moment and tracking back to the early decision (illustration to follow).

The client reexperiences the original scene and feeling state and
   brings to awareness the decision made in the original scene.

The client completes the original scene by expressing explicitly
   what was left unexpressed in the early scene.

The client makes a new decision and expresses this new decision in
   the fantasized original scene.

The client anchors the new decision by stating it clearly and
   matter-of-factly in contact with the therapist and/or the group.

The client or therapist reinforces the new decision by restating it
   periodically during the course of treatment.

This *process* outlines the steps of making a redecision. All elements
must be present to ensure effectiveness. However, the order of events
may vary. Further, the contact between therapist and client must be
authentic and free-flowing, not "techniquey" or forced. The therapist is responsible for both maintaining authentic contact and covering all the steps of the redecision process.

Discovery and Treatment of Lethal Injunctions

Case One illustrates the general intake procedure where lethal injunctions are not relevant (how you check it out). Case Two illustrates intake procedures where lethal injunctions are relevant and
redecision techniques are implemented.

Case One

This is an example of checking out the existence of lethal injunctions during intake process.

Therapist: Are you or have you ever been suicidal or homicidal, or thought you might go crazy?

Client: Mmmmm . . . no.

Therapist: I noticed you hesitated and said "mmm." What was that about?

Client: Well, I have had the idea of suicide cross my mind at times, but I have never entertained it long.

Therapist: O.K. Will you say to me, "I will not kill myself or someone else or go crazy no matter what."

Client: Yes. [pause] You mean now?

Therapist: Yes. Say out loud, "I will not kill myself or anyone else or go crazy no matter what."

Client: O.K. I will not kill myself or anyone else, or go crazy no matter what.

Therapist: What do you feel?

Client: I don't know—nothing much.

Therapist: Make eye contact with me and say it again.

Client: [looks at the therapist] I will not kill myself or anyone else, or go crazy no matter what. [pause] I feel sort of curious, like, what's this about?

Therapist: We'll get to that. What are you aware of in your body?

Client: Well, I'm aware of my heart beating and I guess I feel a little more open and clear that I won't ever do that.

Therapist: Good. It's good to know that you aren't in danger of self-destructive activity, and both you and I need to know that you are not in these kinds of dangers in order for therapy to proceed. If you ever have any of these kinds of thoughts in or out of therapy will you tell me or some other professional?

Client: Yes.

Therapist: Thoughts of suicide, homicide, and insanity block the therapeutic process, and if they are present or come up, they have to be cleared away in order to proceed with your therapy. That's why we raise these questions in the intake interview. Any questions?

Client: No. It does sort-of feel good to know I wouldn't destroy myself.

Therapist: Yes; it does.

In this case, redecision was not indicated, but redecision theory guided the process. In gestalt terms, the process made the implicit explicit. In transactional analytic terms the Adult ego state made an explicit statement and the Child ego state experienced relief and freedom. For the therapist, explicit statements and reports of relief are clear indicators that it is all right to proceed with therapy.

Case Two

This is an annotated case scenario, created out of multiple experiences of using the redecision process to demonstrate the steps of the redecision process in dealing with lethal injunctions.

Therapist: Have you ever had suicidal, homicidal, or insanity worries or thoughts?

Client: Yes, sometimes, but it's no real problem today.

Therapist: Tell me about them.

At this point the therapist needs to hear the story, no matter how ancient, so that she or he can assess the situation. Especially, we need to know the extent to which the thoughts were developed into an operational plan, as well as the frequency of the thoughts. The fact that the idea of suicide, homicide, or insanity will cross someone's mind is not unusual; however, for the person to benefit fully from therapy it is important that he or she make a clear explicit decision not to entertain or advance such thoughts. Therefore, a "yes" answer to the above question indicates the need for clinical assessment. If, as in

Case One above, such ideation on the part of the client was casual and minimal, a clear statement from the client and evidence of affectual relief is sufficient indication to proceed. However, as you listen to the detail of the story of past or present suicidal, homicidal, or insanity ideation you will need to decide on a treatment procedure to remove the threat. (It is always best to err on the side of caution.) After hearing the story and making the assessment, proceed as follows:

Therapist: Recall the time when you last thought about suicide/ homicide/insanity and describe it to me. [This should be stated as a matter-of-fact (Adult) direction.]

Client: It was after I broke up with a girlfriend at her initiative about two years ago. I thought, what's the use, I'll never have the kind of relationship I want—I might as well kill myself.

Therapist: What did you do then? [The therapist wants to begin to get an idea of the sequence of events—what went on before, during, and after the suicidal thoughts.]

Client: I don't know, it just sort of went away. I was depressed for a while, and then I just went on with my life.

Therapist: Are you depressed now?

Client: A little.

Therapist: How long have you been a little depressed?

Client: I don't know. I guess I've been a little depressed ever since that breakup.

Therapist: Tell me about a time in adolescence when you were depressed.

Client: I don't remember any particular time.

Therapist: What was the first thing you flashed on when I asked the question?

Frequently, when this type of intervention is made, the client will not have a clear memory of the same feeling; she or he will have an automatic "flash" that is indicative of an intuitive awareness. If she or he does have such an intuitive flash, you will want to deal with it as follows. If she or he doesn't, you may skip this part of the process.

Client: Well, I don't think it fits, but I thought of my dog. About the time I graduated from high school my dog died. He was my pal and I guess I thought I'd never have another friend like him.

Here the client is showing some sadness and the therapist is aware that he is still mourning the loss. This grief will need to be finished at some point in the therapy. However, to deal with it at this point could be disruptive to the process of getting a clear decision to live and remove any threat of suicide.

Therapist: It sounds like you still miss your dog. But tell me what happened after the dog died.
Client: Life just went on — got busy making plans for the summer.
Therapist: Was it a sad time?
Client: Yeah. I spent the whole summer working and running around with my friends and I remember that I thought this should be a happy time before college. But it wasn't.

Here the therapist is seeing a distinct pattern: a loss, failure to get closure, and low-grade ongoing depression. The next step is to get the client in touch with an "early scene." This is the scene where the idea was originally established for this way of dealing with loss.

Therapist: Tell me about an early time in your life when you were depressed.
Client: [long pause] I guess that would be when my grandmother died. I was the only one at home when my grandfather called. He asked me to tell my mother to come quickly. I rode my bike to church where she was at choir practice and told Mother that Grandma was ill and Grandpa wanted her to come right away. She became hysterical and hurried away and left me standing all alone at the church. Later that night she called and I overheard her say to my grandfather, "What shall we tell the kids?" She told me everything was O.K. and to go to bed, she'd be home later. Somehow I knew it wasn't true but I didn't say

anything. The next morning she told me that Grandma had died. I just acted nonchalant. But I was real sad.

Therapist: What happened then?

Client: I just went on—feeling sad and not telling anyone.

Here we have a pertinent early scene—the experience where the client's protocol for dealing with loss was established. The therapist can imagine the client deciding that what he thought and needed was unimportant. The strategy for the therapist now that the protocol is evident is to get the client to reexperience the scene and discover the decision.

Therapist: I want you to recall that scene. Imagine your mother telling you that your grandmother died. How old are you? What do you think and feel?

Client: It was a long time ago. I was 9.

Therapist: Yes, but it appears to be still fresh to you.

Client: Yeah . . . I feel like I'm 9 years old and nobody cares about me. [The client is looking sad at this point.]

Therapist: Feel the sadness and tell me what you are thinking.

Client: [looking very sad] I really loved Grandma. She used to sit with me on the porch swing and give me treats. I remember I called her graham cracker and she was offended. I didn't mean it that way. I was just letting her know how much I liked being with her. Like I liked graham crackers. When Mother told me she was dead I thought, who will be so good to me? Yeah. She was dead and there wouldn't be anyone to be close to like her. I felt sad.

Therapist: Do you feel sad now?

Client: Yeah. I am sad when I think about it.

Therapist: Stay with the sadness and imagine your mother in front of you. Tell her what's going on inside.

Client: Mom. [pause] I can't tell her.

Therapist: Say, "Mom, I can't tell you what I feel because. . . ."

Client: Mom, I can't tell you what I feel because you're so sad. Without Grandma, I don't have anybody. I wish I had died too.

Therapist: Say that again: "I wish I had died too."

Client: [tearing some] Mom, I wish I had died too. You are too sad to help me and I don't have anybody.

Here the therapist will want to give the client time to feel the feelings and hear that decision and express the feeling. Then the therapist will set up the scene for a new decision as follows:

Therapist: Will you tell your mom what you need and want?

Client: I will, but it won't do any good.

Therapist: Say it anyway. Imagine your mother in front of you and say, "I know it won't do any good but I feel . . . and I want. . . ."

Client: I know it won't do any good, but I feel all alone and helpless and I know that no one will ever love me like Grandma. I need someone to take care of me, and you can't and no one will. I wish I had died like Grandma. [Here the therapist hears an implicit decision to kill him or herself: If I didn't exist I wouldn't feel this pain. I'm all alone and nobody cares.]

At this point the decision becomes clear to the therapist, and the client has said what he is thinking and feeling in the original scene. It is now appropriate to call for a redecision. To do this the therapist will need to provide rational (Adult) information to the client.

Therapist: Do you see the similarity in these three scenes? You suffer a loss, you don't reach out for comfort, repress your thoughts and feelings, and decide that all is hopeless—that you might as well die?

Client: Yeah . . . the dynamics seem the same. I guess I decided that since I can't get what I want I should just die.

Therapist: That's how it sounds to me. Would you like to change that decision?

Client: Yeah. I don't want to die or kill myself. I want to live and be happy. That's why I'm here.

Therapist: That's why I'm here too! Now, imagine your mother in front of you and say that to her.

Here the therapist will want to make sure that the affect and the words of the client are congruent.

Client: Mom, I know that you were suffering when your mother died, but I needed you. I needed you to understand that Grandma was my only source of comfort during those days. You and Dad were fighting, and I was all alone. I needed to be taken care of . . . I needed someone to talk to, and since you weren't there for me, I decided I would be better off dead. [pause] So I decided to be tough, even if it killed me. That was a long time ago. Now I am going to live. I will not destroy myself.

Therapist: Say that again.

Client: I am going to live. I will not destroy myself.

Therapist: No matter what?

Client: I will not destroy myself, no matter what. I will live.

Therapist: What are you feeling?

Client: I'm a little sad but mostly happy. I feel excited.

Therapist: What's going on in your body?

Client: I'm breathing easy. I feel my chest moving. I feel kind of proud.

The report of relief is the prime indicator of a new decision. When this occurs the therapist needs to move the client out of the past scene and into the present. If the therapeutic work is being done in a group setting, have the client announce his decision to the group; if the work is in individual treatment, have the client make eye contact with you and announce the new decision.

Therapist: Look around the group. Look at the expressions on people's faces. Be aware of the empathy they feel for you and the happiness in their faces and say to them, "I will not destroy myself no matter what. I will live."

Client: [looks at the group] I will not destroy myself. I will live.

Therapist: I will not destroy myself no matter what. I will live no matter what.

Client: I will not destroy myself no matter what. I will live no matter what. That feels real good.

Therapist: It feels good to us, too. Look at how moved the people in the room are. By letting us know what you are feeling and thinking *we* can be helpful to you. By making a decision to live *you* can be helpful to you. Is there anything else you want to say to the group?

Client: Just thank you—thank you for being here.

Therapist: Thank *you* for being here—you have helped us all.

At this point the redecision is complete. You will want to instruct the client to bring this decision to mind any time he feels depressed. You may also want to give the group members the opportunity to congratulate the client for the work.

Lethal Injunctions and Further Clinical Work

Coming out of this redecision work are several other significant pieces of therapeutic work that will need to be addressed in the course of therapy: closing the scenes with his girlfriend, his grandmother, and his dog by saying goodbye. The issues with his mother around her unavailability will also need to be addressed in the course of treatment. However, *the decision not to destroy himself has to be made first.* The other issues will come up or may be brought up by the therapist. One further note: It is probably not best to pursue further work during this session, as it would tend to dissipate the intensity of the redecision.

Redecision Process and Procedures
for Dealing with Lethal Injunctions

Whether at intake or in the course of treatment, when lethal injunctions are encountered either in the client's narrative or in the therapist's intuition it is imperative that the therapist obtain a clear, congruent statement from the client that she or he will not kill him- or herself or anyone else, or go crazy accidentally or intentionally, no matter what. It is imperative for both the client's and the therapist's protection. If you cannot get a clear decision from the client to live and a decision not to obey lethal injunctions it will be necessary to provide the client with protection, that is, to hospitalize the client or make a satisfactory arrangement for the client's safety before you end contact.

Dealing With Client Resistance

Frequently the client will say, "I can't say that." The therapist counters with, "You can! Are you saying you won't?" This often leads to, "I can but I won't mean it." The therapist says, "Will you say the words 'I will not kill myself no matter what'? It doesn't matter whether you believe it just now." This may take some time and work but your objective is to get the person to say the words aloud. After you have been successful in getting the client to say the words, check out the feelings: if relief is not reported, have him or her say it again and again until she or he reports some relief. You may have to deal with many diversions and varying levels of resistance as you proceed. You may have to matter-of-factly tell the client that a decision to live is imperative before therapy can proceed. You may have to tell the client that you will not let him or her out of your office until she or he has made a decision to live. Whatever you have to do, hang tough. Your ace in the hole is that the client's natural healthy self *wants* to live and *needs* an ally. You will have to gain the confidence of that most natural part of the client (the Natural Child ego state). Whatever it takes, the therapist has to gain the confidence of the client and become an ally with the natural healthy self and elicit a decision to live. This is the basis of the therapeutic alliance.

The Redecision Process

1. Begins with a feeling in the present
2. Establishes the scenario that resulted in the feeling
3. Identifies a time (scene) when those same feelings were present, in or about adolescence
4. Identifies the events that preceded the feeling and what transpired as a result of the feeling
5. Identifies an early scene, best during the first few years of life where the same feeling was present
   a. Identifies the events that transpired to evoke the feeling
   b. Identifies the action and/or decision that was a result of the feelings
6. Brings this sequence to the client's awareness
7. Sets the stage for the client to reenter the scene, feeling its full impact and expressing the feelings and thoughts that were repressed in the original scene
8. Calls for a redecision—a decision not to kill self or others or go crazy
9. Provides the client a process to reinforce the new decision in contact with others in the here and now
10. Instructs the client to recall this decision anytime she or he feels the old familiar feeling and/or slips into lethal ideation
11. Directs the client to make an agreement to contact you or another therapist if suicidal, homicidal, or insanity ideation becomes an issue in the future.

Post Script

Lethal ideation is the result of the "script" in transactional analysis, and while becoming a trained transactional analyst is a matter of personal choice, almost all therapeutic persuasions acknowledge the existence of scripts as they account for pathological activity. Lethal activities are viewed by all therapies and psychological theories as pathological. Therefore, no matter what your theoretical orientation, it is important to have a systematic and effective method of dealing with lethal ideation and activity. Redecision therapy is the best and most effective way the author knows to deal with these issues. Regardless of your theoretical orientation, adding a thorough understanding of redecision processes to your intervention techniques will deepen your effectiveness.

References

Phillips, R. D. (1975). *Structural Symbiotic Systems*. Chapel Hill, NC: privately published.

5

Childhood Scenes in Redecision Therapy

Mary McClure Goulding, M.S.W.

Clients make redecisions when they are stuck in childhood decisions that are hurtful or impede growth in their current lives. These redecisions are often made in the context of an early childhood scene.

Sometimes these scenes actually occurred, and sometimes they are the client's beliefs about what occurred. In the field of psychotherapy, the controversies about real and false memory syndrome arise because therapists think they must judge the validity of each scene a client reports. Therapists are not detectives, judges, or members of juries. Their job has never been to discover truth. Their function is to help clients deal as well as possible with their own present lives. Past scenes are helpful in this task.

In general, I believe my clients, and I know that my belief is not an issue. What is important is that the client recover from the past, real and imagined, and go on to a fulfilling life. I tell a client, "A person who grew up in Dachau deserves to leave the concentration camp. It is appalling to continue to spend one's life in a concentration camp that was abolished years ago. I will work with you so that you can stop living in your personal Dachau. I'll work as fast as I know how, so that you don't have to spend an extra minute in horror or tragedy." Any other goal would shortchange a client.

In transactional analysis terminology, we speak of injunctions, decisions, and redecisions. Injunctions are irrational messages given by parents, other family members, society, and sometimes by fate, as when a parent dies while the child is young. Childhood decisions are made in response to such injunctions. Redecisions are new decisions that change or supplant the early, childhood decisions. Here are some examples of the use of childhood scenes in redecision work with clients:

Injunction: Don't Exist

Decisions: If things don't get better I'll kill myself. I'll kill myself and then you'll be sorry. I am worthless and I might as well be dead.

Necessary redecisions: I will not kill myself. I'll take care of myself. I am not worthless. I am unique and valuable to myself.

Scene: Clients return in imagination to specific, remembered scenes in which they felt unwanted, unloved, or burdensome. One client, who was often physically abused, remembers being beaten for wetting his bed. He wished he'd die. "I wish my father would kill me and get it over with." He reexperiences his childhood agony, and then realizes, "In spite of everything, I survived. I didn't try to kill myself then, and I shouldn't now." He imagines saying to his father, "In spite of what you are doing to me, I am going to keep on living." Reentering the scene as his adult self, the client imagines holding the wounded child of the past and saying, "I am proud that you survived so well under such terrible circumstances. I am not going to kill you. I'll take care of you and be good to you. I'll keep you safe."

Scene: The client chooses a scene of great poverty in his home and imagines returning to it. As a child, he believes that his very presence is too much for them. There are too many children in the family and not enough food. He feels guilt and sadness, and then realizes, "Too many children in one family was not my doing, it was yours, Mom and Dad. I am not responsible for your irresponsibility." Another client, also working with the issue of chronic poverty, said, "Yeah, it was hard for you. You didn't know what to do. We all survived even though life was so hard. Thanks for keeping us alive. And now I will keep me alive."

Each childhood scene is remembered and chosen by the client, who is encouraged first to say and feel what was real at the time the scene took place, and then to make new discoveries within the scene. Sometimes this is done in a single session, and sometimes it takes several sessions.

Injunction: Don't Trust or Don't Be Intimate

Decision: I'll never trust (a man, a woman, anyone) again.

Necessary redecision: I will take my mother's (father's) face off the rest of the world. I will find a man (a woman) whom I can trust and love.

Scene: A client recalls the day her father deserted the family. She brings him back in fantasy and tells him, "Hey, Dad, I've been looking all over the country to find men as worthless as you, and unfortunately I found a lot of them. Only worthless men seemed exciting to me. Well, screw that." Her redecision is, "I am going to look for men who are trustworthy. I know they exist and I know I can find one. I will find one."

Scene: The client is a child, lying on his bed, sobbing. He worked all summer in the cornfields, and now he has discovered that his alcoholic mother has stolen all the money he had saved. As he relives his remembered scene, he experiences his despair, his rage, and his decision never to trust anyone again. He pounds a pillow and shrieks at his mother. When his rage has dissipated, the therapist asks him to recognize his childhood strength and endurance as he worked in those cornfields and feel proud of himself, in spite of what his mother did to him. "Yeah, and that's another decision I made, that I'd do whatever it took to escape those cornfields. That turned out to be a good decision." All his adult life, he has worked hard and success-fully. "I am proud of myself." He sits back, relaxed, and later reports to his therapy group, "I feel myself melting . . . not myself . . . what's melting is my armor. I am softer, and I think I do want love. I will look for love. I think I can accept love now. All women are not my mother."

Injunction: Don't Grow

Decision: I'm too little, too weak, too helpless, or too stupid for adult tasks.

Necessary redecision: I am an adult and function as one.

Scene: The client picks a scene at night before bedtime, when his older brother is doing the client's homework for him. The therapist asks the client to experiment with the scene. "Pretend that you were born first instead of last. How would you be different?" "Well, there's still my mother to do my homework for me. Or my father." The client sighs. "If I am oldest and smartest, it would be fun to know I can do my own work. It must be fun to feel competent." He sighs. Several sessions later, he makes the redecision, "I'm tired of playing around and whining and doing nothing until somebody rescues me. I missed out on feeling smart. I was not stupid! I was lazy! I am tired of believing I am cute and wonderful and the family idiot!" As in all redecision work, personal change in a present scene is also essential in order to make the redecision stick. In a present scene the client says, "I have flunked the licensing exam three times. Now, I am going to sign up for the pre-exam course and I am going to hire a tutor. Not to give me answers, but to help me learn how to learn effectively. That will make a fundamental difference in my life."

Scene: The client remembers a scene in the living room with his mother. She calls him "baby" for the millionth time. He confronts her, "Hey, Ma, you may need a baby, but I am grown up. I am no longer your baby! I am walking out the front door this minute, and crossing the street even though you think that is too dangerous for me, and I'm going to the library and read a book about chess."

Injunction: Don't Be the Sex you Are

Decision: I am a girl in a man's body, so I don't fit anywhere.

Redecision: I accept myself as I am and I fit for me.

Scene: The client is on the school playground, where other boys are calling him "sissy" and physically abusing him. He is crying. He feels his pain, his self-loathing, and then states that their behavior, not his, is loathsome. He says, "No matter what you boys think, I am acceptable as I am." Briefly, he wishes he had the courage to fight them, but then he says, "No, I am a person who doesn't fight physically, and I admire that in myself. I like the part of me that can't fight. I really do. Wow, I still believe I am more female than male, but I'm not ashamed of who I am."

At another session, the client enters the same scene and, as his adult self, leads the child away from his tormentors. He promises to honor and protect the child from now on, and then decides to explore self-defense classes, to *learn* to protect the child inside him.

Decision: I have to be a servant to men, because I am female. I don't want to be a girl.

Redecision: I am a woman and I can choose what jobs I'll do.

Scene: A client is at the family dinner table as a child, helping her mother serve the men and boys. Afterwards, she and her mother will clean the dining room, wash the dishes, and set up the table for the next meal. "I hate this scene! I hate my damned servitude. I spent my childhood being a slave to the men in the family, and that's why I wished I'd been born a boy. What I want to do is throw the food in their faces, those complacent men . . . my uncle, my father, my brothers . . . I will no longer be their slave!" She fantasies throwing the food at them, and then, laughing, walks proudly out of the family home. That evening, she tells her husband, "It's not you I resent, it's the roles I thought we had to play. I don't have to be the family servant, just because I'm female. I am not cooking and serving our food. I earn a good living and so do you. We can hire a maid, cater dinners, or just snack. Or, if you choose to cook, you can. I am not cooking again until . . . unless I choose to cook for pleasure, and I doubt if I'll ever get that healthy. But I am learning that I can like being female, when I separate being a girl from being a slave."

Injunction: Don't Be a Child

Decision: I'll take care of my younger brothers and sisters, and I'll resent them forever.

Redecision: I am not my brother's keeper, or anyone else's.

Scene: The client imagines being in the park with "the little kids," taking care of them until her mother returns from work. After voicing her anger at constant babysitting and her sorrow at missing out on being childlike, she decides, "O.K., kids, you're nice enough and it's not your fault that you are little. But enough's enough. There should be an age when you can take care of yourselves." She imagines all of them, who are now between 30 and 40 years old, sitting together in her living room. She says, "You are on your own. I do mean that. I will no longer burden you with my fine, social worker advice. I won't lend you money. You don't need me and I think we'll be better friends now that I know this."

Injunction: Don't Have Fun

Decision: I'll work hard and never play.

Redecision: I'll learn to have fun.

Scene: It's an every-Saturday scene from childhood. The client and his parents have worked all day, cleaning and gardening. In the scene, the client screams, "This is a terrible way to live! Who cares if there are a few weeds in the garden and a little dirt on the floor? Your problem is you don't know how to have fun and be a child, so you don't let me be a child either. And now here I am, an adult, and I'm just like you. Well, I'm going to change. I don't know how, I really don't. But I am going to start by asking the members of this group to tell me what they do for fun on weekends, and I'll get suggestions from everyone I know. At age 50, I am going to begin to be a child." He went back in fantasy to the backyard where he and his parents are pulling weeds. He says to them, "I'm leaving now. I am going to town to play. I'm going to town to learn what fun is all about." He fantasizes being in town, watching children who are smiling and laughing. He takes time to bounce a ball, to swing, to go to the nearby creek to watch frogs catch flies. Imagining this, he smiles broadly, and chuckles to himself.

In these scenes, the clients played themselves as children and gave themselves new responses. In addition, it may be useful for the client to take the parts of the others in the scenes, in order to understand them better. For example, in a scene in which parents divorce, the client may need to be each parent in order to understand them better and to realize emotionally as well as intellectually that the child actually is not responsible for the behavior of parents.

Another useful technique is to treat the scene as if it were a dream, in which the client plays all roles and accepts the parts of himself that each role exemplifies. The boy who is bullied for being a sissy may need to know the bully in himself. The girl who is a slave to men may discover that she has autocratic aspects to herself and expects others to serve her, just as the men in the family expected her to serve them.

These are very brief samples of ways to use early scenes in redecision psychotherapy. With the therapist's encouragement, clients will find their own specific scenes, experience their original emotions, thoughts, and actions in these scenes, and then use their own words to make their own redecisions. Each scene will be unique, just as the original decisions and the present redecisions are unique.

After redecision work, which may take only a session or two, clients need to practice using their redecisions in their current lives.

Practice is essential, in order to reinforce the decisions. Even though redecision work may be done quickly, the need for reenforcement may continue over a much longer period of time. Clients who redecide to value themselves, to trust and to love others, to learn to play, to function in new and different ways, may continue in therapy as they experience their triumphs and setbacks in their ongoing quest for a more satisfying life.

6

The Importance
of Saying Goodbye

Charles F. Vorkoper, M.S.S.W.

Saying goodbye is an important part of redecision therapy. Goodbye is a Natural Child activity. We all carry within us a healthy and natural process that allows us to let go of our losses. We lose people, things, ideas, ideals, hopes, dreams, locations, and more throughout our lives. Even undesirable parts of our lives may require a tearful goodbye. When we make use of our natural, healing grief process we move past the loss, and our lives are richer and more satisfying. Successful grief work is empowering—the kind of empowerment that is the goal of redecision therapy.

> "I loved,
>> which was purgatory.
> I lost,
>> which was hell.
> and I survived,
>> Heaven!"

[Colgrove, Bloomfield, and McWilliams, 1976, p. 119]

Healthy Goodbyes

Healthy goodbyes are a process in which we let go and get on with life. Each person has a unique process. For one person a flood of tears may be critical to wash the loss from his or her life. For another the process may involve fewer tears and more nurturance from other people. What is critical is that people take the goodbye time to let go of what is lost. Carrying around the ghosts and shrines of the past becomes very heavy, as we shall see.

The complex, healthy goodbye process has been studied by many people. The model most relevant to redecision therapy has been described as a task model (Valente and McIntyre 1996). The goodbye tasks described include: managing feelings, finding meaning, restoring and maintaining integrity, and realigning relationships. These are similar to Lindemann's description of the healthy grief process (Lindemann 1979). He describes three tasks: 1) emancipation from the bondage of the deceased that involves an acceptance of painful and intense emotions; 2) readjustment to the environment in which the deceased (or loss) is missing. In this task the person does an active review of events that preceded the loss. The person also recalls experiences with the deceased (or loss); 3) the formation of new relationships. "This involves a gradual rehearsal and testing of new patterns of interactions and role relationships that can replace some of the functions the deceased fulfilled in the survivor's life" (Lindemann 1979, p. 170).

The Problem When People Don't Say Goodbye

When people do not say goodbye the loss hangs on and interferes with the conduct of life. Sometimes the interference means a dulled life. At other times, interference may take the form of negatively defining life.

In an evening lecture on dreams, Jill asked me to discuss a recurring dream. In her dream a little girl must say goodbye to her father. He is dying. She does not want to say goodbye in the hope that if she never says goodbye he will continue to live. At the end of the dream Jill feels sad. When she awakes she feels confused. She said that the little girl in the dream was about 7 years old. I asked Jill about herself and she reported that she was 57 years old. She lived alone and was basically very lonely. She appeared to be withered, and was very thin with dark eyes (like some of Picasso's paintings). She claimed that she had experienced no major losses in her life. When I asked if her parents were alive she said that her father died when she was young. When she said that she was 7 when he died, the room became very still. Jill's face darkened even more and she became aware that in some ways, her life had paused beginning with her father's death. She said that she did not cry very much at the time of his death but bravely went on with her life. I suggested that it might be the time to find a therapist to help her do her crying.

Jill's life had been on hold for fifty years. Jill and the many people who have not allowed themselves to say goodbye live marginal lives. Jill stands as a symbol for the many clients I have had. They need to say goodbye but their unfinished mourning blocks their energy and their capacity to live full lives.

Erich Lindemann, in his landmark article, "Symptomatology and Management of Acute Grief" (Lindemann 1969), describes two kinds of "morbid grief reactions." The first is a delay or postponement of reaction. This happens when the loss occurs at a time when the person is confronted with important tasks, or when postponement is important to maintain the morale of others. The delay may last for years. The feeling may reappear as a spontaneous eruption. It may begin after another loss or trauma. When the feelings about this new loss begin, the memories of the earlier loss intrude into the grief work about the recent loss. Joe's new wife, Jackie, is threatening to leave him, saying that he is frequently distant to her. Joe responds by becoming depressed, so depressed that he can't go to work and spends most of his time in bed. He talks about ending his life. Jackie, frightened, asks him to call the local suicide and crisis center. He does and the volunteer talks with Joe and finds that the threat of Jackie leaving brings up his feelings about his first wife's suicide. After this suicide, Joe was so busy taking care of the business affairs that the first wife left and her family's turmoil after her death that he never took time to say goodbye. He tried to carry on with his life until Jackie threatened him with a second lost relationship. The crisis center phone volunteer convinced Joe to enter a bereavement group for those who had lost a loved one through suicide. There he was able to say goodbye to his first wife for the first time and was encouraged to enter therapy to help him with his second marriage. Joe's experience is a familiar one to people who work in telephone crisis centers.

When survivors begin to do grief work in a bereavement group or in individual therapy, they frequently talk about their loss as if it happened yesterday, although the actual loss may have occurred years ago. As these individuals work through their grief they frequently experience their loss as further and further in the past. One implication of this delay is that important aspects of the individual's life are paused or suspended until the bereavement work is done. Some people never mourn, and suffer their entire lives. Examples of the effect of this suspension in survivors include difficulty with the expression of emotions, difficulty with concentration, creating distance in relationships and, especially in the case of survivors of suicide, the increased likelihood that they will be suicidal.

Lindemann's second type of morbid grief reaction is distorted reactions. He lists nine behaviors that may imply an underlying unresolved grief reaction (Lindemann 1979). People with these reactions show up frequently in therapists' offices and agencies. They are diagnosed in a variety of ways. It is important that redecision therapists see the reaction as a possible distorted reaction to loss.

1. *Overactivity without a sense of loss.* The activity is frequently similar to activities carried out by the deceased. A son may choose his deceased father's profession and energetically try to do this profession like his father. He stays very busy but the

business never works out as well as it did under his father. He never feels the sadness about the loss of his father.

2. *Acquiring symptoms that belonged to the deceased's last illness.* Mary's father died of colon cancer and now she is diagnosed with ulcerative colitis. Colitis preceded her father's diagnosis of cancer.

3. *Development of psychosomatic conditions.* Lindemann studied ulcerative colitis, rheumatoid arthritis, and asthma and found them linked to distorted grief reactions after a tragic fire in Boston.

4. *Social adjustment changes,* especially a conspicuous alteration in the relationship with friends and relatives—usually progressive social isolation. After Charlie died, Alma spent more and more of her time with her grandchildren on their farm. She spent less and less time with her adult friends. She seemed to be happy with the children but as time went on the children began to ask their mother why their grandmother was so sad.

5. *Furious hostility against specific persons may be present.* People are sometimes angry at the doctor who tried to save their loved one.

6. *Some hide their hostility and become wooden and formal.* After Peter's father left his mother he began to become more serious and developed a formal stance toward teachers and fellow students in school. While everyone was surprised at his great posture, they wondered why he had become so stiff.

7. *There is a loss of patterns of social interaction but an eagerness to have interaction.* Jim talks about wanting to date after his divorce in very excited terms. He rarely manages to arrange a date and when he does get a date, "something comes up." He stays angry and lonely and wonders why he can't get a date. He talks about his divorce very seldomly and none of his friends recalls seeing him cry after his wife left.

8. *The person is active but most of the activities become detrimental to the person's own social and economic existence without any awareness of the negative consequences to self and others.* After his wife's

death, Bob stays very busy all the time at work. He spends much of his time organizing employee events for the company, raising money for the United Way, and being president of the local Rotary Club. He is baffled and disappointed when his employer expresses dissatisfaction with his productivity on the job.

9. *A grief reaction can take the form of a straight, agitated depression with tensions, agitation, insomnia, feelings of worthlessness, bitter self-accusation, and expressed need for punishment.* Such a person may be dangerously suicidal.

Bob and Mary Goulding (Goulding and Goulding 1989) frame the problem of an interfering, unresolved grief reaction in terms of positive intent behind the symptoms. They talk about an "if only" morass following trauma. The continual dwelling on "if only" is an attempt to rewrite history so that the present will not be painful. It is pretense to assume that the person has a second chance. "If only" Mary had visited her mother the mother would not have died. Mary is trying to avoid the pain of her goodbye.

A second device some use to avoid mourning is to try to get over the trauma too quickly. People who use this device try to diminish the significance of the traumatic event by attempting to rush their good-byes. They do not respect that they have a Natural Child way to say goodbye and that way takes its own time—regardless of the person's hurry.

Both of these are self-deceiving ways to avoid a painful experience after trauma. According to the Gouldings (Goulding and Goulding 1979), the problem with these attempted solutions is that people keep a part of their "energy locked in yesterdays. They may refuse intimacy in the present and experience extreme difficulties with current 'hellos' and 'good-byes'" (p. 175).

Assisting Goodbyes

Redecision therapy helps people keep current with saying goodbye through helping people stay aware of their current experience. As people have losses, they are mourned as long as that person's goodbye process requires. In redecision group therapy, the group offers an effective mourning support system during the group session and between therapy sessions. Group members are encouraged to express their feelings and receive support for getting their personal needs met during a time when they are saying goodbye. An important part of this process is to ask the group members to create a unique goodbye experience for each person. Mourning individuals are encouraged to have their feelings in safety as they are experiencing their loss, to find meaning in the loss for them, to sustain their personal sense of integrity, and to find new patterns of relationships.

Redecision therapy uses a variety of methods to assist people with unsaid goodbyes to the losses of the past—the ones to which they are devoting personal energy (Goulding and Goulding 1979). Their formula has five steps:

1. Being clear about the fact of the loss
2. Dealing with unfinished business with the lost person or other loss, including expressing regrets and appreciations
3. Having a goodbye ceremony, frequently using a funeral and burial ceremony
4. Briefly and simply informing the client about the mourning that is going on and its purpose
5. Saying hello to today.

The following exchanges take place in several ongoing redecision group sessions. The context of each group session is slightly different for each exchange. The examples are brought together to illustrate the flow of work with someone whose life is affected by an unsaid goodbye. There are times when this work is done during one session. Usually it takes more than one.

Step 1 — The Fact of the Loss

Jack was a 35-year-old engineer. His father died when he was a teenager. His mother remarried a few years after the death of his father. Because he liked this new man in his life he does not remember a lot of sadness about losing his father. Now he has come to therapy to deal with his depression. In the examples that follow, the aspect of his depression that he is working on is the way he deals with his stepchildren.

Jack: I get so angry when they act just like their father.
Therapist: Talk about what it's like for you to be angry like this.
Jack: I didn't act like that when my mother remarried. I adjusted and went on with my new father.
Therapist: Just like your first father did not die.
Jack: He was dead and I had a new father. Why should I carry on with all those feelings?
Therapist: Jack, your father died. There is no substitute for him. He is dead and lost.
Jack: [his eyes beginning to water] I know.

Step 2 — Dealing with Unfinished Business

Therapist: Is there anything you would like to say to him right now? If so, put your father in that chair [points to an empty chair].
Jack: [crying throughout] Goodbye, Dad. I still miss you. Why did you have to die?
Therapist: Now will you move to Dad's chair and hear your father's response?
Jack: [for father] Jack, I'm sorry for you. I did not want to leave you. My heart was so bad that I could not live.
Therapist: [motioning Jack back to his seat] Respond to your father.
Jack: I regret that you had heart trouble. Why didn't you take care of yourself? I want you to be healthy and alive. [cries]

Therapist: [with gestures encourages Jack to continue to change chairs throughout his conversation with father] Hear father's response.

Jack: [as father] The doctors couldn't help me, Jack. I'm sorry.

Jack: [as himself] Thanks for telling me you're sorry. I didn't know you felt that way. I thought you didn't care.

Therapist: Jack, tell your father what you appreciated about your life together.

Jack: Dad, I loved all the trips we took together. And when you were there in the stands when I played baseball. I especially remember you saying goodnight every night you were at home. I felt so safe and happy in my bed. Thanks, Dad. [is silent for a moment, then continues] I could never tell him how lonely I was because he worked such long hours and was out of town on business trips so much.

Therapist: Tell him now.

Jack: [to father] Every time you left home or worked late, I thought you would never come back and I used to lay awake at night wishing you would be there to say goodnight. Sometimes I would wait up, hoping I would be awake when you came home. I felt so lonely. You never noticed how lonely I was.

Therapist: Dad, will you respond to Jack?

Jack: [in father's chair] I was so caught up with my business during the day. I thought about you a lot but I just kept going.

Therapist: [motioning him back to Jack's chair] Jack, tell Dad about your regrets.

Jack: Dad, I regret that I never told you how much I loved you. I wanted to many times but I got scared, or somebody interrupted.

Jack: [in father's chair] I'm sorry there wasn't time in our lives, son. But I hear you say that now and I feel warm and wonderful.

Jack: [in Jack's chair] Thanks, Dad.

Therapist: Jack, have you finished with Dad for now?

Jack: Yes. I'm finished. I'm feeling sort of peaceful now.

Step 3—Have a Goodbye Ceremony

(in another later session)

> *Jack:* I've been thinking about my father a lot this past week. It's weird—like he is still around. I feel like he is a ghost. I want to finish my goodbyes with him.
>
> *Therapist:* Tell him goodbye now. I want you to imagine that he is here in his casket in this room. You can say what you need to say to him now. Stand next to the casket and talk to him.
>
> *Jack:* [crying] Dad, I needed you and you were not there. [He becomes aware of other aspects of his relationship with his father and shares them with his dad. After Jack has finished speaking, the therapist continues.]
>
> *Therapist:* When you are ready, say to him "You are dead, Dad," and say goodbye in a way that feels right to you.
>
> *Jack:* You are dead, dad. Goodbye [stands silently, crying].
>
> *Therapist:* Imagine the burial ceremony and go through this now, using words to describe what you are doing.

Jack continues to cry as he describes his father's burial. After he finishes the group members spontaneously get up and hug him. After receiving everyone's hugs, Jack sits down and appears ready to go on.

Step 4—Inform About the Goodbye Process

> *Therapist:* Jack, I think you have had an important experience saying goodbye to your father today and you may continue to feel some sadness for a time.

Jack's tears gradually cease and he acknowledges what has been said nonverbally.

Step 5—Say Hello to Today

Therapist: Look around you at the other members of this group [he does]. Think about what you want from them right now.

Jack: I want them all to tell me I will be all right.

Therapist: Will you look at each person and let them tell you how you will be all right with them? [He does and group members respond warmly and reassuringly to Jack.]

Jack: [Everyone is silent for a while when he sits down.] Thank you.

Therapist: Be aware, Jack, that we are here for you.

Jack: I know that now.

Jack has some more work to do. He will feel rushes of sadness in a variety of settings. He will feel sad on anniversaries of his father's death and perhaps other anniversaries significant for him. But now he begins to respond to the present needs of his stepchildren. They are no longer him. He no longer gets into angry speeches with them and willingly listens to them and is happy to tuck them in bed at night lovingly. His relationship with his wife has improved and he reports being able to communicate with her much better.

When they do enough of the grief work, patients have energy for their present lives. They may use this energy to do further redecision work. I use the word "enough" to mean that I am not implying that this is the end of their sadness about this loss. Grieving, even of arrested grief, may go on for a long time. It can go on while the patient is doing other things in therapy and in life. Redecision therapists stay aware that this grieving may come up from time to time. When this happens, the response is to encourage the natural grief process and to get support and affirmation for the individual to continue.

There are many ways redecision therapists invite patients to unlock "frozen" grief. Some patients come to therapy because they want help dealing with a loss. At other times patients get in touch with unfinished grief when they access childhood memories. They find they want to say goodbye to someone or something important before they proceed further with redecision work. Redecision therapists and clients become aware of unfinished goodbyes as they work in the present moment. People experience feelings of grief and sadness and get unstuck in the present. So long as someone is aware of his or her present experience, he or she will feel any unfinished goodbyes and have the opportunity to finish saying goodbye.

There are a myriad of losses other than death that require saying goodbye. Some that require special attention include losing someone to a suicidal death, a SIDS child, or a divorce. Special programs and support groups exist in many communities for these kinds of problems and can be an important adjunct to therapy. There are other kinds of losses that people often do not recognize as meaningful. Some of these include loss of ideals or dreams, loss of parts of the body or body functions (as in aging), and loss of fantasized biological children or grandchildren (as with infertile couples). Goodbye ceremonies may be useful for these less tangible loss experiences as well.

Cultural issues are important in response to loss. Mourning customs, the significance of certain losses, the amount of emotional expression, the length of the mourning process are a few of the differences between cultures. Orthodox Jewish people have mourning traditions that are a whole family experience. People born in rural America with important European connections and memories frequently expect losses, especially death, to be followed by large, extended family gatherings. When people live a large distance from their families of origin, difficulty with loss is compounded by missing the extended family rituals and gatherings that help mourn losses. George, raised in a large Polish area of Chicago, moved out of state to live with his Italian bride. He felt the family would never accept her and he wanted to find freedom and his own life. When his father died he experienced great pain. In addition to the loss of his father, he was also missing the closeness of his Polish family and neighborhood that would have supported him had he stayed in Chicago. In therapy he found ways to substitute for this family while he did his mourning.

Saying Goodbye to Therapy

It is easy to say that the reason for entering therapy is to leave. However, leaving is frequently difficult. In group therapy patients have gotten familiar with an environment where they are accepted, where there is hope, where there are lots of positive strokes, and where others are changing as they want to change.

This experience was particularly poignant for me after the October I spent at Mt. Madonna with Bob and Mary Goulding in 1975. My month there was wonderful. I still have memories about the warmth, the training, the caring, the wonderful therapy, the delightful people, the beauty of the place. I even left with two people I came to like during the month to get to the airport. That was a splendid trip. When I did get home, I stayed on a kind of high for a while and then became depressed. It took me a while to be present where I lived with my spouse and my work. I mourned the experience at Mt. Madonna. I lost my "month." There have been Octobers since then when I have had an anniversary experience—sadness about my "month."

Because leaving therapy is a loss, it must be given attention. Endings in individual or family redecision therapy are best planned by patient and therapist. In time-limited groups, ending should be planned with a closing exercise or ceremony. This is prepared for in a previous session. In my open-ended groups I have made it a practice to ask patients to give three weeks notice when leaving therapy, announced at the beginning of the session. This notice gives the patient the opportunity to say goodbye to the experience and the people in the group as well as the therapist. This is done even though many patients come back to group for more work at a later time; the present leaving is an end—a loss. I ask patients to decide how they will say goodbye and make a plan to do so. At the last session I make sure that their plan gets top billing and they have a chance to say goodbye as they planned. This gives the other group members an opportunity to deal with their loss as well. They are losing a group member who has shared in significant ways in their lives. One of the reasons for doing this is to use this opportunity to teach people how to say goodbye to the losses in their lives. They can then stay current with their goodbyes.

Releasing the energy people tie up in holding on to unsaid goodbyes is experienced as very powerful. People report feeling lighter, more free, joyous, energetic, and centered. To have unsaid goodbyes means to live life referring to the past and to a sad event in the past. To say goodbye means to be free to live in the present. Sometimes patients report that they feel newborn. They are like an infant, unfettered with losses and ready to be present for life in the world, attracting loving attention from others.

References

Colgrove, M., Bloomfield, H. H., and McWilliams, P. (1976). *How to Survive the Loss of a Love*. New York: Bantam.

Goulding, M. M., and Goulding, R. L. (1979). *Changing Lives through Redecision Therapy*. New York: Brunner/Mazel.

———— (1989). *Not to Worry!* New York: William Morrow.

Lindemann, E. (1979). *Beyond Grief: Studies in Crisis Intervention*. New York: Jason Aronson.

Valente, S. M., and McIntyre, L. (1996). Responding therapeutically to bereavement and grief. *Nursing and Allied Healthweek— Dallas/Fort Worth*, April 22, pp. 5–6.

7

Accessing the Natural Child as the Key to Redecision Therapy

Vann S. Joines, Ph.D.

As a practitioner and trainer in redecision therapy for over twenty years, I have been intrigued with what facilitates and shortens the redecision process. Having trained with Bob and Mary Goulding and observed their work over many years, I became aware of what skill they had in helping clients access their Natural Child ego state. Once the client was in Natural Child, the therapy process proceeded very quickly and easily. As I watched the Gouldings' work, did therapy myself, and trained other therapists in the redecision process, I began to realize that enabling clients to access and stay in touch with their Natural Child ego state was really the key to redecision therapy.

The Natural Child

Unless something goes wrong in utero, we come into the world as a natural, spontaneous child, which is the core of our being. As long as there is environmental support for our spontaneity, we feel excited. When our caretakers or others around us encounter something in our behavior that feels threatening to them, they withdraw their support. When environmental support for our spontaneity is withdrawn, we feel vulnerable. Thus, spontaneity with environmental support feels exciting; spontaneity without environmental support feels dangerous. As small children, when environmental support is withdrawn, the only way we have of explaining what has happened is to tell ourselves that there is something wrong with our feelings and needs, our behavior, or both. In order to regain the support of those around us, we decide to suppress that spontaneous, natural part of ourselves, with those particular feelings, needs, and behavior. The result is that we adapt our behavior in a way that regains environmental support, but gives up an important part of ourselves. Because we are no longer behaving in a way that feels threatening to the people around us, they resume taking care of us, or at least stop threatening us. From that point on, we feel vulnerable whenever we contemplate behaving in the way that previously resulted in a withdrawal of environmental support. In addition, we tend to work to justify why we shouldn't or couldn't behave in a spontaneous way now, in order to protect ourselves from those vulnerable feelings we experienced in the original situation. The price of our survival has been to relinquish a vital part of ourselves in similar situations: our Natural Child ego state.

Creating a Safe Environment

In order to aid clients in accessing and reclaiming the parts of their Natural Child that they have previously given up or set aside, the redecision therapist creates a "nurturing environment" (McNeel 1977) where it is safe to be spontaneous and experiment with behaviors that feel vulnerable. Creating a nurturing environment begins the moment the client walks in the door, as the therapist focuses on making effective contact with the client and looking for and positively stroking what is right about the client, in order to build on that. An example would be asking the client in the initial interview what he likes best about himself as an individual. The redecision therapist strokes the client for strength and health (McNeel 1977). She stays on the side of the Natural Child in the client by offering nonjudgmental caring and expressing "indignation at past injustices done to the client when he was a child" (McNeel, p. 431). The therapist also interrupts the client's own internal harassment of himself, and helps the client build an internal Nurturing Parent, who will be on his side as well. For example, when a client talks about how awful he is, the therapist might say, "You really are hard on yourself!" The therapist might also invite the client to see himself as a child in a situation in which he was getting a negative reaction from another person, and, from the Adult part of himself, see that he was simply being a normal, natural child. The therapist uses playfulness, humor, and fun to model being in Natural Child herself and to invite the client to feel safe in joining her by moving into his own Natural Child to have fun and enjoy the change process. Explicit procedural rules for confidentiality, safety, and protection are offered to establish clear boundaries.

Empowering Clients

Most clients initially come into therapy feeling like victims, since they felt helpless in childhood to prevent what was happening to them, and had to give up their spontaneity in some way and adapt to what other people around them wanted. The problem is that they are still seeing the world and themselves from that Adapted Child perspective. A goal of the redecision therapist is to help clients realize that they are not victims of life and circumstances, but powerful and autonomous individuals who can now reclaim the power and autonomy they gave up in childhood in order to survive. In accordance with this goal, the therapist listens carefully to clients' language and other ways they may be giving up their power and responsibility (McNeel 1977). Examples would be the client saying, "X happened to me" (instead of "I did X"), "I can't" (instead of "I won't"), "You are making me angry" (instead of "I'm feeling angry at you"). Another example of giving up one's power is talking in a very quiet voice. To assist clients in owning their power and responsibility, the therapist invites them to speak up, and to use the pronoun "I" and active verbs to experience being in charge of their lives rather than experiencing themselves as passive victims. The therapist also helps clients see that they are responsible for themselves, since they are the only ones that will ultimately live with the consequences of what they decide. The emphasis in redecision is always on helping clients take charge of their lives. Attention is paid to each transaction, since every transaction between therapist and client will reinforce either the client's Natural Child autonomy or the client's Adapted Child script (the life plan the individual decided on in childhood in order to survive) (Berne 1972).

The Individual's Internal Stroking Pattern and Use of Energy

When individuals are in their Adapted Child, they are in a closed energy system. The behavior of their Child ego state is used to take care of the needs of their internal Parent ego state rather than their own Natural Child needs. The internal Parent in turn strokes the Child for that behavior. Developmentally, this process began in childhood. As long as the parents did not encounter any behavior in their offspring that was threatening to their own internal Child ego state, they used all three of their ego states (Parent, Adult, and Child) to take care of their offspring. The result was that their offspring felt free to be in a Natural Child ego state and be spontaneous, experiencing unconditional love and support. However, when the parents encountered some behavior in their offspring that was threatening to their internal Child ego state, the parents shifted their energy out of their Parent and Adult and assumed a competitive stance in their Child ego state. For example, when a 13-year-old boy got kicked out of a dancing class for being playful by a substitute instructor who was feeling insecure, the boy's mother severely shamed her son because she was afraid of the embarrassment she would experience in the community. In these situations, the offspring experienced that there was no way to survive a competition with the parent's Child ego state, and therefore adapted their behavior to appease the parent's Child. The 13-year-old decided to be perfect in order to never disappoint his mother again and experience that kind of shame. Once the parents' Child ego state was no longer threatened, the parents shifted their energy back into their Parent and Adult ego states and resumed taking care of their offspring. The only problem was that the care-taking was no longer unconditional, but was at a price. The parents were in effect saying, "I will take care of you, but you owe me not behaving in a way that I feel threatened." The price for the 13-year-old who gave up his playfulness was that he had been depressed ever since. He came to see me in his forties because even though he was very successful, he felt like a failure, felt responsible for everyone around him, never stopped working, and had no joy in life. The good news is that he changed this in one therapy session as he reworked that early scene, reclaimed his okayness as a 13-year-old, gave the responsibility for mother's disappointment back to her, reclaimed his Natural Child, and became playful once more.

In the present, when an individual is in his Adapted Child, he will experience a closed, restricted energy flow in which the internal stroking is from his Adapted Child to his internal Parent and back. The result is anxiety, depression, somatic complaints, acting out, and so on, which become substitute sources of strokes in the place of enjoyable interactions. When the person is in Natural Child, he will experience an open, spontaneous energy flow throughout his personality structure that is not dependent on a certain type of behavior. The result is spontaneous, autonomous behavior. Since the individual learned to survive with his parents by maintaining the closed restricted energy flow, he will attempt to set up the same type of relationship with the therapist as he had with his parents in order to feel safe and ensure his survival. Thus he will behave in Adapted Child ways to elicit the same type of strokes from the therapist that he is used to, until he is sure it is safe to move into Natural Child behavior. For example, the client may be overly compliant, overly rebellious, act helpless, or be guarded and suspicious. Depending on the client's early experience and subsequent experiences with trust, the time required to feel safe in order to move into Natural Child behavior will vary greatly. The therapist's ability to be in her own Natural Child ego state and work from a position of seeing both herself and the client as okay will greatly facilitate this process. Another part of the necessary safety will be created by the therapist negotiating a clear and meaningful contract with the client.

Contracts

When individuals first learn about redecision therapy, they often assume that every piece of therapy should involve a redecision. A lot of preliminary work, however, goes into creating the conditions necessary for a redecision. The first step is formulating a clear contract with the client (Goulding and Goulding 1979). However, there are additional factors that sometimes have to be dealt with in order to get to the point of contracting. The client may not be clear about what she wants to change, or is not sure that change is possible, or is not even aware of what the problem is. Sometimes the client is not yet mentally in the room with the therapist. She is still thinking about the fight she had with her spouse before she left home or the things she left unfinished at the office. Another difficulty may be that she has never developed trust in another person to really care about her feelings and needs.

The redecision therapist starts by making sure that the client is really present and in as full contact with the therapist as possible. Next, the therapist helps the client identify the problem she is experiencing and frame it in a solvable form. Sometimes the client isn't sure what the problem really is and needs some help in identifying the problem. At other times, the client has the problem framed in a way that is unsolvable. Examples of unsolvable problems are trying to change someone else or trying to change in order to please someone else. The client will need help in reframing the problem in a way that it becomes solvable.

Once the client is fully present, in contact with the therapist, clear about what the problem is, has it framed in a way that is solvable, and developed sufficient trust, the next issue is what the client wants to change in order to solve the problem. Frequently, the client, outside his awareness, will be discounting his ability, the therapist's ability, or the solvability of the problem in some way. The way he phrases the problem may convey one message on the social level but imply a different message on the psychological level. An example would be, "I think I want to resolve my anxiety." The psychological implication is that the therapist is supposed to convince him that that is what he wants to do. In order to clarify the issue and make the psychological level congruent with the social level, the therapist can ask, "Is it okay for you to be sure?" Almost invariably, the client who says "I think" has an injunction not to be important or take a firm stand on what he or she wants. Unless the psychological level is congruent with the social level, the behavioral outcome will be determined at the psychological level (Berne 1964) and the therapist ends up being responsible, in the client's mind, for the change.

It is also important in contracting with a client to find out what he wants (Natural Child), as well as what he thinks would be beneficial (Nurturing Parent), while taking into account the reality factors in the situation (Adult). Questions are asked to elicit information from all three ego states. For example, "What do you want to change about yourself today?" "How would that be beneficial to you?" "What would you have to do in order to accomplish that?" In addition, the more behaviorally specific the contract is, the easier it will be for both parties to identify when it is accomplished. For example, "What will we see you doing differently to let us know that you have made this change?" Contracts also make explicit that the therapy process is a mutually agreeable and cooperative one, as both parties agree together on a specific course of action. Negotiating a clear contract will cut through psychological games like "Do Me Something," create a feeling of safety and hopefulness, and increase the possibility of a successful outcome in therapy.

Impasse Clarification

Once a clear contract has been negotiated, the second step is clarifying the *impasse*. Impasse is a term from gestalt therapy representing a conflict between two parts of the self. One part is wanting to move in a spontaneous Natural Child direction, while the other part is wanting to move in the protective Adapted Child direction that the person developed as a child in order to survive. Both desires are positive, but usually the individual will be identified with one side and experience the other side as negative. The issue is helping the client value the positive intent of the protective side and be aware of the additional resources he has for protecting himself in the present. Impasse clarification is assisting the client in owing and experiencing both sides so he experiences having choice and control over each. By having the client experience both sides of the impasse, he can begin to appreciate and value the part of himself that he previously felt negative about and may have been trying to get rid of, not realizing the survival purpose it served in childhood.

For example, a person may want to get rid of the part of himself who feels scared. He wants to spontaneously feel and express his anger, and to set limits with people who are abusive, but when he did so as a child he got severely punished and feared for his life. He learned to feel scared and stay quiet in order to protect himself. Not expressing his anger enabled him to survive as a child. Once he experiences the purpose that part served, and can appreciate that part, he can identify other resources he has available in the present for accomplishing the same purpose of protecting himself. For example, he can experience his ability to take a stand for himself now and not allow anyone to hurt him. Instead of fighting with himself internally, he can move to a cooperative position, with the two sides working together rather than against each other. As he gets the needs met of the part of him who is scared, he can let go of his scare, allow himself to feel his anger, and set appropriate limits in the present.

Energizing the Adult

Whenever clients are in a defensive Adapted Child or Critical Parent ego state, it is very difficult for them to energize their Adult ego state from that position. In order to get them to begin using their Adult, the therapist needs to first get them to shift their energy into Natural Child or Nurturing Parent. Once they have shifted their energy into Natural Child or Nurturing Parent, it is quite easy for them to energize their Adult ego state as well. By working in such a way as to keep clients continually in contact with their Natural Child or Nurturing Parent, the therapist aids the clients in having easy access to their Adult in order to think clearly, problem solve, and assist themselves in making redecisions.

Some of the ways the therapist can keep the client in touch with her Natural Child are to carefully track the client so that the therapist is with her each step of the way, and to make sure the client is being present to herself. Having the client be present to herself involves monitoring the client's pace, breathing, and use of distractions, in order to have her stay in touch with her feelings. When she moves away from her feelings, it is important to bring her back by commenting on that. Another important way to keep the client in touch with her Natural Child is for the therapist to work from his Natural Child by staying in touch with his feelings, using humor, and being playful. The therapist needs to be emotionally available to the client and empathically connected in order to have one foot in the client's world and be able to feel what it is like to be in the client's shoes. The therapist also needs to have one foot on the outside so he can also be objective. By having one foot in each place, the therapist can simultaneously experience the situation from both perspectives and know what needs to be done each step along the way.

Stroking the Rebellious Child

Occasionally, a client will be heavily entrenched in an Adapted Child position and refuse to move out of that. While it may not be possible to get him to shift his energy directly into a Natural Child position, it is often possible to first help him shift his energy into his Rebellious Child by stroking him for how good he is at staying in the Adapted Child position. When his Rebellious Child is stroked, he will often begin to laugh and then shift his energy into Natural Child. An example would be a client who doesn't answer questions directly but responds in a tangential way that requires the therapist to ask additional questions. The therapist can say in a playful way, "You are really good at not answering my questions!" Often the client will begin laughing and then answer directly.

Sometimes it will take a while for the client to shift his energy. An example would be a client who, when the therapist offers an intervention to move in a positive direction, goes further in a negative direction. The therapist may need to spend some time discouraging the client from changing by pointing out how well he has mastered the position he is in and suggesting that he shouldn't give it up lightly. It is also useful to point out all the problems he will have to deal with if he moves out of the position. In cautioning or discouraging the client from changing, the therapist takes over the resistant position and allows the client to free his energy and move in a positive direction.

Redecision Work

Having helped the client fully experience both sides of the impasse, the third step is facilitating a redecision. Assisting a client in making a redecision is a somewhat paradoxical process. Redecisions are facilitated by helping the client fully own and experience the early decision she made in childhood that may now be limiting her in some way. Clients are often unaware of the early decisions they made, and the importance of those decisions in taking care of themselves as children. In order to bring the early decision into awareness, the therapist asks the client for a specific example of the problem she is experiencing in the present. Next, the therapist asks the client to be in the situation as if it were now and to report what she is feeling, what she is saying about the other person(s), what she is saying about herself, and what she is saying about her destiny. The therapist then asks if that is a familiar position and who she was in that position with as a child. When the client describes the early scene, she is asked to be there as if it were now. As the therapist listens to the early scene and the messages the client is receiving, he asks the client what she is deciding she will do in response. When the client reports the early decision, she is asked to say that to the person(s) involved in the early scene, and to tell them what her fantasy is concerning what will happen next. As the client fully experiences and owns the decision she made and her fantasy about it, she begins to experience a sense of power and satisfaction at her cleverness and creativity as a child. She stops feeling like a victim and begins to experience her autonomy as she shifts her energy from Adapted Child to Natural Child. The paradoxical part is that the redecision is made spontaneously by the Natural Child as she fully experiences and owns the early decision she made and appreciates how clever and useful it was in taking care of herself, given the situation she was in. Again, humor, playfulness, and Natural Child energy on the therapist's part are very useful in assisting the client to access and stay with her own Natural Child energy.

Case Example:
Cure of a Snake Phobia in a Twenty-Minute Session

In a recent marathon, I was working with a woman whose contract was to cure her snake phobia. She was now in her sixties and had had the phobia since she was a small child. Whenever she saw a snake or a picture of a snake, she would become terrified. By accessing her Natural Child energy, she was able to resolve the phobia in a single brief session.

Therapist: When did you first experience this?

Client: Maybe 4 or 5 years old.

Therapist: And where are you and what's going on?

Client: Actually, always my mother told me . . . she had a snake phobia. She is so afraid of a snake . . . so every time she would say, "Watch if you are going into that field! A snake might be there!" and "Watch if you are going into the countryside, you'll have a snake there!" We had a kind of a snake shop when I was a child . . . in our town. They were selling a kind of Chinese medicine, or rather some Chinese stuff, and there was a window with many snakes . . . and the Chinese believed that snakes make a man's sexual power increase . . . so they dry them and make a powder and make some medicine and drink it . . . that kind of a shop. So my mother was always very cautious and anxious about passing in front of that shop. She always took the other side of the road. She would take me and just run! [makes running motion with her hands] So I did not have a snake bite me, no experience like that, but I am very scared about snakes.

Therapist: Well, what I hear is that it is Mother's scare, that she invited you to carry, and are you wanting to give that back to her?

Client: Yes, I want to.

Therapist: Okay, how about we put a chair out here [in front of the client] and you want to ask her what this is all about?

Client: Ask my mother?

Therapist: Yes . . . what this is all about, that she scares herself about a snake shop.

Client: [imagining mother in the chair] Mother, why are you so scared of snakes? You are too scared. You have any experience . . . a snake bite you or something?

Therapist: Now switch. [client switches chairs]

Client: [as Mother] Oh, no . . . no, but I really . . . [turns up her nose] I just . . . I don't like snakes . . . the shape [makes an elongated shape with her hands] . . . and the way it moves. [shivers] I cannot stand it!

Therapist: Tell her where you learned to think like that. As Mother, tell your daughter where you learned to think like that.

Client: [as Mother] Well, I cannot remember, but when I was a child, I lived on a mountain side once, for a short time, and in this area were lots of snakes and some boy put . . . my mother's cousin . . . put a snake in my bed [looks anxious and breathes very shallowly] . . . and I was so surprised and so scared that the only thing I could remember . . . since then I have never gotten to see snakes . . . oh . . . oh. [shivers] It was a long time ago. It was long, a really long time ago, but still I remember that, and so I have dreaded snakes.

Therapist: "I have been scaring myself ever since!" [client looks at therapist quizzically] As Mother will you tell your daughter, "I've been scaring myself ever since."

Client: [as Mother] Oh, yes, I've been scaring myself ever since.

Therapist: Are you ready to be yourself?

Client: [nods and switches chairs]

Therapist: So, as yourself, what do you want to tell Mother?

Client: As a child or right now?

Therapist: Right now.

Client: I'm glad you told me. For a long time I have forgotten about that story, but when I sat here [points to the other chair], I remembered that a long, long time ago she told me so, and [to mother] I'm glad you told me . . . and it was your experience . . . and I didn't have any experience myself because you protected me and scared me. I know some snakes are poisonous but that others are not.

Therapist: Are there any poisonous snakes where you live?

Client: Yes.

Therapist: How many?

Client: Only one.

Therapist: You know what it looks like?

Client: Yes. [describes it] But in the city we don't have any snakes . . . only we have to be very careful when we go to the countryside . . . some places in the mountains.

Therapist: At age 5, when your mother told you this story, what did you feel?

Client: I think I was so scared [voice sounds anxious] . . . and the same thing might happen to me . . . but luckily it's never happened. [laughs] But still I can't stand the shape and the way it moves. I can't look at them even in a zoo.

Therapist: Okay. You do the hula, right? [she had mentioned this earlier]

Client: What?

Therapist: You do Hawaiian dances?

Client: Yes. [laughs]

Therapist: Okay. So I want you to see a little snake crawling out of the corner over there with a grass skirt on, doing the hula. [she begins to laugh, I and the group laugh with her, and she puts her hands together and looks delighted like a 5-year-old child] Just see it coming across the floor here doing the hula. [she, I, and the group laugh harder and she continues to look delighted]

Client: Oh! With a lei, and a grass skirt! [laughs and makes a hula motion, then gets up an begins to do the hula with the fantasy snake while I and the group laugh and enjoy her delightfulness, and she enjoys herself. She then points to the snake and laughs] Nice one! Thank you.

Therapist: You're welcome! [laughing]

Client: Okay, so if I feel scared, I will see this snake doing the dance. [laughing and continuing to make a hula motion]

Therapist: Yes, so any time you see one, just imagine this snake with the little grass skirt on. [laughing with her]

Client: Oh. Okay. [laughing]

Therapist: And you want to give Mother's scare back to her and let that be hers? And you can enjoy watching them do the hula.

Client: Yes! So, I give my fear back to you! [motions to Mother] but thank you anyway. [laughs and I and the group laugh with her]

Therapist: Nice work!

Client: Thank you.

Therapist: So you can watch snakes and they may teach you a thing or two! [laughter]

Following this work, I asked the client if she would be willing to draw a picture of the snake she saw doing the hula, with the lei and grass skirt. She agreed and later shared the picture with the group with a lot of humor and enjoyment. One of the members of the group also brought her a toy snake the next day that looked very real but was dressed in a grass skirt. She took the snake without reservation and played with it, laughing and showing it to the rest of the group. She also kept it with her all that day. The next step will be for her to go see live snakes in a zoo.

Two important parts of the redecision process are anchoring the redecision and supporting and stroking the new behavior. Using an image like the snake wearing a grass skirt and doing the hula is a way of anchoring the redecision. It is a way for the Natural Child to hold onto the redecision. The Child's response is to laugh rather than to be scared. The group joining in the laughter and playfulness supports and strokes the new behavior of feeling comfortable with snakes and using one's Adult to differentiate between poisonous and nonpoisonous ones rather than having a phobic response to snakes in general. The ultimate goal is always to implement the new behavior in one's life.

I think this case is a good illustration of how accessing the Natural Child, by using humor and playfulness, can greatly speed up the therapeutic process and make change fun and enjoyable!

The Natural Child ego state is the source of power, creativity, and spontaneity. Therefore, the real power for change in therapy is in the Natural Child. When we help clients access and maintain their Natural Child energy, they are empowered for change. As clients shift their energy from Adapted Child to Natural Child, they experience their own autonomy and the freedom to choose what they want for themselves in the present. No longer do they feel like victims, but experience their capacity to take charge of their own lives. Accessing the Natural Child is clearly the key to redecision therapy.

References

Berne, E. (1964). *Games People Play*. New York: Grove.
———— (1972). *What Do You Say After You Say Hello?* New York: Grove.
Goulding, R. and Goulding, M. (1979). *Changing Lives through Redecision Therapy*. New York: Brunner/Mazel.
McNeel, J. (1977). The seven components of redecision therapy. In *Transactional Analysis After Eric Berne: Teaching and Practices of Three TA Schools,* ed. G. Barnes, pp. 425–441. New York: Harper & Row.

II

Practice

8

Using Redecision Therapy In Groups

Eugene M. Kerfoot, Ph.D.

Introduction

Redecision therapy was created over three decades ago as a new approach to brief group therapy. Its procedures center on individual work, so it can also be employed effectively in individual therapy, although its most powerful use is within a redecision group framework.

The importance of this approach was demonstrated very early in a study of group leader behavior and outcomes (Lieberman et al. 1973). The transactional analysis group led by Bob Goulding used innovative procedures that included moderate use of executive function, and affective stimulation coupled with timely cognitive feedback. Irving Yalom recently reported that Goulding's group achieved the highest therapy gains in the study (Yalom 1992).

From those early days, using TA's elegantly simple and comprehensive model of personality, coupled with experiential methods from gestalt therapy and other models, Mary and Bob Goulding systematically and creatively added new concepts and procedures to fashion a distinct and powerful approach that remains state-of-the-art brief group therapy.

Entering a Redecision Group

Selection

Screening and selection procedures start a process that ends with entrance into a group. These procedures usually involve one or more face-to-face contacts between therapists and potential clients, so both can begin to learn what a therapy relationship with the other would be like. Therapists obtain background data, including a general health history, previous therapy experience, and family composition. It is important to discuss informed consent issues, such as confidentiality and its exceptions, client rights, therapy procedures, payment of fees, attendance, and behavior limits—mainly distinctions between the value of expressing feelings and prohibitions against violence or threats of violence.

Therapists listen to initial complaints and consider them in relation to solutions clients initially may propose. The overall objective is for clients to become able to make informed decisions about entering a redecision group and for therapists to decide whether to recommend entry. An agreement about these matters marks the official beginning of a therapeutic alliance.

Criteria for Exclusion

Most people can benefit from group work, so interview procedures pretty much constitute a self-selection process in which clients decide whether this particular kind of group therapy appears to offer what they want.

Criteria for exclusion are simple, sensible, and flexible. A relatively small number of people, such as active alcoholics, drug abusers, sociopathic individuals, those with significant organic brain damage, or people who are chronically psychotic or acutely suicidal for the most part are not appropriate candidates for outpatient groups. Some of these may do well with appropriate preparation that includes development of well-defined and targeted therapeutic arrangements, for instance, effective no-suicide, no-homicide, or no-psychosis contracts (Goulding and Goulding 1979). Others may require arrangements such as daycare or inpatient groups that are suited for their particular needs.

Travelers and Travel Agents

Beyond establishing a general alliance, it is important to explain to potential clients how redecision work is unique. A redecision therapist is a kind of travel agent, and clients are travelers about to embark upon a trip. Clients need to know that they have exclusive rights to pick their destinations, and they receive the interesting news that their travel agent believes they have within them enough power and other necessary resources to go the distance. Clients hear that the travel agent's job is to facilitate their journey. While agents don't pick destinations, they are experts on means of travel, likely routes, and possible shortcuts, as well as potential hazards and roadblocks that may be encountered, and as guides will be there for the whole trip.

Dimensions of Groups

Group approaches can be described in terms of three dimensions or levels of therapeutic work: a self-change or intrapersonal level, a level associated with dynamics or properties of groups, and an interpersonal or relationship level. In the material that follows, redecision therapy's use of these dimensions will be discussed and contrasted with other models.

It also should be noted that increasingly redecision therapists (Joines 1977, Kerfoot 1995, McClendon and Kadis 1983) have integrated these three dimensions of group therapy into broader systems perspectives.

Therapy Procedures

Intrapersonal Work

Redecision therapy essentially is individual, self-change work that is done in a group. It is structured to take place one person at a time in discrete episodes, usually no more than about a half hour in duration. A client ordinarily works toward one of a few outcomes: successful completion of a redecision, partial completion, such as contract clarification, or becoming stuck in an impasse. At one of these points the work is ended either by the client or the leader, and another member of the group takes a turn. Repeated episodes of individual work are the major kind of work that takes place in the group.

When people become stuck in an impasse, it is time for the therapist to stop the work. This is a therapy judgment, but almost always a fairly easy one to make. Naturally, the best ending place is after a redecision; the second best stopping place is when someone is firmly stuck and not going to complete the work at that time.

While someone is doing individual work, other group members usually are observers, although they play a vital role later, providing reinforcement and opportunities for practice (Gladfelter 1992). While observing, group members learn how change involves more than cognitive activities, and that redecisions contain basic affective elements initiated from a Free Child ego state.

> Sam's initial complaint was "I'm angry. I work all the time and never have any fun." After appropriate contract clarification work, the therapist asked, "When you were a little kid, working a lot, feeling angry and not having any fun, what was the scene?" In an early scene, Sam relived a decision in which not having fun became a way of life. The work culminated in an experiential,

emotionally charged redecision to enjoy his life more, followed by experimenting and practicing the change in transactions with group members. For instance, with some hesitance he asked Tom to have lunch with him. To his surprise, Tom, who was working on becoming more outgoing, readily accepted, and the two began to take lunch together fairly regularly after their morning group session.

Redecision work illustrates that often early decisions at one time were solutions to problems that in present life again have become problems because the old solutions, for various reasons, no longer work well enough (Kerfoot 1985). Sam, for instance, said "working all the time just doesn't get it for me any more; if I don't change now, I'm going to burn out."

Group Properties and Dynamics

Bion's (1960) basic assumption group theories reflect the kind of group dynamics that have led analytic (Kauff 1993) and object relations group therapists (Rutan and Alonso 1978) to identify the *group* as a client to be treated in addition to the treatment of individual patients. Psychodynamic approaches tend toward long-term therapy, and their treatment goals of insight and preparation for change are well served by the richness of group dynamic themes.

In redecision therapy, however, the group is never the client. The primary goal of therapy is self-change, work that must be done directly by clients who claim active ownership of their problems.

Redecision and Psychodynamic Procedures

From the perspective of transactional analysis theory, Eric Berne (1966) described psychoanalysis methodologically as a form of structural analysis in which transference and countertransference responses are recognizable as cross-transactions. Redecision therapists do not focus on the analysis of transactions, nor do they utilize interpretation or employ constructs such as transference, counter-transference, or projective identification as do psychodynamic therapists. Redecision self-change procedures involve people resolving their projections in gestalt-like dialogues that take place in their internal self-system (Kerfoot 1995).

> Sue's contract was to be more open, instead of remaining detached and lonely. When she said "I don't think that Marilyn [another group member] likes me," the therapist asked her to speak directly to her image of Marilyn; unsurprisingly, the Marilyn in her head (her internal image of Marilyn) turned out to be a good deal like her mother, which led to early scene work in which Sue resolved her loneliness.

> During a training group, a beginning leader asked a client colleague who was working on a dream in which he was describing a drum, "Do you think the drum might be your mother?" but before his client could answer, Bob Goulding's voice came booming out from a nearby room where Bob was taking a break, "Let him be his own damned drum!" which pretty much says it all. Again, therapist facilitation is not based on interpreting or analyzing client behavior, interventions that from a redecision perspective would be intrusions on a client's work.

The Interpersonal Level

Redecision therapy uses its understanding of transactions to facilitate interpersonal (i.e., relationship) work, which involves change contracts or agreements negotiated by members with each other to develop mutually desired behaviors, as in Sam and Tom's work described earlier.

Self-Change and Relationship Change

Interpersonal work exists at a different systems level than individual, intrapersonal work, and often flows from and follows individual change. Since relationship work provides opportunities to practice basic redecisions in the group, such work also is important in helping to make change durable.

> Louise entered group with her husband, Bill, complaining that he didn't love her. Both wanted to become closer, and closeness became a relationship contract goal. It turned out that at an underlying level, Louise believed she was unlovable, an early life decision. Before she could fully carry out her part of the relationship work with Bill, it was crucial for her to develop and work through, partly in early scene work, a self-change contract to love and accept herself. Bill, of course, had his own self-change and relationship work to do, mainly centering on issues of experiencing and expressing his feelings. Their separate self-change work was at a more basic systems level than their relationship work, and both needed to do the self work before they could satisfactorily work through the relationship level work, although there was overlap between the two.

Values in the Group: Norms

Redecision theorists and interpersonal theorists, such as Yalom (1985), agree on the usefulness for group work of desired values or norms, such as openness, trust, and self-disclosure. In redecision groups, taking responsibility and active support for changes in others are of special value, and while there are no official expectations for such behavior, the focus on self-potency and the procedures used in this kind of therapy can become powerful modeling experiences and, in their own fashion, group members often choose to develop such kinds of behavior. The creation of an environment for change is important for redecision work (Goulding 1972), and supportive norms clearly play a part in the development and maintenance of such an environment.

Desirable norms, like all other behavior, develop from individual conduct, and the potency of clients and therapists in determining their own behavior is not discounted or attributed to external forces that might be assumed to "make" people behave in certain ways.

The Here and Now

It is very important for group members to become able to focus attention in the present, the here and now, both in real-life transactions with other group members and intrapersonally in self-system dialogues. They learn how to treat events that are taking place elsewhere as if they were happening here and now, and to treat past experiences in the same fashion. For instance, instead of talking about other group members, people speak directly to each other, and instead of gossiping about those not present, people use imagery to speak directly to internal representations of them. Such behaviors facilitate therapy work and are useful in confronting denial.

Denial

Some of the most important work takes place when clients subvert therapy goals by denying ownership of feelings, thoughts, and actions. Denial is reflected in comments like "you made me feel," "a thought came to me," or "I'll try." Therapists confront denials in order to foster autonomy. For instance, when someone says, "I can't tell Uncle Joe that I'm angry with him," the therapist may ask the client to visualize Uncle Joe and say, "I won't tell you what I'm feeling." Bob Goulding sometimes would signal that a confrontation was on the way by ringing his cowbell, a playful and potent intervention.

Stroking for Change, Nonstroking for Nonchange

Strokes are powerful sources of stimulation and motivation, and the giving and receiving of them is essential for well-being. Everything that people say or do has a recognition/stroke value, and appropriate positive stroking is an especially important therapy activity. Positive strokes can range from smiles or words of approval to applauding, hugging, or cheering. Strokes support change, are given after successful work is completed, and are most effective when given soon after a redecision. Leaders provide a model for stroking, and their strokes, either verbal, such as "good work, Bob," or giving someone a hug, can be particularly important.

Some people do not want to be touched or to have much notice taken of them in any fashion, and it is crucially important to respect everyone's boundaries and preferences by not forcing on people recognition that they do not want. That said, over time even those who are quite reticent eventually become more active in stroking. And since stroking begins at home, it is important for people to remember to stroke themselves for completing their own work.

For several reasons, strokes are contraindicated after work that is incomplete or ends in an impasse, even when someone ends up feeling uncomfortable, such as hurt or sad. First, it is important for clients to accept and exercise their ability to be in charge of feelings. Not responding to a client's discomfort may seem harsh and uncaring. However, the clinical result of withholding strokes has been consistently positive, since stroking someone who is stuck in an impasse is likely to be experienced at an underlying level as support for not changing.

Rackets

The uncomfortable feeling that accompanies an impasse often has a stereotypic quality, sometimes termed a *racket* (Goulding and Goulding 1979). Racket feelings may play an significant role in establishing and maintaining early life decisions and are important to identify and resolve as a part of the redecision work. Outside of the context of actual therapy work, of course, it is appropriate for group members and leaders to be supportive of each other when experiencing difficult life situations.

Scenes

Very often, work takes place in stage-like dramas called scenes, set up by therapist and client. These include present scenes, recent scenes, early scenes, imaginary scenes, and combinations. Since ego states are coherent experiential patterns, not unorganized bits of stimulation, therapy dramas staged within the self-system, using ego state components that give and accept injunctions and make decisions, are intuitively appropriate ways to structure active self-change work.

Group Leaders

Single or Co-leaders

Redecision groups sometimes have a single leader, but there are many advantages to co-therapy. Co-leaders model equality, one is not another's assistant, and they complement each other in various ways. A leader who is not actively working is free to see what else is going on in the group and can listen in a detached way to the therapy dialogue. Leaders can change roles at any time, and may take over, relinquish, or share active leadership.

Friedman (1989) has noted the popularity of co-therapy in many group approaches, and has pointed out various difficulties that may come about when the co-therapy relationship is not fully functional.

The redecision model lends itself to healthy cooperation because the client's contract is the major guide for therapist interventions rather than, for instance, interventions based on more subjective constructs, such as transference, countertransference, or projective identification. In addition, redecision training emphasizes peer group work, with considerable attention paid to the co-leadership model. Trainees learn early and often how to deal with personal and procedural co-therapy issues.

As to the usefulness of co-therapy, the work of highly skilled co-therapists, such as Mary and Bob Goulding, clearly reveals the significant benefits of collaboration. It also is useful for clients at times to see therapists express healthy disagreements and conflicts, and resolve them in ways that add value to the therapy process. Finally, co-therapy is stimulating and synergistic work, is surprisingly often fun to do, and helps to keep leaders alert and refreshed.

Making Change Permanent

Redecision therapy is not about pathology or illness. Its goal is not insight or preparation for change. It is about active change that is carried out by clients who experience from inside their power to change themselves. Redecisions are real—and only a beginning. It is not wise for people to assume that once they make a redecision, the change will remain automatically in place. Even the essential and powerful vitality of the Free Child, who generates a redecision, is not enough to guarantee permanence, and there is no magic involved in maintaining new habits and skills. To make change enduring, redecisions must be incorporated in new behavior patterns through experiment and practice.

Long ago, Epictetus said "regular running makes us better runners" (Lebell 1995, p. 112). Practice does the trick, just as it did back in childhood days when learning to ride a bicycle or skip rope, and for much the same reasons: the new behavior, initiated from the childlike free self, is desirable and attainable and supports autonomy. The redecision message is: change what you want to change, change now, and practice till the cows come home.

Group Applications

Redecision group work takes place in diverse settings with many kinds of clients, and uses many formats. Below is a sampling that illustrates the variety of group applications.

Ongoing Groups

Ongoing groups are open-ended and convenient, offering easy entry and simple departure. Such groups usually meet on a weekly basis, so there are repeated opportunities to make changes and work them through over a suitable time with plenty of opportunities for practice in the group.

Time-limited Workshops and Marathons

Workshops and marathons are designed for short, intensive, and concentrated work, a format that for many people is the treatment of choice and for others is a useful adjunct to their ongoing therapy (Goulding 1977). A potent dimension is added when people live together for several days in a residential workshop, an arrangement that allows for many naturalistic opportunities to practice changes outside of group sessions. In addition to the usual dimensions of ongoing groups, intensive workshops have another vital component: a structured closure, allowing people to bring to a useful end what most likely has been an intense therapy experience. Adequate closure time is needed to review that has been accomplished, identify unfinished business, and make concrete plans for carrying out redecisions at home with family and friends. Finally, saying goodbye to other participants allows people emotionally to finish what is over, and move more fully into the future.

Family Groups

A comprehensive, theoretical, and methodological approach to family therapy based on principles of general systems theory has been developed by Ruth McClendon and Les Kadis (1983). There are three stages in their family therapy model: an initial evaluative and diagnostic stage, followed by script analysis and redecision work, leading to a third and final stage in which reintegration of a new family system takes place.

Treatment of Youthful Offenders

A number of institutional programs have been devised for the treatment of youthful offenders. Paul McCormick developed one of the most thorough of these, a system-wide small group treatment program for institutionalized delinquent boys in the California Youth Authority. In conjunction with this program, McCormick (1971) designed various measures, including a script check list, for diagnostic and treatment planning.

A two-part group treatment program for institutionalized delinquent adolescents was developed at an Oklahoma Department of Public Welfare Institution for juvenile offenders (Kerfoot 1969). Monthly multiple family group sessions centered on relationship issues in the family. These were coupled with weekly small group sessions involving the residents which focused on self-change issues. While both kinds of work were useful, their combined use yielded better results than either practiced separately.

Couples Groups

Ellyn Bader and Pete Pearson (1988) originated a creative and effective program for couple therapy that uses redecision work as part of a comprehensive treatment approach. Their program is based on a developmental model of behavior that connects stages of human development with corresponding stages in the development of couple relationships.

Therapy Training in Graduate Education

In the last several years, at least two programs incorporating redecision and transactional analysis principles have been developed in academic settings. Lessler (1977) developed a program at the Southeastern Institute, and in 1990 John Gladfelter and the present author developed a group therapy training program for graduate students enrolled in the Fielding Institute's psychology program.

This transactional analysis/redecision therapy training program (TART) was designed using Western Institute for Group and Family Therapy (WIGFT) training principles and methods that have been adjusted to accommodate an academic environment. For example, contracts for personal and professional change are defined in terms of competencies or abilities, and competency-based rating procedures have been developed to evaluate student progress and effectiveness.

Management Consultation

Management consultants (Kerfoot 1995) have applied transactional analysis theory and redecision group methods and theory to address a variety of management issues, including conflict resolution, professional development, organizational effectiveness, and team building. Richardson (1992) has paid particular attention to the human element in organizations in addressing management problems.

References

Bader, E., and Pearson, P. T. (1988). *In Quest of the Mythical Mate: A Developmental Approach to Diagnosis and Treatment in Couples Therapy*. New York: Brunner/Mazel.

Berne, E. (1966). *Principles of Group Treatment*. New York: Random House.

Bion, W. R. (1960). *Experiences in Groups*. New York: Basic Books.

Friedman, W. (1989). *Practical Group Therapy*. San Francisco: Jossey/Bass.

Gladfelter, J. (1992). Redecision therapy. *International Journal of Group Psychotherapy* 42(3): 319–333.

Goulding, M. (1992). *Sweet Love Remembered*. San Francisco: TA Press.

Goulding, M., and Goulding, R. (1979). *Changing Lives through Redecision Therapy*. New York: Brunner/Mazel.

Goulding, R. (1972). New directions in transactional analysis: creating an environment for redecision and change. In *Progress in Group and Family Therapy*, ed. C. Sager and H. Kaplan, pp. 105–134. New York: Brunner/Mazel.

———— (1977). No magic at Mt. Madonna: redecisions in marathon therapy. In *Transactional Analysis After Eric Berne*, ed. G. Barnes, pp. 77–94. New York: Harper & Row.

Joines, V. S. (1977). An integrated systems perspective. In *Transactional Analysis After Eric Berne*, ed. G. Barnes, pp. 257–269. New York: Harper & Row.

Kauff, P. (1993). The contribution of analytic group therapy to the psychoanalytic process. In *Group Therapy in Clinical Practice*, ed. A. Alonso and H. E. Swiller, pp. 3–28. Washington, DC: American Psychiatric Press.

Kerfoot, E. (1969). *Effects of institutionalization on children*. Paper presented at The Department of Institutions, Social and Rehabilitative Services Conference on Groups, Tecumseh, OK, June.

———— (1985). *The undefined self*. Paper presented at the International Redecision Conference, Asilomar, CA, May.

Kerfoot, G. (1995). Self systems and relationship systems: achieving lasting change. *Transactional Analysis Journal* 25:316–318.

Lebell, S. (1994). *Epictetus, The Art of Living*. New York: Harper-Collins.

Lessler, K. (1977). A graduate program in psychotherapy. In *Transactional Analysis After Eric Berne*, ed. G. Barnes, pp. 146–158. New York: Harper & Row.

Lieberman, A. M., Yalom, I. D., and Miles, M. B. (1973). *Encounter Groups: First Facts*. New York: Basic Books.

McClendon, R., and Kadis, L. (1983). *Chocolate Pudding*. New York: Science and Behavior Books.

McCormick, P. (1971). *Guide for the Use of the Life Script Questionnaire*. San Francisco: Transactional Publications.

Richardson, G. (1992). *The human element: success or failure of a merger*. Paper presented at the International Air Transport Association Meeting, Brussels, Belgium, May.

Rutan, J. S., and Alonso, A. (1978). Some guidelines for group thera-
    pists. *Group* 4:40–50.
Yalom, I. D. (1985). *The Theory and Practice of Group Psychotherapy*,
    3rd ed. New York: Basic Books.
————— (1992). Memorial service for Robert Goulding. American
    Group Psychotherapy Association Conference, New York City,
    February 20.

9

Treating Depression

Curtis A. Steele, M.D. and
Nancy Porter-Steele, Ph.D.

Basic Healthiness

Hippocrates in the fifth century B.C. taught that health was a natural condition and that illness was a deviation. Redecision therapy takes the same view: that healthiness is natural, that healing is a normal process, and that the therapist's job is to remove obstacles to healing.

In many cases, the tendency toward depression has been cured through redecision therapy. When faced with the depressed patient, all too often professionals assume that something in the basic makeup of the person, physically or mentally, is the cause, and that nothing can be done other than provide support to a crippled being. They look for the pathology as if it were a flaw in the basic character, rather than looking beyond that to the innate healthiness. There is a form of one-upmanship that arises in the process, lending itself to elitist thinking: "I'm O.K., you're Not-O.K., but if you follow my treatment plan you too can become O.K." The experiences of redecision therapists, however, again and again validate the view that people are fundamentally healthy. This basic healthiness is assumed, can be discovered, and can be used in the process of psychotherapy to help patients free themselves from depression.

Diagnosing Depression, and Considerations Regarding Interventions

What we call depression is not a unitary disease. Increasingly more has been learned about the brain and behavior, and biological therapies have added major advancements in treating patients who suffer from certain types of depression. When someone complains of being depressed, I always ask, "What do you mean by that?" People may mean many different things by the word depression.

Depression can be an illness by itself such as bipolar disorder, major depressive disorder, or dysthymic disorder, or it may be a symptom of some other issue or illness, such as an infection, an undiagnosed malignancy, an endocrine problem, an allergy, an environmental hypersensitivity, alcoholism (overt or crypto), a stress-related problem, or a state of unacknowledged grief. There are so many possible causes that it's very important from the outset not to follow the assumptions made in the first consultation, but to do a careful assessment to determine just what we may be dealing with, and to be ready to modify that assessment as further experience and diagnostic evidence arise.

Many of the people who come to psychotherapists, whether on their own or referred, have dysthymic disorder. This used to be called "neurotic depression." From the redecision therapy perspective it is understood to arise from early childhood decisions; from other perspectives it has been considered to come from a variety of endogenous and exogenous sources. Many psychotherapists have thought that antidepressant therapy was neither appropriate nor useful with these people. However, the advent of a new class of medications called selective serotonin reuptake inhibitors (SSRIs) has changed that view. With these drugs it is often possible to increase a person's available energy and elevate his or her mood so that redecision therapy can be used to change habitual patterns of thinking, feeling, and behaving more rapidly and effectively than if we'd used psychotherapy alone. People with dysthymia who refuse to consider the use of medication may benefit from psychotherapy, but often require longer and more laborious efforts on the part of both therapist and patient. For the nonmedical redecision therapist it's very important to have consultation with a physician who has an open mind to possible diagnoses and is skilled in the use of antidepressant medication. Examples of some of the complexity of diagnosing and treating depression follow.

Karen a 26-year-old school teacher, sought group therapy for chronic depressed mood. Initial assessment indicated a pattern of suffering typical of dysthymia. She entered a treatment group and worked diligently in each session, but didn't get relief. Then abruptly one weekend she became manic and the true nature of her illness, a bipolar disorder, became evident. After starting on lithium, her mania cleared, and so did her feelings of depression. She felt so well that it was mutually agreed that she didn't need further psychotherapy. Follow-up over the next four years confirmed this.

Sam, an experienced psychotherapist, requested antidepressant medication for a persistent depressed mood and low energy level that had not responded to psychotherapy. His physician couldn't find any medical reason for his listlessness. He didn't respond to antidepressant medication and continued to feel sub par. Months later he began to notice difficulty swallowing and a malignancy of his esophagus was found. As sometimes happens, an occult malignancy lay behind his depressed feelings.

Mary, a 36-year-old environmental designer, reported she was chronically depressed, had a history of years of intermittent recreational drug abuse, impulsive unprotected sex with men she'd pick up in bars, and periodic intense suicidal ideation with wrist cutting and pill overdose. Her impulse to self-harm was so strong that she felt powerless in the face of it. However, after only two weeks on fluoxatine (Prozac) she was able to control this behavior, to participate fully in psychotherapy, and to identify and change early childhood decisions. Previously, in the grip of powerful impulses to act, she had been unable to utilize psychotherapy despite repeated attempts. She now was able to work successfully using redecision therapy to a satisfying conclusion, whereas previously, despite years of effort, nothing had changed.

These case examples indicate the need for a broad view in the assessment and treatment of depression. They do not in any way discount the importance of redecision therapy, the single most powerful method we have found to help people change the quality and direction of their lives. Like any method, it must be used appropriately.

Self-Responsibility, Habitual Bad Feelings, and Early Decisions

With redecision therapy, as you have seen earlier in this book, the patient's own power is a given. If I'm depressed, I may be using my own power to depress myself. If so, I've taken on depression as a habitual pattern, and I use my thinking, my interactions with others, my body posture, my voice tone—all my abilities—in the process of recreating depression over and over again. Not in my Adult awareness, of course! I would never deliberately create such suffering for myself.

How did I start such a habit? Our experience in twenty-some years has verified what Bob and Mary Goulding taught us, that depression as a habitual emotion probably indicates a "Don't exist" injunction/decision. Let's take Norma as an example.

Norma was a well-educated woman in her late thirties. She had a good job in a technical field. Her marriage had recently ended, and she felt primarily relieved about that, as it had been a difficult relationship and she had seen no possibility of improving it. Her children seemed to be doing well; she wasn't worried about them. Nevertheless, Norma frequently became very depressed, and dragged herself through her days as if made of wet clay.

In therapy, she'd made a contract to give up depressing herself. On the way to that, she'd accepted that she was the one in charge of her depression—not to *blame*, but in charge.

The therapist explored with Norma her grieving process, her attitudes toward her work and success, her support network, and other current issues and found nothing suggesting reactive depression, adjustment disorder, physical maladies, bipolar disorder, or such. Furthermore, Norma reported having felt depressed off and on for many years. Following the Gouldings' pointer, the therapist suspected "Don't exist" and chose to use Mary Goulding's method of "following the habit feelings back" (Goulding 1973).

Therapist: What's a recent time that you were feeling depressed? Tell it in present tense, let it be happening right now. Where are you? Who else is there?

Norma tells a recent experience. When she strays from immediacy, the therapist reminds her to stay in present tense and to describe sensory detail, so they'll both learn as much as they can from the telling. Norma gets deeply into the direct experience of depressing herself, of her body feelings and the thoughts that go with them.

Therapist: Now, staying in touch with those feelings and thoughts, go back in time, maybe five years, maybe ten, maybe to your teens, or even earlier, to whatever scene comes up.

Many patients go back gradually, through four or five or six scenes, before arriving at an early one. We've chosen Norma for this chapter because she jumped right back and we can write more succinctly about her than about most.

Norma: I'm 4 years old. I'm in the yard outside my uncle's house. I'm wandering around the yard by myself, feeling bad. I'm thinking how my mother is always mad at me, and my father doesn't say anything to me, and I don't know what to do. I'm thinking maybe I'll die. It's a quick flash, but it's like I'm seeing them looking down at me, seeing me dead, feeling sorry, and then everything's O.K.

This is a typical early decision scene, in this instance a decision not to exist, not to be physically alive. To the child, it makes sense that dying is the way to solve devastating problems that are entirely beyond a child's realistic power to solve. It's normal and healthy for a child to use magical thinking. So Norma at four thinks that when she's dead, her parents or somebody will understand the problems and fix everything, and they'll all live happily ever after.

A child doesn't understand the finality of death. Children's magical thinking is like fairy-tale logic. This doesn't indicate anything wrong with the child at all. In fact, the decision to die, to kill oneself, or whatever the child's particular version is, represents an expression of the basic healthy wish to solve problems and have everything and everyone be O.K. Yet, having decided, the child feels even worse. Some intuitive understanding of self-destructiveness is operating, despite the magical thinking.

Jen, in a recent therapy group, working to eliminate her depression, reexperienced a scene at age 7 in which she dug a big hole in the snow and decided, "I'm never coming out of this hole." Jen, too, expected that when she was dead her parents would change their ways.

Sometimes the child makes the decision to die out of compassion that's been engaged too early in life: "I'm a burden to my mother (or father, or whoever). They'll be so much happier if I'm not around for them to have to take care of."

John sought therapy for recurrent suicidal impulses that he had not acted on, but which kept him miserable and alarmed. He was asked to follow the bad feeling back to the earliest time he could remember. He went to age 4 and described in present tense how his drunken parents were violently quarreling in the kitchen. He was crying and trying to get them to stop, but without success. He decided that he was the problem, and that if he hadn't been born his mother would be happy and would get along with his father. He began a pattern of thinking and feeling in which getting rid of himself appeared to be a solution to problems. If things got bad enough he would kill himself. After recognizing the childhood origin of his pattern, he was asked if his mother was happy at the present time. He responded, "No, she's divorced, all the kids have grown up and she's still unhappy." A group member pointed out that John wasn't the cause of his mother's misery. Knowing what he now knew about his mother, he agreed that she would probably have been unhappy even if he hadn't been born. John suddenly realized he wasn't the problem and the expression on his face was wonderful to behold. He decided he wasn't going to kill himself no matter what problems arose in his life. In that single session he changed, and was subsequently free of the depressive feelings and suicidal thoughts that had bothered him for so long.

Because the early decision is stored in the Adapted Child ego state, our grownup patient's Adult isn't ordinarily aware of it, and finds it illogical when first becoming acquainted with it. Parent ego states are likely to discount the entire situation: "Don't be silly. There's no reason for that." We often spend some time helping the patient get in touch with the good intention behind the early decision, the fundamentally healthy wish to solve problems, that went awry because she or he was too young to have effective methods for confronting such problems.

It's more than twenty years since Norma's redecision about the "Don't exist," and she hasn't been depressed since. Jen's redecision has yet to be tested over time and we think she has some more injunctions to deal with. Experience has taught us that a person with a "Don't exist" early decision usually has taken on several others. Redeciding the "Don't exist" brings great relief. Complete relief, though, may await redeciding the other injunction(s).

Multiple Early Decisions

Working with depression, in addition to the "Don't exist," we most often find three other areas of early decisions:

> "Don't feel (or don't express feelings)." This includes especially anger. Furthermore, when anger is prohibited, often awareness of one's needs and wants is, too.
> "Don't separate (don't grow, don't be grown up, don't think for yourself, don't attend to your needs but attend to mine)."
> "Don't succeed."

Charles was a successful therapist who nonetheless was often unsure of himself, was excessively competitive with peers, and became depressed especially when things were going well for him. In therapy he confronted his father, for whom Charles as a little boy could never do things well enough, and decided that from now on he was going to do things for himself and that he would be the judge of his own success. A chronic and recurrent pattern of depressing himself slipped away unnoticed until pointed out months later by his mate.

Any or all of the possible injunctions could be behind a depression habit. From habitual stomachaches to panic to irritability habits, including depression, a child chooses the particular kind of suffering based on a variety of factors. When we were training with them, the Gouldings pointed out several:

Copying a role model (I'm like my uncle, or like the heroine of my favorite story).

Taking on what hasn't already been chosen within the family (my mother's the only one who gets to be angry; sister gets to be scared; father's the withdrawn one. I can be depressed).

Continuing what brings attention (when I'm depressed, someone tries to comfort me; otherwise they don't have any time for me).

Using what appears to be a magical power (when I'm depressed, I'm protected from anybody making me feel any worse).

In any of the above examples, the choice, instead of depression, could have been any other emotion or body symptom.

The particular injunction is not necessarily a factor in settling on an habitual bad feeling. We're stressing that though a few injunctions seem especially likely to be present when the patient is depressed, there may be quite different injunctions instead or in addition to these. The therapist should keep an open mind to learn what injunctions this particular patient has accepted, and what this person's own decisions about those injunctions were.

Closing the Escape Hatches

Because depression is so often associated with "Don't exist," the redecision process nearly always involves one or another method of closing the escape hatches, which Denton Roberts, earlier in this volume, discusses as "the no-suicide/no-homicide contract." We have developed our style for doing this work after the example of Harry Boyd (1980). Harry wanted to eliminate self-destructive options early in therapy, and in his teaching about the process he emphasized removing the dramatic quality from these options to help people feel less attached to them. Even if depression isn't the problem we're working with, we usually go through our checklist of escape hatches within a few sessions of meeting a patient for the first time. Here's how we do it:

> *Therapist:* I'm going to go through a standard checklist with you now. I'll read off six statements, one at a time. I ask you to repeat each statement. Say it out loud, so that each part of your personality can hear you and respond. The most important part is that you pay attention to your internal experience as you're saying the statement aloud. It may be body sensations, or emotions, or words, or sounds, or images. Whatever happens, let it tell you how true the statement is for you today. Give me an answer in percentage, like "that's a hundred percent true," or "that's about twenty-five percent." I'll explain more about this later.
>
> First statement: I won't kill myself, on purpose or by accident, and I won't set it up for someone else to kill me.

The patient repeats the statement aloud. Sometimes the patient has a lot to say in connection with the statement, sometimes not. An occasional patient for whom 'Don't Feel' is an important injunction will quickly report 100% for every statement. If this isn't really accurate, the therapist can usually notice incongruence and other clues to the suppression taking place. The therapist records the percentage answer to each statement in the chart.

> *Therapist:* Second statement: No matter how angry I may get, I won't kill or physically harm anyone.
>
> Third statement: Knowingly or unknowingly, I won't shorten my life to prove anything to anyone.
>
> Fourth statement: Knowingly or unknowingly, I won't make myself ill.
>
> I have to explain this next statement, because it's easily misunderstood. It's going to say, "When I have crazy thoughts or feelings, I won't act on them." In this statement, "crazy" is

not the slang word, a word for being silly or a little out of line. In this case "crazy" means something so irresponsible that if you did it, somebody would have to take over your life, put you in the hospital or some such thing. And we say *"When* I have crazy thoughts or feelings . . ." because we assume that the human mind is capable of any thought or feeling, and that's no problem. It's only what we do about the thoughts or feelings that matters.

So, the fifth statement, then, is: When I have crazy thoughts or feelings, I won't act on them.

Finally, the sixth statement: Knowingly or unknowingly, I won't arrange my life to end up lonely.

We've often found a child had decided to run off and be a hermit or the equivalent as a form of nonsurvival. Intuitively, the child knows she or he couldn't survive that way, and it's the same as dying. People with this version of the "Don't exist" decision are especially unlikely to allow themselves good close relationships, and redeciding the "Don't be close" decision won't be enough until the escape hatch has been closed.

After the patient has gone through all six statements and discovered how true each is today, we usually explain the notion of escape hatches as decisions that children make under stress to try to solve problems. The label escape hatch is used because it looks like a way out to the child. People intuitively recognize this; it's familiar to their Child ego states. Their Adult ego states recognize that the method won't actually solve anything. Of course sometimes the Adult isn't available or is confused, and then it's necessary to engage the Adult and clarify the reality before undertaking redecision work.

If the percentage truth for some of the six statements is already very high, 90 percent or so, we may invite simply saying the statement again with the intention that every part of the personality will agree to make it 100 percent. Some people can close an escape hatch as easily and quickly as that, and feel the relief. (We absolutely agree that number one, killing oneself, is to be closed before the others.)

In any event, we take closing the escape hatches as the necessary ground to prepare for the success of all the other work we may do with the patient. If I'm carrying around a plan for solving my problems that involves death, whether mine or others', there's no way I'm going to cease being miserable some of the time, no matter what else I change in therapy.

The method for making the redecision, once the issue is clarified, as Vann Joines's earlier chapter highlights, is any method that accesses the Natural Child and results in the Natural Child confirming that he or she's willing to give up the original decision in favor of a new one.

Norma had followed the habitual feeling back, and discovered an early scene in which she made her decision. Then the therapist guided her in using the empty chair method, putting her mother and father in the chairs. From her Natural Child, supported by her Adult as well as all ego states of the therapist, she told these projected parents that she wasn't going to kill herself, no matter what.

Jen had discovered her early scene in an immediate response to the therapist's question, "Since when have you been feeling this way?" When the early decision had been recognized, at the therapist's suggestion Jen used her own current grownup Adult and Parent ego states to reenter the hole in the snow with her Child, physically arranging her arms so that she could feel herself holding the Child. She told her Child, "You're a wonderful little girl. You've been trying for so long to make things O.K. by staying in your hole, even if you died. I want you to know that you don't have to do it that way any more. I want you to agree to keep yourself alive." The Child was delighted to agree. To anchor the redecision, the therapist invited Jen to project her parents in front of her and tell them, "I'm not going to kill myself, even if you don't change." This she did with gusto!

A technique we've played with quite a lot lately is a delight for people who easily access the Child. Having established the contract and clarified the early decision that is to be redecided, we say to the patient, "Gather around you all the little children that you once were. Imagine the tiny baby who can't even turn over yet. And the little one who is just starting to wriggle around the mattress a little. The little one who's starting to sit up. . . ." We continue, in order, through developmental stages, until entering school, at which point we say simply "the first grader, the child in second grade, and so forth, up into your teens. You don't have to actually see them, but when you have a sense that they're all here, let me know. Now, tell them all hello, and tell them you're glad they're with you." For a few patients, this brings up a big resistance: "I'm *not* glad." In this instance, we have to apologize for having chosen a method that doesn't fit for the person right now, and shift to another method. When the patient *does* tell the children he or she's glad they're here, the next step is for the patient to say, "I'm speaking to you as the grown-up me. I wasn't around when you really were little, but I'm here now, I'm grown-up, and I have lots of abilities. I will be taking care of you from now on, and I want you to know that as the grown-up I will not do anything that will undermine our life or our health."

After giving the "children" a chance to respond to this, the patient continues, "I want you to agree that no matter what happens, you *also* will not do anything that will endanger our life or our health."

The therapist instructs the patient to discover how the various children are responding, and especially explore if there are objections. When a "child" is objecting, the patient thanks the child for speaking up and says, "What's the good intention of your objection? What *positive* do you want to do, as you object?"

The individual creativity of every person results in a great variety of possibilities here. The job of the therapist becomes one of guiding the patient to negotiate with each projected Child so that all good *purposes* can be served, but by using *methods* that will be satisfactory in the present, instead of the well-intended but destructive methods originally decided. When a number of different Child ego states have objections, this work may extend over several sessions.

At the end of each piece of work, whether there's more to do or not, the patient gathers all the "children" back in, using physical extension of her or his arms to add to the reality of the experience.

Other Comments on Redecision Process with Depression

Except for the prevalence of the "Don't exist" injunction, redecision work with depressed patients is not different from redecision work with patients whose habitual feeling is anxiety, anger, confusion, or a physical symptom. As with the other kinds of symptoms, the therapist persists in defining the patient's self-responsibility and power, until the patient connects with the reality of it. There's no reinforcement for continuing to feel bad (no "Poor you" about the habitual feeling, the symptom), and no support for the patient's self-criticism, but consistent reinforcement for all healthy activities and here-and-now feelings that the patient presents. A contract to give up the distressing habitual feeling is arrived at. The distress itself is used to discover the early decision. With guidance and encouragement from the therapist, the patient creates a situation in which the Natural Child can let go of the old decision and proclaim a new, healthy one. Intellectualizing is avoided for at least 24 hours afterward, so that the decision can be integrated in the person's natural intuitive process. Feeling good is a great reward in itself, and feeling good is celebrated and reinforced by the therapist and, in group therapy, by other members of the group.

Most patients need work both for the Child and for the Parent ego states. Sometimes a Parent ego state persists in putting the Child down, although redecisions in the Child have been successful. Some patients lack a good Parent, and will feel like a lost child until they incorporate one. We rely on work such as Muriel James's (1974, 1981) self-reparenting, and on our own new work (Porter-Steele and Steele 1994) with healing the inner Parent, to address these issues.

Case Example

Bennett, a family physician, was badly depressed, and suicidal to the point that he kept a loaded handgun under his pillow. Now and again he would remove the clip and practice dry-firing it at his head. He had a slowly progressive neurological disease that he knew would eventually cripple him. His marriage was tumultuous and miserable. His children were unhappy and misbehaving. He was adamant that he would kill himself before he would be confined to a wheelchair or become dependent on others.

In a therapy group Bennett was very reluctant to make a no-suicide agreement, as his decision seemed to him to be entirely rational. Following vigorous therapeutic confrontation he was willing to make only a one-day-at-a-time decision to stay alive. Later, he was feeling somewhat better as a result and was willing to explore the childhood origins of his suicidal behavior. The therapist asked him to follow the depressed feeling back in time to the earliest scene that came up. Bennett arrived at a time when he was 1 year old, riding on a train with his mother. He could see the little plastic box of colored candies on the seat beside him. And Mother had disappeared! He was surrounded by a crowd of strangers and was terrified.

Bennett couldn't stand his state of panic. "Are you making a decision what you're going to do?" the therapist asked.

"I'll die, I'll kill myself, I don't know how, but I have to, I can't stand this. I will never ever let myself feel this bad again."

"Come back to your Adult now. Bennett, you've just discovered that you made the decision to kill yourself when you were only a year old. Are you ready now to change that decision?"

Bennett paused. "No! I'll kill myself before I'll let myself be dependent on other people."

After some reflection, the therapist responded. "Bennett, until now you've been guided toward killing yourself by a decision made by a 1-year-old child. If you change that early decision now, it won't mean that you can't make a new, Adult decision later, if you want to at a future time. The issue is, are you going to continue to have your life and death determined by a terrified 1-year-old?"

Bennett was unwilling to be controlled by an infant, and he promptly proceeded with a redecision, qualifying it by emphasizing that he reserved the right to make a decision to suicide if his neurological disorder became severe enough, but it would be an Adult decision. A few weeks later he told us he'd realized "The only time I think about suicide now is when I realize I'm not thinking about suicide any more!"

That was more than a dozen years ago. Bennett's neurological disease has taken its terrible toll. He's progressively become more paralyzed, and had many losses of function. He hasn't been depressed or suicidal. He went through a difficult divorce. He watched, unable to intervene, as some of his children made serious mistakes in their lives. He married again, a woman who is cheerful and energetic in working with his disabilities. He modified his work situation so that he could continue working in a different way when his physical limitations prevented former activities. He had a long convalescence after an illness, and used it to study his religion. His community has honored him prominently. He's kept in touch with us, and provides a stirring inspiration in every dimension of the human spirit.

References

Boyd, H.S., and Cowles-Boyd, L. (1980). Blocking tragic scripts. *Transactional Analysis Journal* 10(3): 227–229.

Goulding, M. (1973). Personal communication.

James, M. (1974). Self-reparenting theory and process. *Transactional Analysis Journal* 4(3): 32–39.

——— (1981). *Breaking Free: Self-Reparenting for a New Life*. New York: Addison-Wesley.

Porter-Steele, N., and Steele, C. A. (1994). Healing the inner parent: bringing the wisdom of the ancestors into psychotherapy. In *Social Systems & TA. The Maastricht Papers. Selections from the 20th EATA Conference*, ed. P. Lapworth, pp. 138–142. Maastricht: European Association for Transactional Analysis.

10

The Treatment of Panic Disorder and Agoraphobia

Dean S. Janoff, Ph.D.

Introduction

It is a privilege to write this chapter on panic disorder and redecision therapy for two reasons. First, too little is commonly understood about the importance of psychological decisions made by young children concerning their emotional safety, danger, and anxiety. These decisions are subtle ways of knowing that are intricately woven into a child's identity and are observable later in his or her life through action, feeling, imagery, and beliefs. These early lessons regarding emotional and physical safety play an influential role in how a person perceives and copes with significant physiological arousal later in life. The development of panic disorder is intimately connected to one's deepest thoughts and feelings about his or her body, physical sensations, safety boundaries, and physical and emotional security.

Secondly, within the circle of mental health professionals there is an ongoing debate on the proper focus of treatment for anxiety disorders. Specifically, most clinical research supports the use of psychoactive medication and/or a cognitive-behavioral approach (Mattick et al. 1990, National Institutes of Health 1991), both of which focus on reduction of panic symptoms. Little or no evidence exists in the literature for effective treatment that includes the resolution of early childhood conflicts as an important part of a specific, behavior-change panic disorder treatment program (National Institute of Mental Health 1993, Roy-Byrne and Katon 1987). Further, there is a growing awareness among professionals and the public that general psychotherapy, while beneficial in many other contexts, is not the treatment of choice for panic attacks (Andrews et al. 1994). Unfortunately, professionals and the public alike remain unaware of redecision therapy: A brief, solution-focused approach that contracts to help people change their experience of physical symptoms as well as longstanding, maladaptive beliefs and feelings based on early emotional and cognitive learning. An example follows which illustrates a panic attack and the development of panic disorder with agoraphobia.

Development of Panic Disorder: The Case of Patti

Patti was not all that different from many of her friends when it came to the things she enjoyed most in her life—friendships, travel, and adventure. She was bright, successful in her college coursework, and was dating an extremely likable young man. She had plans of traveling to Europe for the entire summer with her boyfriend, Stephan, until she had her first panic attack.

Patti was driving with Stephan to visit her parents. She was in the midst of preparing him to meet her mother and father when she began to notice an uncomfortable sensation in her stomach. She didn't say anything at first, although the traffic was heavy and she became increasingly worried that she could no longer concentrate on her driving. Her mind began racing back and forth from her parents to her increasing nausea in her stomach to her boyfriend and to her difficulty driving. Finally, Stephan inquired,

"Hey, Patti, are you all right? You look pale and frightened." It was true. Patti was now feeling very frightened! She thought she was losing her mind and began to pull off the freeway explaining, "Don't worry, I'm fine. I just need to stop for a moment." However, Patti was in fact feeling more and more frightened and uncomfortable. Her heart began to palpitate, her face was fully flushed, her hands and feet tingled, and she felt as if she could not breathe in enough air. Finally, in desperation, Patti began sobbing loudly and yelling that she needed to get to a hospital soon or she might die. Stephan responded immediately and drove to the nearest telephone and called for an emergency ambulance.

Three-and-a-half hours later, Patti and Stephan were sitting in a hospital emergency room listening to a young, on-call internist's diagnosis: "I think you just had an anxiety attack. Your heart and lungs are normal, no EEG abnormalities. In fact, you seem in great health. The medications I gave you will help you to relax and sleep. I really wouldn't worry about this; it is unlikely to happen again. You may want to consult a school counselor when you go back if you feel the need to." Stephan was quite relieved and said so, but privately Patti worried about her future health as they left the hospital for the rest of their weekend.

The anxiety or panic attack described above is familiar to more than 3 million Americans. The National Institute of Mental Health (1993) estimates that 1.6 percent of the population currently suffers from panic disorder or will develop it in their lifetimes (Regier and Robbins 1991). In any given month, approximately 1 million people have panic disorder, and women are twice as likely as men to develop this problem (Regier et al. 1988). People with panic disorder experience unexpected and repeated episodes of intense fear accompanied by a set of unexplained physical symptoms, such as heart palpitations, shortness of breath, chest pains, trembling, or tingling sensations. The good news is that panic disorder is a highly treatable mental health problem. However, it is also true that panic disorder is often undiagnosed, misdiagnosed or improperly treated when correctly diagnosed (ADAA Reporter 1993, National Institute of Mental Health 1993).

In addition to its diagnosis and treatment, the etiology of panic disorder and agoraphobia has been the subject of considerable study and debate (Pasnau and Brystritsky 1990, Taylor and Arnow 1988). Most experts have agreed on a "contributing factors" model to explain the development of panic disorder. The primary factors are genetic predisposition, biochemical irregularities, history of childhood trauma, and conditioning—the pairing of high autonomic arousal with specific places, situations, or internal sensations (National Institute of Health 1991).

Today, there is no way of adequately measuring the exact influence of any or all of the above factors in the etiology of panic disorder. However, we do know that psychological factors are always present in the development of panic disorder and agoraphobia (Barlow 1988). These psychological factors can be divided into: 1) early life experiences (often in one's family) that result in the development of maladaptive beliefs concerning danger, bodily function, disease, and the ability to predict and control one's life in positive ways; and 2) immediate or recent misinterpretation of bodily sensation or situational events that acts either as a trigger or a reaction to a panic attack.

In the Eye of the Tiger: High Anxiety, Panic, and Avoidance

In the panic attack described above, Patti's body responded physiologically as if she were in real danger—as if she were being attacked by a tiger. But where was this tiger, or real danger? By imagining that she was in danger, Patti elicited the so-called "fight or flight" physiological response. This danger mechanism serves as an automatic and comprehensive physiological response to crisis. Fortunately, this danger response takes place quickly, without conscious effort, and results in many important changes. A range of hormones (ACTH, ADH, TSH) from the pituitary gland and neural impulses from the hypothalamus and other structures near the base of the brain control the process. The joint effect of hormonal and neural factors is to render one's physiology ready to defend against physical danger and damage. This high level of sympathetic nervous system activity increases metabolism, muscle tension, blood pressure, and blood flow to skeletal muscles, and directs energy away from maintenance and long-term protective processes (e.g., the immune system), all in an effort to avoid or escape danger.

The perception or anticipation of an attacking tiger also stimulates the fight or flight response system. This ability to anticipate danger can work against us in several important ways. First, it is possible to misattribute danger to a benign event or situation. In this case, the fight or flight system is triggered when, in fact, there is not any real danger to manage, for example, "I thought I heard a car speeding around the corner and my heart nearly jumped out of my body." Second, this major physiological event (fight or flight) can be easily conditioned or associated with a variety of daily situations. Examples include loud noises, a room full of people, wide-open spaces, driving on the freeway, interpersonal conflicts, or an increase in body temperature. Third, once this type of conditioning is in place, the fight or flight response may be triggered when the person sees or imagines the feared situation. In fact, most of our "dangerous situations" in life are only perceived psychological threats (e.g., fear of dying, suffocating, losing one's mind, embarrassment) as opposed to a literal and/or imminent threat to one's physical being. Finally, an important problem associated with conditioned fear is that many people will desperately try to avoid or escape the undesired experience. Repetitive avoidance or agoraphobia is often the real damage caused by panic disorder, namely that one's sense of safety, and therefore activity, can become increasingly limited to the point of becoming literally housebound.

Before we describe redecision therapy with panic and agoraphobia, let us finish the story of how panic disorder developed in the case of Patti.

Three months transpired before Patti's second panic attack. This time it happened in a shopping mall just after having an argument with Stephan over the phone. She and Stephan had not been getting along since the weekend at home with her parents. Although they had several recent verbal fights in which she had felt quite upset, she had not been close to a panic attack. Out of the blue it came—the same symptoms, with the same thoughts of dying or losing her mind. Patti again rushed herself to the local emergency room and was again told that nothing physically appeared wrong with her. This time she was prescribed a longer-acting antianxiety medication. Feeling frustrated and scared, she again left the hospital knowing something was indeed wrong with her, even if the doctor could not tell her what it was.

The next twelve months were a blur in Patti's mind. She and Stephan had several more major blowups and finally decided to part ways. Patti began having weekly and then daily panic attacks. Her school work had noticeably deteriorated and she began withdrawing from even her closest friends. Her anxiety symptoms seemed present all the time: tightness in her chest, fluctuating heart rate, tingling sensations, fatigue, and frustration with her constant worry about when and where she would next be "attacked by panic." Patti's self-esteem plummeted and she felt increasingly ashamed of herself, which led to further isolation and more shame. Eventually, Patti began to avoid situations in which she feared becoming emotionally upset or that she thought might trigger anxiety and panic.

Within one year's time, Patti found herself without faith in her health, her future, her doctors, or her friends. Her family seemed concerned that she was having problems, but they could not understand why she couldn't stop worrying about every little thing. It seemed as if Patti's life had fallen into a million pieces, and she had no idea why or, more importantly, what she could do to feel whole again. She spent the next two years going from one medical specialist to another. Even eight months in personal counseling produced little change in her daily panic attacks.

Patti's situation is typical of panic patients as the disorder develops and many solutions are tried. It was more than three-and-a-half years of suffering before Patti received the appropriate help she needed. She attended a public lecture on panic disorder at a local hospital, which led to her initiating treatment with the author. Her treatment began with a detailed clinical evaluation (Barlow and Craske 1988) and specific education about panic disorder: the physiology of anxiety; the connection between physical sensation, thoughts, images, and feelings; the importance of early childhood family transactions as a "blueprint" for later beliefs about emotional and physical well-being. In addition, Patti was referred for a medical examination and evaluation for the possible use of appropriate medication for treatment of panic.

All in the Family: Early Childhood Decisions Regarding Safety, Danger, and Bodily Sensations

Patti's redecision work began in her second session.

Therapist: What do you want to change about yourself?
Patti: I want to feel safe again.
Therapist: How would you feel different if you felt safe again?
Patti: I would not have this feeling of tenseness in the pit of my stomach or this tingling in my hands that I'm feeling right now. I would feel more relaxed and able to concentrate throughout the day.
Therapist: Do you remember feeling unsafe as a child?

Without hesitation, Patti began to describe a typical family interaction around the dinner table that revealed important information about her early learning regarding fear, anxiety, and loss of control.

Therapist: Start at the beginning and describe this family scene in the present tense, as if it were happening right now.

Patti: I'm sitting at the dinner table with my parents and my brother and sister. I am already feeling tense, as I do every night. Others look tense, too, but no one is saying anything about it. My father and mother are talking now. He looks rageful, and she sounds angry as they begin to argue.

Therapist: And what are you experiencing now as they begin to argue?

Patti: I'm feeling scared, anxious, and unsafe. Their arguing continues to the point where they are now yelling at each other. My father snaps and jumps towards my mother, swinging wildly at her face. I scream for him to stop. My heart is racing, blood is pulsating in my head, and I'm feeling incredibly scared. My mother runs into the bathroom and locks the door. I can hear her sobbing loudly and uncontrollably. I look at my father with fear and disdain. He yells at me, "What the hell are you looking at? You better get out of here before I smack you!" I run to my bedroom crying, feeling scared and ashamed.

Therapist: Yes, and in your bedroom now, what are you doing and thinking?

Patti: I'm sitting on my bed, holding myself and rocking slightly. I'm crying and thinking that my family is awful. I feel lost. My stomach hurts. I hope that my brother and sister are safe. I'm shaking with fear. After a long while, I fall asleep exhausted.

Patti now spontaneously jumps to a new scene—the next morning at the breakfast table with her family.

Patti: Everyone is sitting in his or her usual seat, with the usual tension in my father's face and my mother's voice. No one dares to mention the previous evening's battle. My stomach is tight, my heart is racing, my hands feel tingly as I look around the table. Finally, I can't stand it anymore and ask to leave. I tell my parents that I am feeling very sick and close to throwing up. I go to my room. The last thing I want to do is to go to school.

Therapist: You look very sad right now.

Patti: Yes, I'm feeling so ashamed and unloved by either of my parents. [beginning to sob] I'm so worried about the future. Maybe this is all my fault!

What did Patti learn about her bodily sensations from the experiences described in the family mealtime scenes? First, Patti learned that strong physical sensation (fear and anxiety) was followed by feeling hopeless and unloved by her parents. Second, she learned that feeling threatened or in danger was consistently followed by feeling bad about herself. Finally, she learned that feelings and strong bodily sensations were to be denied or at least never discussed.

Imagine how these early childhood learnings (i.e., decisions) may have helped Patti to survive in her family. In Patti's family it was helpful to know that intense emotion was often followed by verbal threats and rage. This knowledge enabled her to begin preparing for what was coming next. However, a decision that there is always a connection between strong emotional expression and negative consequences could (and did) prove problematic later on in her life. Further, children often make themselves responsible for the bad feelings and conflicts of their parents ("I must be bad" vs. "my parents are angry people"). After many similar family transactions, Patti decided that she was not supposed to be a happy person in life and that intimacy led to conflict, anxiety, and loss of control.

The Minefield of Early Decisions: Developing Cognitions of Danger, Fear, and Anxiety

Negative childhood decisions, originally adaptive, become a psychological minefield activated later in one's life by specific events that are directly or indirectly reminiscent of early childhood experiences. In panic disorder with agoraphobia, early decisions regarding danger, fear, and bodily sensation are of particular importance. For example, Patti decided that the world was not safe for her, based on the violent and unpredictable emotional explosions she experienced within her family. She learned that whenever she felt a moderate level of physical sensation (e. g., heart beats faster, muscles tighten in her chest, neck, and shoulders, breathing becomes constricted, or a tingling sensation is noticeable), danger must be right around the corner. Or, as the folktale goes, the eye of the tiger is near! If this cycle of experience with the same interpretation of danger is repeated again and again, we have someone who is ripe for a panic attack and/or high levels of anxious apprehension. Similarly, children make decisions regarding their relative self-efficacy in the world (Bandura 1977). Significant low self-efficacy can also lead, later in one's life, to an inability to tolerate minimal levels of physical sensation without evoking thoughts of inadequacy, self-doubt, danger, or feelings of anxiety.

Understanding the Development of Panic Attacks, Anxious Apprehension, and Agoraphobic Avoidance in the Mind of the Adapted Child

If you have ever watched a 1-year-old play, you have witnessed what Eric Berne (1961) referred to as the Free Child. At this age, children have no idea that they should be any different than they are. They express their emotions freely, without restraint. As the child grows, his or her parents, relatives, teachers, and others begin the process of socialization. This is where Berne saw the appearance of the Adapted Child; who begins to understand how to survive in a world of competing demands. In Patti's case, her Adapted Child found solutions to the negative decisions she made about herself in relation to her parent's conflicts. These solutions helped Patti adapt to the fact that her parents were not available to support her true needs for nurturance and closeness. By blaming herself ("Something must be wrong with me that my parents ignore my needs so."), Patti was able to take action to try to be a better, more lovable child. To realize that her parents were, in fact, neither prepared to sustain an intimate relationship with each other nor able to provide enough emotionally for their children was too complicated and overwhelming for Patti to understand. Alternatively, Patti's Free Child might well have blurted out such truisms as, "You are not really interested in me," or "I'm really mad at you," which certainly would have been met with strong criticism and the threat of physical reprisal. So Patti increasingly relied on her Adapted Child to find ways to survive her family life.

The Toxic Elixir of Anxiety and Early Childhood Decisions

The Gouldings (1979) have listed a number of typical negative early childhood decisions formulated through traumatic and/or dysfunctional family interactions. The following injunctions and counterinjunctions play a significant role in one's ability to cope with anxiety: "Don't be," "Don't be important," "Don't succeed," "Don't be you," "Don't be sane or well," "Don't belong" (examples of injunctions); and "Be strong," "Be perfect," "Please me," "Feel what I feel," "Work harder" (examples of counterinjunctions). All of the above messages may be reinforced when a child is confronted with a situation that creates anxiety. In fact, as children are challenged with novel or conflicted experiences, a normal feeling of anxiety will occur that evokes many of the important beliefs (decisions) about him- or herself. The feeling of anxiety or fear coupled with a strong negative belief about oneself (e. g., "Don't succeed") can easily lead to further self-doubt, increased anxiety, and perhaps, ultimately, uncontrollable fear. Remember, thoughts of increasing danger or feelings of fear stimulate the sympathetic nervous system (fight or flight response), which triggers further anxiety, fear, and negative beliefs or decisions about oneself.

When the above sequence of negative thoughts and feelings occurs over and over, the developing path of misattributing danger to normal events (actually a threat to one's internal sense of self-control or health) is cemented into a person's way of perceiving his or her world. Not only can internal sensations (e. g., increased heart rate) lead to the conclusion of danger (e. g., "I'm having a heart attack"), but external events such as job promotion can also trigger an internal voice (injunction) that says, "I'm not able to succeed," which can lead to panic. Over time, misattributing danger to a variety of normal events erodes one's ability to use one's perceptions accurately.

The Disappearing Free Child
in Anxious Apprehension and Agoraphobic Avoidance

As already stated, the Adapted Child works hard to figure out ways to survive traumatic childhood experiences. The Free Child's tantrums or legitimate expression of fear and anger may initiate further abuse, as opposed to emotional closeness. The Adapted Child begins to find a way to survive early negative decisions by choosing (with little or no awareness) to work harder, escape, or avoid altogether situations that stimulate the old feelings and beliefs. Anxiety is the vehicle for avoidance or escape behavior. The Adapted Child begins to anticipate danger (anxious apprehension) and learns adeptly how to initiate escape or avoidance responses. The main clue to danger for the Adapted Child is significant sympathetic nervous system arousal, that is, increased heart rate, muscle tension, and so on. Meanwhile the Free Child begins to disappear as he or she learns that there is no support for natural coping responses to frightening experiences. Patti's parents responded to her natural reaction to tension at the dinner table by ignoring or punishing her. She (her Adapted Child) figured out how to survive—escape the situation next time by feeling sick. These solutions are brilliant in childhood but, unfortunately, lead to real problems later as an adult.

Establishing a Contract for Change
in Redecision Work with Panic Disorder

"What do you want to change about yourself today?" is the question posed by the redecision therapist. Usually, the patient with panic disorder responds, "I want to stop having panic attacks." However, with further questioning it often becomes obvious that the patient's previously attempted solutions have included both escape and avoidance behaviors. Therefore it is necessary to distinguish between change (stopping the panic attacks) and all other behaviors that are attempts to avoid or escape a panic attack. For example, a patient may have tried to stop panicking by avoiding driving on certain roads where panic is expected. Alternatively, the patient may have tried to escape the onset of panic by looking for and finding a freeway exit. However, in both of these attempted solutions the problem is once again reinforced. Lasting change means redeciding about the belief that actual danger is always connected to sympathetic nervous system arousal.

Change in the redecision model is paradoxical in that panic attacks disappear the instant they are no longer feared. Sympathetic arousal may continue (heart rate increase, sweaty palms, tingling sensations, tight chest, etc.) but when the person is willing and able to tolerate these sensations, there is no further need to panic. The same situations (e. g., driving on certain roads, riding in an elevator, traveling a long way from home) may continue to elicit a physiological response via classical conditioning. Pavlov (1927) and his dogs demonstrated a long time ago that conditioned responses take time to extinguish. Eventually, without an actual or an anticipated panic attack the old sensations will disappear. Most patients with panic disorder know somewhere in the back of their mind this is true, but their anxiety continues—why?

In order for panic attacks to cease once and for all, many patients will need to confront (redecide) their early childhood decisions regarding safety, danger, and physical sensation (Janoff 1996a). Thus, the therapeutic contract for change must go beyond the patient's commitment to befriend anxiety (learning to tolerate uncomfortable sensations vs. avoiding or escaping) to completing redecisions that support a positive, competent, powerful, and deserving sense of oneself. Without the relevant redecision work, anxiety management strategies may give way to the natural outcome of a continual eroding sense of self—fear in the present and anxiety about the future.

The redecision therapist must assess and direct the patient to a workable contract for change. Redecisions are made about how the patient will choose to think, feel or behave differently. The contract must include: 1) commitment to tolerating uncomfortable sensations, thoughts and images; and 2) commitment to all redecisions necessary to promote a deserving sense of self, for example, "I deserve to be free of my imagined, unrealistic danger and resulting fear and anxiety." The redecision therapist will use education, sensory awareness exercises, gestalt chair work (Perls 1969), and experimentation to help the patient realize his or her goals once the proper therapeutic contract for change is in place.

Making Redecisions: Accessing the Free Child through Images and Memories

Completing redecisions is the work of the Adult and Free Child ego states (Stewart and Joines 1987). The decision to change must be appropriate in the current adult world as well as satisfying the needs of the Free Child. The relevant redecision work is completed by having the patient, in the therapy session, replay early childhood scenes in which both anxiety and a negative sense of self were present. In the case of Patti, she was asked to recall many childhood scenes in which violent anger evoked considerable fear, anxiety, and a negative sense of self. In the therapy session described earlier, Patti was instructed how to set up a dialogue with her mother and father in which she communicated her true feelings regarding their conflicts with each other.

> *Therapist:* Patti, I would like you to imagine your mother and father sitting in these two chairs. Please tell them how you are feeling right now.

Patti: [after a moment of adjusting to their "presence" and continuing to sob] I feel so bad about myself. I'm scared, I don't know how I will survive! [crying loudly] My whole body is buzzing.

Therapist: Tell them both what you want from them right now.

Patti: I want you to help me, instead of hitting each other! I want you to stop scaring me. I want you to hold me. [crying and moving to a fetal position]

Therapist: [pause] Patti, look at your parents now. How are they responding to you?

Patti: I don't know . . . , they look kind of confused, scared.

Therapist: Yes, and are they going to help you right now?

Patti: No, they really haven't got a clue, about me or themselves. [rotates herself towards her parents, tightening her neck and facial muscles]

Therapist: What are you feeling in your body now?

Patti: I feel tense, my heart is beating fast. . . . I'm hot. . . . I'm feeling angry and sad. I'm angry and sad that I feel so hopeless!

Therapist: [pause] Patti, I would like you to come and stand over here, next to me. [both therapist and Patti move to stand outside of the chairs, so that Patti can begin to activate her Adult ego state] Tell me about how bad this little girl is feeling.

Patti: She's feeling really bad, like her parents don't love her.

Therapist: Yes, she thinks so. And she is scared of their violence, isn't she?

Patti: Oh, definitely! She doesn't know how to stop their fighting and screaming at each other.

Therapist: Do you really think she can stop their fighting?

Patti: No. . . . she can't solve their problems.

Therapist: Do you think she is really as bad as she feels about herself?

Patti: No, absolutely not! She's just stuck in this family for now. She copes pretty well considering how upset she feels.

Therapist: She *is* excellent at coping! In fact, I think she is more
    amazing than you give her credit.

Patti: [beginning to smile] Yeah, she is really amazing!

In this excerpt, Patti expressed how frightened she was by her
parents' anger and how much she really needed their attention and
love. Patti realized that both of her parents felt helpless, and that they
were unprepared to change. After this work in her early childhood
scene, Patti was ready to make new decisions regarding her parents
and herself. Her redecisions included: "I am lovable just the way I
am," "My fear and anxiety were due to a real threat against my
physical and emotional security," "I am not currently nor do I choose
to ever again live with anyone who threatens my physical or emotional security," "Strong physical sensation *can* be fun and pleasurable," and "I was not completely safe then, I am now!"

Moving from Past to Present: How Redecision Work Affects Anxiety in Adult Life

Patti made an important shift in her stance about her parents, herself,
and the world around her. She felt more empowered and deserving
of a life free from inhibiting anxiety. She was now ready to benefit
from gestalt awareness training (Janoff 1996b) and the many important cognitive-behavioral techniques for understanding and managing anxiety in her present life (Barlow and Craske 1988). In further
therapy sessions, she gained confidence in knowing that her physical
sensations were not dangerous ("no tigers here!"), which in turn
changed the way she thought about her previous panic attacks. "I can
see now that I was never in any real danger even when I panicked.
Rather, I just scared myself with my old feelings and thoughts about
how out of control I imagined I was, which of course only magnified
my fear and anxiety." Patti concluded, "You know, I can't even
imagine being panicked if I were to have an anxiety attack. I'd be
uncomfortable for sure, but I'd survive!"

Anchoring Redecisions in the Context of Current Experience

With Patti's redecision work in place, she was ready to learn how to experience her bodily sensations in a new way. Patti was asked to complete graduated exposure exercises which stimulated the very physical sensations she originally tried so desperately to avoid. Hyperventilating, spinning around in a chair, and sitting in a small, enclosed closet with the lights out served as excellent exposure exercises. Initially, she felt a substantial amount of physiological arousal (heart rate increase, difficulty breathing, hands and feet tingling, increased body temperature, tightening in her stomach, neck and shoulders) as well as the old thoughts about possible danger. However, she also was instructed on exactly what to expect for each exercise. Patti began to tolerate each activity with less fear, less physiological arousal, and an increased sense of power and mastery. She understood quickly how her fearful thinking was triggered by her physiological sensations and that feeling uncomfortable was not always an indication of real danger.

Initially, the exposure exercises were completed in the therapist's office where Patti's ongoing thoughts, feelings, and sensations were carefully monitored. Patti's awareness of herself, her body, and her many strengths grew in leaps and bounds as she completed the exercises. Next, Patti was instructed to practice her new learning in different contexts between therapy sessions. First, Patti chose to tell a close friend whom she had been avoiding how she had been feeling hurt and angry for several months over a previous argument. Patti reported feeling "anxious, heart pounding, and tight all over" as she began the confrontation. However, she learned that she could now tolerate her strong physical sensations even when taking an emotional risk with someone she cared about. The following week, Patti made a trip home to visit her parents. She expected to feel a wide range of uncomfortable bodily sensations and feelings throughout the visit. She was right! Both her memories of upsetting family events and her ongoing interactions with her parents evoked strong feelings and mental images. Patti reported that her old negative self-image lurked in the background during the entire visit. "I cycled through one wave of uncomfortable sensations after another, all the while remembering what I had decided about me, my past, and my parents. I never came close to panicking, although I was exhausted at the end of each day."

Through these and other planned experiences, Patti was able to anchor her redecisions and new skills in experiencing her physical sensations to her present life. Patti noticed how often her feelings and sensations changed over the course of each day. At the end of thirteen treatment sessions, Patti had been panic-free for two months. At an eight-month follow-up, Patti still had not had another panic attack and was very excited about her progress and a new relationship she had recently begun.

Conclusion

In the case of Patti described above, and in many similar cases, a variety of factors contribute to the overall success in treatment, including: accurate information about panic disorder; education regarding the physiology of anxiety and the physical causes of panic-like symptoms; consideration of an appropriate medication; therapeutic focus on the psychological issues of control, relative safety, and their origins in early childhood decisions; and very specific awareness training in observing sensations, cognitions, and subtle avoidance behavior. The goal of the present chapter was to highlight the use of redecision therapy in the context of treating panic disorder. A rabbi was said to have once remarked, when asked about the medicinal powers of chicken soup, "Chicken soup does not cure illness, chicken soup cures the patient." When Bob and Mary Goulding (1978) wrote *The Power is in the Patient*, they understood the wisdom of the rabbi; redecision therapy helps the patient reclaim a sense of power, dignity and self-worth. The patient cures the illness, not the therapy. Many patients seek professional help to be "treated" for panic disorder.

Their sense of powerlessness is acute. Redecision therapy helps people to fight back with new decisions about how to think, feel, and behave differently. "I'm turning tigers into kittens," was how one patient put it after his triumph over panic.

References

ADAA Reporter (1993). HARP study shows medical problems, under-use of behavioral treatment. *Anxiety Disorders Association of America*, IV(1).

Andrews, G., Crino, R., Lampe, L., et al. (1994). *The Treatment of Anxiety Disorders: Clinician's Guide and Patient Manuals*. New York: Cambridge University Press.

Bandura, A. (1977). Self-efficacy: toward a unifying theory of behavioural change. *Psychological Review* 84:191–215.

Barlow, D. H. (1988). *Anxiety and Its Disorders: The Nature and Treatment of Anxiety and Panic*. New York: Guilford.

Barlow, D. H., and Craske, M. G. (1988). *Mastery of Your Anxiety and Panic*. Albany, NY: Graywind.

Berne, E. (1961). *Transactional Analysis in Psychotherapy*. New York: Grove.

Goulding, R., and Goulding, M. (1978). *The Power is in the Patient*. San Francisco: TA Press.

––––––– (1979). *Changing Lives through Redecision Therapy*. New York: Brunner/Mazel.

Janoff, D. S. (1996a). *Group treatment of panic disorder and agoraphobia*. Workshop presented at American Group Psychotherapy Association annual meeting, San Francisco, CA.

––––––– (1996b). *Integrating gestalt and cognitive-behavioral therapy for panic disorder and agoraphobia*. Workshop presented at Anxiety Disorders Association of America annual meeting, Orlando, FL.

Mattick, R. P., Andrews, G., Hadzi-Pavlovic, D., and Christensen, H. (1990). Treatment of panic disorder and agoraphobia: an integrative review. *Journal of Nervous and Mental Disorders* 178:567–576.

National Institute of Mental Health (1993). *Panic Disorder in the Medical Setting*. (NIH Publication No. 93–3482.) Washington, DC: U.S. Government Printing Office.

National Institutes of Health (1991). *Treatment of panic disorder*. (NIH consensus development conference statement), vol. 9, no. 2. Bethesda, MD: National Institutes of Health.

Pasnau, R. O., and Bystritsky, A. (1990). An overview of anxiety disorders. *Bulletin of the Menninger Clinic* 54:977–986.

Pavlov, I. P. (1927). *Conditioned Reflexes*, trans. G. V. Anrep. London: Oxford University Press.

Perls, F. (1973). *The Gestalt Approach and Eyewitness to Therapy*. Palo Alto, CA: Science and Behavior Books.

Regier, D. A., Boyd, J. H., and Burke, J. D. (1988). One-month prevalence of mental disorders in the United States. *Archives of General Psychiatry* 45:977–986.

Regier, D. A., and Robins, L. N. (1991). *The NIMH Epidemiologic Catchment Area Study*. New York: Free Press.

Roy-Byrne, P. P., and Katon, W. (1987). An update on the treatment of anxiety disorders. *Hospital and Community Psychiatry* 38:835–843.

Stewart, I., and Joines, V. (1987). *T.A. Today: A New Introduction of Transactional Analysis*. England: Lifespace.

Taylor, C. B., and Arnow, B. (1988). *The Nature and Treatment of Anxiety Disorders*. London: Collier-Macmillan.

11

The Treatment of Bulimia

Linda Carmicle, Ph.D.

Introduction

Modern women have tragically fallen prey to the belief system that equates feminine beauty with gauntness. Many women in Western cultures have adopted bulimic behavior in an attempt to cope with societal demands for the perfect body. There are estimates that more than 13 percent of college women are bulimic (Goldfarb et al. 1985). A 1994 survey of fitness instructors found that one-third of the female respondents and one-tenth of the males reported having an eating disorder (Stedman 1996). Bulimia can be a deadly disorder that creates dangerous physiological and psychological consequences. Although bulimia has affected women for centuries, it was not defined in the *Diagnostic and Statistical Manual* until 1980. There is still a great paucity in professional literature about the diagnosis and treatment of bulimia, with very little knowledge of male bulimics.

The current climate in health care demands knowledge of brief therapies. Redecision therapy is an efficient modality to treat this life-threatening disease. It is a methodology that addresses early decisions and enables patients to make changes in the present. Redecision therapy is fast-paced and very productive, as it deals with both the affective and cognitive aspects of psychological growth.

I have been concerned about the psychological and societal causation of bulimic behavior. My interest in eating disorders grew as a result of clinical work with patients, some of whom came to therapy presenting problems of depression or anxiety. Overconcern with appearance and body weight emerge early in the therapy, and eventually lead to the discovery of bulimic behaviors.

I often find that the depressed, perfectionistic young women who "just want to feel better" have really chosen me for a therapist because they learned that I specialize in the treatment of bulimia. I believe patients and their families have been alerted to the dangers of eating disorders. Within the last three or four years, some patients have been coming to therapy specifically for the treatment of bulimia. There are fewer cases reported in men (Brownwell and Foreyt 1986), and in the ten years that I have worked with eating disorder clients, I have only seen three male bulimics. Because popular trends demand a male to be big and strong, I think steroid abuse may be the male counterpart to eating disorders in females.

Early Child ego decisions concerning self-worth, awareness of biological and emotional needs, and perception of family expectations have contributed to bulimia. The desire for the perfect body leads to rigid dieting, starvation, and hunger. This can cause the cycle of binge eating, purging, and guilt. Although a patient may view giving up binge eating as the goal in therapy, treatment of bulimia is far more complex. Recovery from bulimia consists of many change contracts that involve: educating the Adult ego state about nutrition and body size; teaching the Child ego state to accept and value the self regardless of physical appearance; instructing the Parent ego state to nurture appropriately by healthy caretaking of the body and emotions.

Treatment generally lasts from six months to two years. The duration of therapy will depend on the severity of the disease and the treatment modality (Garner and Garfinkel 1985). Without effective treatment, a patient may suffer with an eating disorder her entire life. Hospitalization of at least thirty days in a good eating disorder unit will often decrease treatment time. New eating habits can be established while patients work through the psychological causes of the disease. However, current insurance plans rarely cover hospitalization for eating disorders and many good facilities have closed.

It is my opinion that redecision therapy is especially effective with bulimic patients because it incorporates cognitive aspects of behavior, uses gestalt experiential exercises, and teaches self-nurturing. The literature is unanimous about the lack of self-nurturance in this population (Garner and Garfinkel 1985, Johnson and Connors 1987). Furthermore, significant improvements have been reported in cognitive-behavioral groups (Johnson and Connors 1987), as well as an experimental group using gestalt techniques (Boskind-White and White 1983). Group treatment has been found to be very effective with eating disorder patients (Johnson and Connors 1987). Lieberman, Yalom, and Miles (1973) noted the importance of both cognition and affect in their research on group therapy involving a variety of modalities. Out of the 17 groups they studied, the most successful group was led by Bob Goulding.

Definition of Bulimia

Bulimia is a Greek word that means "great hunger" or "ox hunger" (Boskind-White 1983, p. 19). The second edition of the *Diagnostic and Statistical Manual* identified bulimia as binge eating, and did not refer to the purging. The purgative practices in bulimia were ignored in the literature until 1976. However, the *DSM-IV* (1994) includes both purging and binge eating in the definition of bulimia, as well as defining purging and nonpurging types of bulimia nervosa. The purging type misuses laxatives, diuretics, or enemas, as well as vomiting, in an effort to control her weight. The nonpurging type may employ fasting or excessive exercise as compensatory behaviors rather than vomiting or other methods of expulsion (*DSM-IV* 1994).

Physiological Factors in Bulimia

The vomiting, laxatives, and diuretic abuse and dietary chaos practiced by bulimic women can have life-threatening consequences.
Dehydration, malnutrition, hair loss, brittle nails, fatigue, insomnia,
constipation, edema, bloating, and abdominal pain are all possible
problems. A more serious consequence of binge eating can be pan-
creatitis. Frequent vomiting can cause swelling and pain in the
salivary glands, dental problems, and depletion of stomach acids and
electrolytes. The loss of potassium, sodium, and chloride can result in
heart attack (Johnson and Connors 1987).

The weight gain and binging in bulimia may be a result of constant dieting, which ultimately slows the metabolism, causing one to
gain weight more easily. Food restriction by bulimic women sets
them up for a binge, as the body is actually starving. Onset occurs in
adolescence and the purging behavior generally commences a year or
so after the origin of the bingeing episodes (Fairburn et al. 1982).

Theoretical Perspectives

Although accounts of binge eating in young women date back to the
nineteenth century, it was not until the 1970s that the binge/purge
cycle began to receive attention in the professional journals. Before
then, bulimia was sometimes considered to be one of the symptoms of
anorexia and was not treated as a different disorder.

Normal-weight women in Western societies have demonstrated a
fear of being fat (Goldfarb et al. 1985). Overweight people are often
discriminated against in our perfectionistic culture. Advertising promotes extreme slenderness as the ideal. Shopping malls display a
multitude of high-fashion apparel on slender mannequins in shops
that surround food courts filled with savory, fragrant, fattening
foods. Consequently, the profusion of appetizing advertisements and
a fast-paced, high-stress society have contributed to overeating (Gar-

ner and Garfinkel 1985). The ambivalence in the Child of the bulimic woman alternately accepts and rejects the Parent message to be perfect. The Adapted Child is attempting to have the perfect body image, while the stressed, hungry Free Child binges on food to lower the anxiety and silence the Parent.

I strongly believe that eating disorders are intertwined with gender conflicts and the search for identity. There appears to be a parallel between the rise of eating disorders and the feminist struggles of the twentieth century (Orbach 1978). A woman today must be slim, intelligent, successful in a career, a loving wife and mother, and submissive to men (Wolf 1991). This emphasizes a woman's need to "Be perfect," "Try hard," "Please me," and "Be strong."

Women have become obsessed with being thin as a way of obtaining meaning in their lives. They have assimilated "Don't be you," "Please me," and "Be what I want you to be" into their life scripts. These women have exaggerated the stereotypical feminine role and this obsessive pursuit of thinness has cost them self-worth and individuality. Eating disorders are symptoms in female developmental crises and conflict in the process of mother/daughter separation (Chernin 1985). The Child ego state of a parent has passed on the dangerous injunctions of "Don't grow up" and "Don't be you" to the Child ego state of the daughter. At the same time, the mother's Parent has told the child to "Be strong," "Be perfect," and "Try hard."

Hilde Bruch (1978), a physician and psychoanalyst, was a pioneer in the field of eating disorders. Bruch described three fundamental characteristics of patients with eating disorders that I have seen in most bulimic patients. They are: a distortion of body image; deep feelings of being ineffective, and the inability to determine hunger, satiety, and emotional conditions. Thus a child incorporates "Don't feel," "Don't succeed," "Don't be you," "Don't want what you want," and many other harmful messages that will need to be redecided in therapy.

Table 11-1 presents the negative messages (injunctions and counterinjunctions) that I have observed in the Child ego of eating disorder patients. Although these may be observed in many other groups, they are commonly found in people with eating disorders.

Table 11-1.

NEGATIVE MESSAGES IN THE CHILD EGO STATE OF EATING DISORDER PATIENTS

	Anorexia *Addiction to Thinness*	Bulimia *Addiction to Food and Thinness* (Purging/Nonpurging)	Morbid Obesity *Addiction to Food*
Injunction	Don't be Don't be you Don't feel Don't succeed Don't grow up Don't be sexual	Don't be Don't be you Don't feel Don't succeed Don't be sexual	Don't be Don't be you Don't feel Don't succeed Don't be sexual
Counter-injunctions	Be righteous Be stoic Please others Be persistent Look perfect Be perfect Try hard	Be sexual Grow up/be a child Please others Be strong Look good Be perfect Try hard	 Grow up/be a child Please others Be strong Be perfect Try hard

Anorexia: weight loss of at least 25 percent of ideal body weight.

Bulimia: weight is close to ideal, but is maintained by vomiting, use of laxatives/diuretics, excessive exercise, or restrictive dieting.

Obesity: weighing at least 20 percent more than ideal body weight. May have characteristics like either nonpurging bulimic or morbidly obese.

Morbidly Obese: weighing at least 100 percent more than ideal body weight.

Purging and Nonpurging Bulimics

The more important and distinguishing symptom in bulimia is the gorging and not the purging (Garfinkel et al. 1987). As discussed previously, the *DSM-IV* has defined purging and nonpurging types of bulimia. Nonpurgers do not vomit or abuse laxatives, but rather restrict food and/or exercise excessively. I have found several differences between these two categories of bulimia (Carmicle 1995). The most important is that the purger appears to have a more critical and undernurturing Parent ego state than the nonpurger.

Current eating disorder literature is unanimous about the role of mother, food, early infant bonding, love, and bulimia. It states that the binge is taking in mother and the purge is rejecting mother (Shulman 1991). My 1991 research indicated that both purging and nonpurging bulimic women experience a paucity of maternal nurturing. However, I found that nonpurging bulimic women perceived fathers to be more loving and less domineering than purging women perceived their fathers (Carmicle 1992). Therefore, I believe bingeing is taking in mother but purging is a symbolic rejection of the father.

For example, April perceived her father as very domineering, sarcastic, and critical of both her and her mother. She thought that her mother was nurturing even though she experienced her mother as her equal. They banded together against a father who was verbally abusive. April was a purging bulimic who vomited almost daily when she began treatment. A great deal of her work in therapy consisted of placing her father in the empty chair while she released her anger toward him and gained a feeling of potency. It was only after much work with her father that she began to realize she received very little nurturing from her mother, and actually felt she needed to protect her. There will be a more detailed discussion of April in the treatment section of this article.

In contrast, Sara, a nonpurging bulimic, said that while both of her parents were somewhat critical of her, her mother was impossible to please. However, her father was very proud of her high marks in school and appeared to respect her intellectually. They shared a common interest in literature and science and often visited museums together. The bulk of Sara's therapy consisted of dealing with the negative messages from her mother. In redecision work Sara stopped trying to please her mother and began to feel her own emotions. By giving up "Please me," "Be perfect," "Don't be you," and "Don't feel," she was able to create a nurturing Parent ego state, and no longer had to bury negative feelings with food.

Redecision Therapy and Bulimia

A series of decisions made at an early age by the Child ego state results in individual life scripts or dramas (Goulding and Goulding 1978). Three of the major life dramas described by Claude Steiner (1974), depression, madness, and drug addiction, can be found in patients with bulimia. Bulimia involves an addiction to food and to an ideal body size. The constant preoccupation with food and the disapproval of one's body leads to anger and depression. The addictive behavior of binge eating and undoing, or purging, results in chaotic behavior that is a type of madness.

In redecision terms, the Adult ego state of a bulimic patient is discredited by her Child ego state. She has accepted the negative injunctions from her parent's Child ego state: "Don't be you," "Don't feel," "Don't grow up," and "Don't think." At the same time, her Parent ego has adopted the counterinjunctions from her parents telling her to "Be perfect," "Try hard," and "Grow up." These conflicting messages keep her in a state of confusion. Most bulimic patients have many memories of contradictions concerning food. They must eat Mother's cooking to show that she is appreciated, but then they are told how it will make them fat.

Treatment

A bulimic patient often enters therapy because of depression or relationship problems. The preoccupation with food and body size interferes with healthy interpersonal interactions. Generally, some form of confrontation by friend, family, or professional has taken place before the bulimic is ready to face the eating disorder. The contract stage can be very tricky as the patient may attempt to make a social contract around what she thinks she *should* do. "I want to stick to a diet," or "My mother is worried about my vomiting, so I guess I should give it up."

At this stage I will be very specific with the patient about what she *wants* to change. She may then say, "I just want to feel better about myself," or "Stop being ruled by the scales." I will then invite her to define "feel better," or ask her to help me understand what it means to be "ruled by the scales." We will continue to narrow the contract to clarify a measurable, observable feeling or behavior that the patient truly *wants* to change. The therapist also needs to be aware of dangerous or harmful contracts.

An example of this would be Mary's proposed contract. She was a dance major in college and discharged a great deal of energy throughout the day. Mary stuck to a very rigid food plan and her proposed contract was to never eat more than 1,000 calories a day. Although this may appear to be an appropriate contract, current nutritional information concedes that this is much too low (Ornish 1993, Sheats 1992). Mary's Adult ego was contaminated with erroneous information about nutrition. She agreed to consult a dietitian, and in a subsequent session contracted to stick to the recommended food plan.

One of the primary functions in the therapeutic process is to decontaminate the Adult ego state. In TA terms, the Adult of the bulimic patient is contaminated by erroneous beliefs regarding food and diet. Decontamination will replace fictitious, imaginary Child and Parent information with factual knowledge. Part of this may be achieved by education.

A multidisciplinary approach is needed with a bulimic population. As cited in the example above, I often refer bulimic patients for nutritional counseling. It is important that those of us working with eating disorders have some knowledge of healthy eating patterns so we can evaluate the competency of the professional we use for dietary support. Someone needs to be a food policeman for these patients and it is better that a dietitian or nutritionist play that role. The therapist may lose the ability to support autonomous change if we attempt to control food intake.

These patients also need to be monitored by a physician who understands eating disorders. If they are vomiting or using laxatives daily, they may need hospitalization. Antidepressants are often helpful, especially the drugs used in treating obsessive/compulsive disorders (Hyman and Arana 1987). Overeaters Anonymous is a good support system for some patients; however, the bulimic's fear of fat will often keep her from bonding with very obese members. An organization called Anorexia Nervosa and Related Eating Disorders (ANAD) caters to anorexia and bulimia, but is still quite hard to find in many areas. If the family is cooperative, schedule a few family sessions to discourage their enabling behavior.

Bulimic patients do well in a redecision group. Accepting positive strokes from the therapist and other group members can be a valuable model for developing a nurturing Parent ego state in the patient. Treatment will involve a series of contracts around changing eating habits, accepting the body and self, learning to play, and establishing appropriate nurturing behavior. Giving up commands to "Be perfect," "Please others," "Stop feeling," will free the Child ego state, which will enable responsible, spontaneous behavior.

An example is April, described earlier, who ate very little at mealtimes, but would binge between meals and then purge. Her redecision work follows:

Therapist: April, what do you want to change about yourself today?

April: I want to stop gorging on junk food between meals.

Therapist: How will you be different if you stop gorging on junk food?

April: I'll stop feeling helpless and sad.

Therapist: What do you say in your head about you when you gorge?

April: That I'm stupid and can't do anything right.

Therapist: And what do you tell yourself about other people when you gorge?

April: That they think I am stupid, sloppy, fat, and ugly.

Therapist: You are a little kid and you feel helpless and sad. You are telling yourself that you are stupid and can't do anything right, and someone is calling you stupid, fat, sloppy, and ugly. What's the early scene?

April: We are at the dinner table, I am very hungry, the food is good, and I begin to eat rather fast. My father starts criticizing my manners, and says I am stupid and sloppy, and that I am becoming fat and ugly.

Therapist: What happens next?

April: I think Mom tried to say something, but he yelled at her and I then ran to my room in tears. It seemed like a long time later when Mom slipped in with some cookies and hot chocolate. She told me not to let my father know that she had brought the food or we would both be in trouble.

Therapist: And then what did you feel?

April: Confused. I wanted the food, but felt it would be wrong to eat, that I would get Mom in trouble, but I ate anyway, and then felt really sad, stupid, and angry at my father.

Therapist: Your father is over there in the chair. Tell him how you feel.

April: [in a loud, angry voice] I'm hungry and you won't let me eat.

Therapist: Be your father and answer April.

April: [as Father in the other chair] I just wanted you to have good manners and not be as fat as your mother.

Therapist: Be April and respond.

April: [returns to the first chair and looks at the therapist] That's what it's about, he was always criticizing Mom about her weight, and stupid mistakes she would make.

Therapist: So tell him that.

April: [looking at the chair] I'm not Mommy, I'm not fat, and I'm not stupid. My teacher says I'm really good at math and reading. [with lots of animation] I'm not stupid, I'm not stupid, I'm not stupid. [April's strong emotions indicated that she has made a redecision to no longer feel stupid, and this is one step toward reprogramming the negative parent tapes.]

Therapist: And what will you tell yourself so you will not feel stupid? [This is a way to anchor the redecision.]

April: I am not my Mother, I have a good education, good job, and I can balance my own checkbook.

Therapist: Good work.

This was a turning point for April. Even though the work seemed to take a very different route than expected, she learned a great deal about the confusing messages in her childhood. Father wanted her to be perfect and please him. Neither parent was comfortable with her feelings and April reported she always left the room when she started to cry. April was frightened of her father's anger and in turn was afraid to feel or express her own anger. She realized how this scene had set up secret binges between meals and invoked the negative emotions. Later work involved April putting her mother in the empty chair and expressing her feelings about her mother's inability to protect her, as well as involving her in clandestine food binges. The secret collusion, along with the child being placed in the middle of parental discord, often occurs in this population.

Many bulimic patients have unusual food restrictions and will totally eliminate certain food groups. Mary was stuck in a Type 3 impasse between her Free Child and Adapted Child. Her hungry Free Child binged on fruit, yogurt, and vegetables but would not allow any meats, fats, grains, or starches in her diet. She was from a large family and had memories of meals including many starches and pasta dishes. Around age 12 her Adapted Child learned from relatives that rich pasta dishes were high in calories. She later expanded this idea to include several food groups. Her work involved double-chair dialogue between these two parts of the Child. The patient moved back and forth between two chairs. The Free Child commented, "I'm hungry, you are starving me, I can't get full," while the Adapted Child argued, "You will get fat if you keep eating. Potatoes are bad, cereal is bad, and you can't have them." Resolution involved the Adult ego taking control and proposing an educated compromise to the two clashing Child ego states. This was done by having the patient stand back and observe the two empty chairs. I stood beside her and asked, "What are you going to do with those two children?" As she was still puzzled, I told her that she would need to take control of them. Mary then decided she would have one starch or grain at each meal and told the two children this would curtail the amount of fruit she would eat. It was a long struggle, but Mary found that she did not binge as often when she added grains and in time her eating habits improved.

Once the patient has established the desire to give up the eating disorder, she will need to accept her feelings and take responsibility for appropriate healthy eating. Learning to accept her body and determining when she is physically hungry will be a major challenge. She will need a great deal of guidance in developing her own Nurturing Parent ego while giving up the negative messages from her parent's Child ego. Below is an example of a patient confronting her parent's negative message.

Jane: I often binge on chocolate and then I feel terribly guilty. [looks down and appears very young]

Therapist: Sounds like guilt is an old feeling for you. [patient nods without looking up]

Therapist: Do you want to give up guilt?

Jane: Yes, I feel guilty about so many things.

Therapist: Go back to a time when you were very young and felt guilty.

Jane: I'm 6 years old and Mother has just made chocolate fudge.

Therapist: What are you feeling?

Jane: I'm excited and I take several pieces off the plate.

Therapist: And then?

Jane: Mother looks angry and says, "I don't like to cook candy because you always make a pig of yourself."

Therapist: What are you feeling?

Jane: Hurt, sad, embarrassed.

Therapist: Will you tell your mother how you feel?

Jane: Oh no, she would be hurt and upset.

Therapist: So put your mother in the empty chair and tell her that you will stay hurt and sad so she won't be upset.

Jane: I don't want to do that.

Therapist: What do you want to tell her?

Jane: I don't want you to call me a pig. [patient starts to cry]

Therapist: Tell your mother how you feel when she calls you a pig.

Jane: You are a mean, mean Mommy and I'm angry at you. You should be ashamed of yourself for treating a little kid this way. [patient begins to laugh] I can't believe I said that to her.

Therapist: What do you feel now?

Jane: Relieved. It's her shame and guilt.

Therapist: What will you tell the mother in your head the next time you want chocolate?

Jane: I'm old enough to make my own decisions.

Therapist: Good work!

After Jane had completed her work, Susan, an experienced group member, said, "Jane, while you were working, I had an image of your mother as a chocolate-coated candy pig like the candy bunnies in Easter baskets." Jane laughed and decided the chocolate pig image would be a good anchor to remind her of the redecision.

The work demonstrated above presents one key piece of the puzzle that enabled Jane to gain autonomy and to free herself from the negative messages she accepted as a child. She began to listen to her own internal signals about hunger and satiety, which ultimately stopped her addictive bingeing on chocolate. As Jane made more and more positive redecisions, she further decontaminated or reeducated the Adult and freed the Child. The therapist continued to stroke good work, while inviting Jane to attend to her feelings and to take responsibility for her behavior.

When patients begin to value themselves and accept their own needs and emotions, the Adult can intelligently evaluate external information. Jane had made some good redecisions between her Adapted Child and Critical Parent, which resulted in several months of healthy eating. When she later attended a family reunion, her uncle remarked that the food on her plate would make her fat. Jane went into the bathroom and vomited. She then had to make more redecisions concerning her need to always please others and her refusal to listen to her own body cues around hunger and satiety. It was approximately six weeks before she stopped purging and regained healthy eating behavior.

When treating a patient in relapse, other events are often discovered that lead to more redecisions. Jane's later work involved a scene at a school basketball game when she was about age 13. A classmate told her she couldn't get a boyfriend because she would rather eat hot dogs and get fat than flirt with boys. Jane remembered she was very uncomfortable with her body as she entered puberty and that she had a crush on one of the basketball players. This combination of events created more self-doubt about food, body image, and sexuality. As with most bulimic patients, Jane had to give up the negative messages "Be perfect," 'Don't be sexual," "Please others," and "Stop feeling" in order to become autonomous and free herself from bulimia.

Conclusion

Bulimia is a disease with many facets. It can be physically, socially, and emotionally debilitating. The Adult ego state is filled with erroneous information concerning food and body size. The Child ego state contains many negative messages, and the Parent ego state is critical, with little capacity for nurturing. Bulimic patients are unable to listen to their own body cues concerning hunger and satiety. They are addicted to both food and perfection, and overeat to bury uncomfortable emotions. The guilt feelings following a binge lead to the undoing or purging behavior. Thus, the binge/purge cycle begins with increased depression, self-doubt, pain, and anger. The Adult ego requires nutritional education, the Child ego needs to accept feelings, while the Parent ego becomes a good nurturer.

Redecision therapy is a powerful therapeutic modality that provides the protection, permission, and potency that enable lifesaving changes in bulimic patients. By utilizing both the cognitive and affective aspects of psychological change, the patient is guided toward educated redecisions and self-nurturing behaviors. Although they will experience many struggles between the hungry Free Child and the compliant Adapted Child, these patients will be empowered to give up dangerous societal messages about body size and negative Parental admonishments that curtail autonomy. Redecision therapy will enhance the ability to experience recovery from addiction to food and thinness, as well as the joy of spontaneity.

References

Boskind-White, M., and White, W. C. (1983). *Bulimarexia: The Binge/Purge Cycle*. New York: Norton.

Brownell, K. D., and Foreyt, J.P., eds. (1986). *Handbook of Eating Disorders*. New York: Basic Books.

Bruch, H. (1973). *Eating Disorders*. New York: Basic Books.

———— (1978). *The Golden Cage*. Cambridge, MA: Harvard University Press.

———— (1985). Four decades of eating disorders. In *Handbook of Psychotherapy for Anorexia Nervosa and Bulimia*, ed. D. M. Garner and P. E. Garfinkel, pp. 7–18. New York: Guilford.

Carmicle, L. H. (1992). *The perception of parental love in purging and nonpurging bulimic women* (Doctoral dissertation, Fielding Institute). Santa Barbara, CA.

———— (1995). The perception of parental love in purging and nonpurging bulimic women. *Texas Counseling Association Journal* 23(1):1–8.

Chernin, K. (1985). *The Obsession*. New York: Harper & Row.

Diagnostic and Statistical Manual of Mental Disorders (1994). 4th ed. Washington, DC: American Psychiatric Association.

Fairburn, C. G., Cooper, Z., and Cooper, P. (1986). The clinical features and maintenance of bulimia nervosa. In *Handbook of Eating Disorders*, ed. K. D. Brownell and J. P. Foreyt, pp. 389–404. New York: Basic Books.

Garfinkel, P. M., Garner, D. M., and Goldbloom, D. S. (1987). Eating disorders: implications for the 1990s. *Canadian Journal of Psychiatry* 32(7):624–631.

Garner, D. M., and Garfinkel, P. E., eds. (1985). *Handbook of Psychotherapy for Anorexia Nervosa and Bulimia*. New York: Guilford.

Gilligan, C. (1982). *In a Different Voice: Psychological Theory and Women's Development*. Cambridge, MA: Harvard University Press.

Goldfarb, L. A., Dykens, E. M., and Gerrard, M. (1985). The Goldfarb fear of fat scale. *Journal of Personality Assessment* 49(3):329–332.

Goulding, R. L., and Goulding, M. M. (1978). *The Power is in the Patient*. San Francisco: TA Press.

———— (1979). *Changing Lives through Redecision Therapy*. New York: Brunner/Mazel.

Humphrey, L. L. (1986). Structural analysis of parent–child relationships in eating disorders. *Journal of Abnormal Psychology* 95(4):395–402.

Hyman, S. E., and Arana, G. W. (1987). *Handbook of Psychiatric Drug Therapy*. Boston: Little, Brown.

James, M., and Jongeward, D. (1971). *Born to Win*. Reading, MA: Addison-Wesley.

Johnson, C., and Connors, M. E. (1987). *The Etiology and Treatment of Bulimia*. New York: Basic Books.

Kadis, L. B., ed. (1985). *Redecision Therapy: Expanded Perspectives*. Watsonville, CA: Western Institute for Group and Family Therapy.

Lieberman, M., Yalom, I., and Miles, M. (1973). *Encounter Groups: First Facts*. New York: Basic Books.

Massey, R. F. (1989). Script theory synthesized systematically. *Transactional Analysis Journal* 19(1):14–25.

Orbach, S. (1978). *Fat is a Feminist Issue*. New York: Berkeley.

Ornish, D. (1993). *Eat More, Weigh Less*. New York: HarperCollins.

Sheats, C. (1992). *Lean Bodies*. Fort Worth, TX: Summit Group.

Shulman, D. (1991). A multitiered view of bulimia. *International Journal of Eating Disorders* 10(3):333–343.

Stedman, N. (1996). Where do fitness stars get those bodies? *Fitness,* April, pp. 50–55.

Steiner, C. M. (1974). *Scripts People Live*. New York: Grove.

Stunkard, A. J. (1959). Eating patterns and obesity. *Psychiatric Quarterly* 33:284–292.

Wolf, N. (1991). *The Beauty Myth*. New York: William Morrow.

Wollams, X., and Brown, M. (1979). *The Total Handbook of Transactional Analysis*. Englewood Cliffs, NJ: Prentice-Hall.

12

The Treatment of Post-traumatic Stress Disorder

Vern Massé, M.A.

Although techniques from various disciplines may be used, therapists need a theory to guide them in treating any problem. Redecision therapy is the foundation for my treatment of post-traumatic stress disorder (PTSD). I began treating combat veterans of the Vietnam War in 1981 and have since treated survivors of other military operations of wars. I have also treated survivors of extreme childhood abuse, rape, accidents, and natural disasters. I wrote a chapter for *Redecision Therapy: Expanded Perspectives*, edited by L. Kadis, which was published in 1985. In the intervening ten years my clients have taught me many things.

The Effect of Trauma on Decisions

I make a number of assumptions that guide my work with trauma survivors. These theoretical assumptions include 1) people form decisions from all three ego states, and 2) these decisions are subject to change throughout a person's life. Much of the work done with redecision therapy focuses on early childhood decisions and is based on the premise that as we develop after birth (and possibly before) we gather information about the environment in which we find ourselves and come to some conclusions regarding self, others, and the world. Bob and Mary Goulding (1978) call these conclusions *decisions*. If we live in a relatively safe physical and emotional environment, we continually gather additional information and update our decisions. If we do not live in a safe environment, suffer some trauma, or get information that reinforces our decisions, those early decisions become fixed, unquestioned facts that guide our lives for good or bad.

Our decisions are always subject to change if they do not seem to represent reality. Traumas challenge our view of reality. One of the first beliefs to be challenged is the common belief that "bad things happen to other people." Others are that "you can trust most people" and "the world is generally a safe place."

We like to believe that life is predictable and that we have control over it. When bad things do happen, people often try to make sense of the trauma by feeling that they caused it or could have prevented it from happening. I talk with rape and incest survivors about the difference between behaviors that may have made it easier for someone to victimize them and being responsible for the crime. It is not a good idea to hitchhike in a bikini at 3 A.M. but that does not give anyone the right to rape you. Some people who have repeatedly been victimized feel they were born to be victims. I have them imagine that they were given a baby and told to train it so that it would grow up to be a victim. As they talk to the child and describe how they would treat it and how they would teach it, they become aware that they learned behaviors that make it easier for others to victimize them and they can unlearn those behaviors. Sally was a victim of incest, rape, and she was battered in relationships. She described how to raise a victim. "I would tell you that you don't have any rights, violate you, and then tell you that you liked it. I'd call you a slut if you even looked at a boy. I would point out all your mistakes and ignore anything you did right. I would remind you frequently about how worthless you are." As she did this Sally became tearful and told the child, "You'd grow up like me." I then invited her to be a good and nurturing parent to this child instead. She described to the child how she would love it and teach it how to protect itself and find safe people to be around.

Victimization can result from childhood experiences or from adult events. Soldiers fresh from home often found they could not trust even other American soldiers. New soldiers often got killed or got other soldiers killed because they did not know how to react in combat situations. New soldiers were often shunned by experienced soldiers, so they weren't always told the best ways to survive. One soldier described his first helicopter ride. "I'm wearing my flak jacket and have my helmet on my head. I notice everyone else is wearing tee-shirts and sitting on their flak jackets. Finally I ask someone why. They then explain that if they received fire it will be from the ground up through the floor and wearing a flak jacket is useless. No one was going to volunteer this information."

Rape victims sometimes decide that all men are potential rapists and not to be trusted. This of course makes sense if your only goal is to protect yourself from being raped again. If you never have contact with a man, this would seem to protect against rape. Unfortunately many women are raped by men they had never met. Eliminating half the human race as potential friends and allies is too high a cost for the illusory protection. Women victims of rape and incest may have difficulty working with male therapists due to increased transference as they describe their victimization to the male therapist. Bob Goulding did not want to do anything that increased transference, especially in trauma work. He would have victims of crime describe the trauma, in a two-chair format, to the perpetrator rather than to the therapist. This helped the victim be in the Child ego state instead of providing a factual account from the Adult ego state, while keeping the therapist out of it.

When people experience these kind of extreme traumas, they question the assumptions that guide their lives. In reaction to extreme trauma wherein previously held assumptions are found wanting, a person can spontaneously regress to an earlier developmental age and make new decisions (redecisions) about self, others, and the world. These are not simply Adult decisions but can be decisions involving all ego states. When the person who was raped in an elevator trembles thereafter when they approach elevators, this is not due to an Adult decision that all elevators are unsafe but rather the Child ego state's adaptive decision. Even without trauma, the ego states change as a result of the interaction with the external world. Anyone who has had a child return from college or the Peace Corps can attest to the changes that can result from interactions with the external world.

There are a number of factors that can affect the impact a trauma will have on a person. Some of those factors include: the age of the person (the old and the young are more impacted by trauma), the pre-trauma stability of the person, the duration and severity of the trauma, the support system available to the person, the sense of personal responsibility, and the chances of the trauma recurring. Relatively mild trauma of short duration in a well-functioning adult with a supportive community may not have a lasting impact, while severe trauma of long duration in a young child in a dysfunctional family may cripple him or her. Unfortunately, the real world does not always help victims recover. Rape and incest victims are still sometimes blamed for their own victimization. "If she didn't want it, she wouldn't have dressed that way." A soldier returning from Vietnam on a stretcher at Travis Air Force Base was asked by a pretty girl, "How many babies can you put on a bayonet?" Another soldier came home and was told by his mother, "My son died in Vietnam."

Assessment

When I assess trauma survivors, I attempt to determine how they came to see themselves and the world in which they live. Using a standard clinical interview, I map out in what kind of environment they grew up and what injunctions and counterinjunctions are operating. I want a mental picture of the world in which they grew up. What did their parents do for a living? What did they do for fun?

One veteran's father worked in heavy construction, causing the family to move often. He was always the new kid in school. Not surprisingly he decided it was not safe to get close because "as soon as you do, you leave." Vietnam just reinforced this. I pay particular attention to what changes occurred in survivors after the trauma. For PTSD to be diagnosed, the person must be experiencing something different or more extreme than before the trauma (Diagnostic and Statistical Manual 1994). In war, indecision can be deadly. Soldiers develop "black or white" thinking to eliminate indecision. There are no gray areas; someone is either good or they are bad, they are totally trustworthy or they are totally untrustworthy. If someone who had friends in high school and generally got along with everyone before Vietnam then becomes a social isolate afterwards, it is not difficult to argue that the person changed as a result of Vietnam. On the other hand, I knew one veteran who had been the mascot for the Hell's Angels at age 12 and grew up in a multitude of foster homes. Vietnam appeared to have had little effect on his personality.

Therapeutic Tasks

Even before creating my mental picture of their child and adult environments I must establish rapport. Survivors have had their trust in the world damaged. They feel different and believe that they are different from everyone else, that no one else understands, and that they are outside society as they understood it prior to the trauma. In some ways they are right. Those who have seen death all around them, and know the fragility of human life, experience themselves and life in general differently than those who continue to believe the comforting myth that bad things happen to other people. Trauma survivors may feel more isolated as a result of well-meaning attempts by friends or counselors who express understanding by relating a fictional event from a movie or a real event from experience. Traumatic events are unique events that put their own personal perspective on life. I cannot say, "I understand how you feel," or "I have felt the same way." I must establish some connection with the survivor. I remember one Vietnam veteran reporting that a counselor had told him that in his former employment as a police officer he had been shot at once, so he knew what the veteran was feeling. No one knows what another person feels even if they share the same experience; each person experiences life uniquely.

What I can do is to provide an explanation of post-traumatic stress, that it is a normal, adaptive response to an overwhelming experience. I can relate to survivors what symptoms others have experienced and attempt to normalize a little of what they are experiencing. I talk with them about experiences in my life that may relate, without implying I know what they are feeling or that I am grading how bad their trauma was in relation to others. I talk with them about my experience dealing with people who have survived similar traumas. I must be open and scrupulously honest while maintaining therapeutic boundaries with these clients because they are seeking relief from emotional pain that threatens to overwhelm them, while at the same time on guard and wanting to run from any possible additional pain. Helping trauma victims can be a balancing act. If they get immediate relief of their current pain, they leave treatment before resolving the impasse. If they don't get relief there is no reason for them to continue in treatment. For treatment to be more than a bandaid, they must make a new, healthier decision about themselves, the world, or others. Sometimes people spontaneously redecide while they are processing the trauma by simply verbalizing it over and over. Others need assistance to risk changing what they have come to believe has helped them survive.

I educate survivors about the adaptive process, wherein the person survives by doing whatever appears to work during the traumatic event, including shutting off all unnecessary emotions and then later attempting to place the traumatic event in some understandable context through reexamining it in thoughts and dreams. People may attempt to keep from reexperiencing the trauma by avoidance (e. g., by staying away from places that remind them of the trauma) and heightened awareness (which enables them, for example, to leave situations that resemble the traumatic event). When people experience a trauma, even when the event happens to an entire community (such as in earthquakes), they often feel they are alone in what they are experiencing and are going crazy because they believe they can no longer control their feelings, thoughts, and actions. By putting their current experience in context, it is possible for them to relieve some of this anxiety.

This does not, however, cure the problem. The central problem for survivors is how to put the traumatic event or events into a context that fits into a workable map of their personal world. What changes to their pre-trauma decisions about themselves, others, or the world does this require? The therapist needs to discover what decisions (pre-trauma, trauma, and post-trauma) are in operation that get in the way of the person living a full, happy, and healthy life.

I treated a man who worked in heavy construction building tunnels. One day his assistant was called away to help with another part of the job. A little while later someone else ran over asking for help. When he got to the scene of the accident, all he could see was his assistant's foot sticking out of the dirt. He attempted to get his assistant out but stopped when he discovered that the assistant's head was no longer there. He came for therapy because he was having increasing difficulty returning to work. He felt that he was going to be next and also expressed guilt for letting his assistant go. After assessing that he had no control of where his assistant was sent, he did some two chair work where he talked to the piece of equipment that killed his assistant. He realized that accidents don't just happen but are the result of mistakes. He expressed confidence in his competence and anchored this by saying that every time he saw a piece of heavy equipment he would remind himself of his competence.

After assessing survivors, I get them into as trauma-specific a therapeutic group as I can. This may be a therapist-led group, such as my combat veteran's group, or a self-help group. Being in a group of people who have survived similar traumas helps to further normalize symptoms and provides the usual benefits of group therapy (Berne 1960, Goulding and Goulding 1978, Lieberman et al. 1973).

My choice is to have the survivors' partners and children in their own groups if those resources are available. While I have combined survivors and partners in the same group, my experience suggests that it is more helpful for each to have their own group and to bring the groups together for joint meetings on a regular basis. My group has rules for attendance similar to other such groups. You must have been in Vietnam, although we do have some flexibility for those who served in combat-related fields near by. No weapons are allowed. No violence to people or furniture. All emotions are O.K., but not all behaviors are. Members must have twenty-four hours abstinence from drugs and alcohol prior to group. Within the limits of confidentiality, what is said there stays there.

Intrusive Thoughts and Nightmares

Intrusive thoughts and nightmares are two symptoms that survivors usually experience. These disruptive symptoms distract them from what they need to be doing during the day and keep them from getting restful sleep at night. I see these symptoms as attempts to put the traumas in context. Often the intrusive thoughts are of recollecting all or portions of the trauma over and over, looking for some way to make sense of the event and to prevent a recurrence. Sometimes the thoughts and nightmares are attempts to change the past. One veteran dreams repeatedly of the day an airplane crashed into a building, killing many people. He was standing a hundred yards from the crash and was not injured. He labeled himself as not O.K. because he did not attempt to rescue those inside the building, even though intellectually he knew the resulting fire was so intense as to make any rescue impossible. With each dream he expects himself to act differently. Nightmares can be replays of the traumatic event or can involve scenes they fear could have happened. Often these are worst-case scenarios, for example, a gun jamming or being in a combat situation without a weapon.

I mainly use two techniques to assist survivors with nightmares:

gestalt dream redecision work, as taught by the Gouldings (1978), and dream changing, in which I help clients design changes in recurrent dreams that empower them and give them control. In gestalt dream work, I encourage the person to tell the dream as if it were occurring right now. They describe what they are doing and saying, and what else is happening. I ask them to take the roles of other parts of the dream and tell the dream in the present tense from that perspective. George, a combat veteran, had a recurring dream in which he was being sent back to Vietnam. After telling the dream from his perspective, I asked him be the airplane that was going to fly him back. As the airplane telling the dream, George got in touch with his guilt over leaving his buddies when he returned home. He was then able to say goodbye to them and to the war. In dream change work, I first talk with the person about the nature of dreams. Dreams are not real. Even if the dream reenacts a real event in the past, it is like a video tape; it is not the actual event. Dreams are the person's personal creation and as such are subject to change by that person. Finally, the laws of reality do not apply to dreams, so you can do things and have powers, like flying or invisible protective shields, that don't work in real life. I believe the recurring dream is there for a reason, so I don't suggest that they try to suppress the dream. Trying to not have a dream may only pump more emotional energy into the dream, like "don't think of pink elephants." Recurring dreams that disturb people involve a sense of helplessness; the cure is to empower themselves in the dreams. I ask people to rehearse what change they want to make in their dreams and then to deliberately dream the dream. If they wake up frightened or bothered by the dream, they are to use their creativity to empower themselves in the dreams. A young man, Chad, had a recurring dream of a huge, black, hairy spider trying to get at him. Chad was in a small house, and the spider was on top of the house, trying to grab him through the windows. Through dream changing, Chad at first gave himself an assortment of weapons such as machetes and flamethrowers. This made the dreams less frightening but they did not stop. He then put a magical bracelet on one of the spider's legs that allowed him to control the spider. The spider became his pet and he envisioned himself walking downtown with his huge spider following him as a protector. Chad then was able to talk about being picked on by others and his feelings of helplessness with peers.

Intrusive thoughts are dealt with using two-chair work as taught by the Gouldings (1978) and by confronting cognitive distortions. For example, one veteran of the Vietnam war had recurring nightmares of walking down a trail with a Vietcong sniper waiting to kill him. The veteran would wake up screaming, with the bedsheets soaked with sweat as he is being shot. Working in the scene, he became a tree along the trail, and told both himself and the Vietcong that the war was over and they both could go home now. Both agreed to put down their weapons and go home. The veteran never had the dream again.

Survivor Guilt

Many survivors experience survivor guilt. "Why did I live when others didn't?" They also feel guilt about what they did or did not do during the trauma. They have a view of themselves that may have been damaged by the realities of a traumatic event. I provide an invitation for them to relate their experiences as one would during a critical incident debriefing: What did you do, what did you think, and what did you feel during the trauma? Survivors need to tell about their experiences over and over. As they hear themselves, they can come to have compassion for their helplessness and their forced-choice situations. I help them to look at who was responsible and to share responsibility for mistakes while not denying them. If a soldier shelled his own people or a friendly village by mistake, he made an error, but others were involved too. He got the coordinates from someone, and someone else was supposed to double-check them. He probably was an 18-year-old kid, scared stiff, in a foreign land fighting a war he didn't ask for. Survivors often judge themselves much more harshly than they judge others. Using two-chair work and self-reparenting techniques, I encourage them to build a more nurturing Parent ego state while stroking the Parent ego system for wanting to protect the survivor from further traumas. I may ask a veteran to imagine that he is the father of a baby boy. I take him through the growing up of his son and have him give appropriate nurturing as the child develops. I then ask him to see his son in the same situation as he was in and talk to the boy. After that, he is invited to tell himself what he had just told his son.

Covering Fear with Anger

Survivors, especially combat veterans, may cover their fears with anger. In Vietnam it was useful to be scared prior to a firefight, but when in a firefight it was much more useful to suppress the fear and get angry to mobilize the energy necessary to survive. Many continue to feel anger instead of other emotions. Anger has a sense of power and control, whereas fear and sadness feel weak, vulnerable, and out of control. Being out of control in Vietnam could endanger life.

Many veterans tell me that they have no control over their rage but rather go from calm to rage in a split second that is outside of their awareness. I tell them that although it feels that way to them, that is not how it works. Those veterans have dissociated themselves from their feelings to the point that only very strong emotions break through their defenses. When you ask them how they feel, they respond with "fine," which translates to "I am feeling normal for me." It is important for them to understand that normal to them may not be normal to others and if they normally are full of rage it does not take a large stressor for them to go from "fine" to rage. I ask these veterans to imagine that they have a thermometer inside them on which the bottom number is zero and they are at perfect peace; the top number is ten, where they will kill the next person they come across. I teach them to associate various body sensations with different numbers on the scale. They then practice taking inventory of their thermometer number and discover that their normal is usually about six on the scale, and that it takes very little additional stress to bump them up to rage. If they have support people around them whom they are willing to trust, I suggest they ask the other person to give them feedback on what they observe that indicates to them that the veteran is angry or upset. The veteran himself may be so out of touch with what is happening physically that he may have great difficulty identifying body sensations. I then teach them various behavioral options from which to choose, depending on where they are on the scale. To start with, I divide the thermometer into four sections. The bottom section, 0 to approximately 3, is the "no problem" section. The next section, from 4 to 6, is the "problem but no damage" section. In this section the veteran can use assertiveness and other problem solving techniques. The next section, 6 to 8, is where relationships are damaged. The veteran may make verbal threats or say other things that damage relationships. In treatment, the veteran learns to utilize short time-outs and abdominal breathing, to analyze whether his thinking is calming him down or winding him up and then correct his thinking. He has guaranteed his partner (at a calmer time) that if he needs to take a time-out, he will not hurt himself or others, will come back, and will deal with the problems (although if he begins to lose control he may need to take additional time-outs). This prearrangement is important to prevent the partner from attempting to stop him from taking a time-out, resulting in an escalation of the situation. The highest levels, 8 to 10, are where physical damage to self and others occur. This is the "get out of Dodge" section. Here the veteran must get out of the situation until he is able to deal with it in a rational manner. The veteran is encouraged to ask himself three questions: Is my life or are my family's lives being threatened right now? What do I want to happen from this in the long run? What can I do to create the ending I want? These questions allow him to get out of the emotional Child ego state and into the nonemotional Adult ego state. If the answer to the first question is "no" then violence is not an option. The words "right now," "long run," and "ending I want" are important. The veteran can imagine a myriad of possible dangers that could happen and needs to focus on what is happening, not what may happen. While in the Child ego state, immediate gratification is high on the list of choices and immediate violence will discharge a whole lot of built-up tension. The veteran needs to look at long-range outcomes. Planning an ending he wants not only uses the Adult ego state, it also engages the Child ego state to feel some sense of power and control in the situation. Without this reality check many veterans have difficulty differentiating between possible and actual danger. While this does not cure the problem, it helps them live better in society.

Part of working with the anger is working with any homicidal or suicidal ideation present. No-suicide and no-homicide contracts are often necessary. One interesting case involved a veteran with a lot of fear that he covered with rage. He agreed to a no-homicide/no-suicide contract but continued to have violent dreams wherein he would end up standing at the foot of the bed that he shared with his wife, with a shotgun in his hands, contemplating whether to shoot her or not. He came in with his wife for a session, and she reported that she had awakened in the middle of the night and found him standing at the foot of the bed with the shotgun. The veteran did some dream work and agreed not to harm anyone, even in his dreams. That was more than five years ago, and he reports he no longer has a need for weapons in his home and the dream has not recurred.

Grief Work

I encourage survivors to grieve their losses, which may include the loss of their innocence, their teen years, and many friends, and to say their goodbyes. I encourage them to celebrate being able to feel and to confront their belief that if they feel, they will go crazy or never stop crying. Many veterans came back from the war feeling as if they left part of themselves in Vietnam. I tell them that the part of themselves that they left in Vietnam was their ability to feel.

Grief work can take many forms. For war veterans grieving a fellow soldier's death, the goal is to establish the permanence of the comrade's death, to examine leftover survival guilt, and to confront irrational beliefs such as, "If I accept my friend's death, then I will forget him and his death will be meaningless." Grieving other losses, such as the survivor's youth and innocence, is important. Veterans who have not grieved and accepted their loss of youth and innocence may remain stuck, acting in many ways as if they were still adolescents. Two-chair work can create opportunities for expressing long-suppressed emotions and making new decisions. Going back to the scene in which the friend died or the veteran killed someone is the most impactful way to heal combat losses. One veteran came to group because, although he was successful in most areas of his life, he suffered from recurrent depression and his marriage was shaky. He had been wounded in a firefight that took the lives of three of his friends. After several months in the group, he described the firefight and then was able to visualize his three friends and say goodbye. I always ask the person to express his feelings to the loved ones before they died. I do not want to support the myth that the person is not dead and is either looking out for them or waiting for them. No matter how comforting that may seem, if they believe the dead person is waiting for them suicide may become a way to be reunited with the person, or the survivor may just mark time waiting to die and rejoin his loved one. When the survivors express their feelings, I encourage them to express a range of feelings: anger, loss, guilt, and so on. I end with them saying what they will remember and how knowing that person has enriched their current life. Doing something in memory for those who died—such as writing a poem, working with children, or planting a tree—can help the survivor remember in a positive way those left behind.

Substance Abuse and Social Support

Alcohol and other drug use is prevalent with the survivors I see. Depressant drugs such as alcohol are used to further numb emotions and to suppress dreams. While I do not require abstinence, I ask group members not to attend group while under the influence of alcohol or other drugs. I provide education regarding chemical dependency and the difficulty of experiencing feelings while taking depressant drugs. Many members of our veteran's support group also attend 12-step meetings and encourage other members to go with them. Veterans using drugs with a long half-life, like marijuana, frequently have a difficult time letting go of the drug. They may not have been drug free in more than twenty years.

Most of the Vietnam veterans I see have few friends, even among other veterans, and have had little in the way of a social support system. The support group is the beginning of their socialization. The group provides a place where they can test out friendships and get feedback regarding reality. The facilitator must confront prejudices and other distortions of reality while giving the veteran permission to challenge back. In this way they begin to question long-held beliefs while developing social skills. The group has formed a nonprofit corporation, raising funds through car washes and Christmas tree sales to pay for trips to the Vietnam Veteran's Memorial in Washington, DC. Participation in these activities by veterans and their families furthers their socialization skills and helps to build a community of support. The trips themselves are intense as the veterans face their losses and say their goodbyes.

Conclusion

Treatment with survivors consists of first helping them to understand what they are experiencing and to normalize their symptoms. Next, survivors need tools with which to cope. As the last step in the process, they make new decisions about self, others, and the world that allow them to live full lives.

References

Berne, E. (1966). *Principles of Group Treatment*. New York: Oxford University Press.

Diagnostic and Statistical Manual of Mental Disorders (1994). 4th ed. Washington, DC: American Psychiatric Association.

Goulding, R., and Goulding, M. (1978). *Changing Lives through Redecision Therapy*. New York: Brunner/Mazel.

Kadis, L. (1985). *Redecision Therapy: Expanded Perspectives*. Watsonville, CA: Western Institute of Group and Family Therapy.

Lieberman, M., Yalom, I., and Miles, M. (1973). *Encounter Groups: First Facts*. New York: Basic Books.

13

The Abusive Spouse

James K. Speer, M.S.S.W.

Introduction

Domestic violence is a very complex problem, involving diverse causes and contexts. Effective therapy for this group of perpetrators as a whole is still a much-studied question. Success rates for batterers (15 to 25 percent) is about the same as in substance abuse programs, says Richard Gelles (1994), director of The Family Violence Research Program at the University of Rhode Island. He also advocates more shelters, stronger criminal justice interventions, and more effective men's programs.

As part of my practice, I facilitate a weekly men's group of spouse abusers. The program began in 1989 with five clients. Some clients were self-referred, the others mandated by the judicial system. The group of men has always remained small (4 to 10 participants) and new members are continually added as experienced members complete the program. This method of treatment, as opposed to a closed group, offers the participant the chance to associate with more experienced clients. This provides the facilitator and the participant with added dynamics of behavior shaping as newer participants become exposed to desired changes in longer-term participants. The average participant attends the group for 21 weeks. To date our program has treated 188 men and 2 women. We have experienced very few repeat offenders (less than 5 percent) in court-mandated clients. Actually, this is a rough estimate of success and does not necessarily mean that spousal battery is nonexistent in clients who complete the program.

The program content has remained largely psychoeducational. The Duluth model (Pence and Paymar 1993) remains the core of program content, with frequent opportunities to digress to redecision work as participants become more self-revealing of thoughts, feelings, and controlling behaviors. The Duluth model is aimed at keeping men thinking reflectively and raising their consciousness of stereotypical beliefs of men's and women's roles. Cultural and personal facilitators of battering are examined through video and discussion. Video vignettes of couples are used to demonstrate ways men use power and control to dominate relationships. The intent of this material is to teach batterers that abusive behavior is well-rehearsed, has underlying intents, and is based on their personal beliefs about dominance and control. The use of redecision therapy adds an extra dimension to treatment. It explores early decision making and its influence on present behavior.

The setting is a large room of a local church. The door is locked 15 minutes after the designated starting time to discourage tardiness. Participants are to arrive alcohol and drug free. If I detect either, I dismiss the client and report this to his probation officer. I communicate with probation officers weekly and talk about it openly in group. I report all violations of their entry contract in which they agree to fully participate in the group. I also report to probation officers any continued abuse of their partners or their children. I frequently tell anonymous stories of the numerous times I have initiated revocation of probation. Leverage is my best ally and necessary for client progress toward real behavior change. In my experience, most men who have spent time in jail are more amenable to change.

Personality Types of Men Who Batter

Men who perpetrate violence on their female partners and children present a variety of personality disorders that manifest an array of thinking errors (e. g., entitlement—my needs and wants come first); information processing errors (e. g., feeling criticized when he is held accountable); affective reactions that are out of proportion to the situational context (e. g., emotions stronger or weaker than called for by the situation); and behavior that is socially and legally unacceptable (e. g., raping his partner when turned down for sex). Additionally, there is evidence of criminal thought process and an overlay of alcohol and drug abuse/addiction problems. In an unpublished study (Speer 1994) of 59 batterers in the Kerrville, Texas, Batterers Intervention and Prevention Program (BIPP) who were given the Minnesota Multiphasic Personality Inventory (MMPI), one half had alcohol/drug problems and one quarter had an active criminal thought process.

From this study four DSM personality disorders clearly emerge to clinically classify men who physically and verbally abuse women and their children: Narcissistic, Antisocial, Compulsive, and Paranoid. All present with some degree of overlapping traits. Lorna Smith Benjamin's book (1993) describes the dysfunctional interpersonal characteristics of these four personality types as "attack," "blame," and "control." I find this interpersonal style of communicating a common thread with batterers.

The participants in our batterers treatment programs are 80 percent court mandated. This often means that a willingness to change behavior is nonexistent. The batterer gives the appearance of wanting to change, but usually this is because his behavior has come to the attention of the police department. Getting a firm contract for change with nonvoluntary clients often hinges on the clinician's leverage and the client's discontent with the judicial system being involved in his life.

The criminal personality subset of batterers are very entrenched in their style of behavior. They are the masters of the con. Stanton Samenow (1989) points out that the antisocial person does not regard his victim as a thinking, feeling human being. "Even in day-to-day interactions, that do not in any way involve an arrestable act, the anti-social youngster [or adult] does not put himself in the place of others" (p. 56). He or she is the hub of the wheel, never one of the spokes. I find this group sometimes to be interested in a behavioral change contract that has to do with not being hassled by me or the police rather than for any guilt about what has happened to the victim. They see themselves as the victims, so a contract for change needs to be centered on helping them get their autonomy back. If getting back autonomy can equate to a cessation in hitting their partners or children, then we both win. Behavior is changed out of convenience. Call it a reverse con job that leaves room for any feelings toward the victim partner to catch up or surface later.

A Redecision Therapy View of the Problem

Redecision therapy is built upon the clinician's understanding of the interpersonal childhood experiences of the client and the early decisions that were made that underpin the client's thinking and behavior patterns as an adult. Understanding the early decisions of the Adapted Child ego state are crucial for corrective action as an adult. Children do not choose the environments in which they are raised, or the adults present, but they are responsible for their responses to each. Early childhood decisions are often made with inadequate adult information available. Once in adulthood, as Mary Goulding (1979) points out, an individual can rewrite his own script with the help of a strong Parent ego state that he builds for himself.

The principal life positions, as described in *Transactional Analysis in Brief* (Woollams 1976), most visible in abusers are "I am okay with me and you are not okay with me," and "I am not okay with me and you are not okay with me." Children assuming either life posture usually have grown up with one or both parents modeling behaviors of abusiveness and neglect. These children are parented not from the Adult or Nurturing Parent ego state in the parent, but primarily from the Child ego state in the parent. When children are parented in this manner, they receive many more negative than positive strokes. They don't get permission from parents to develop their full capacities. They get parental injunctions that set the stage for a "loser" script.

A particularly lethal injunction is "Don't be." When children are verbally and physically assaulted as punishment, they learn not to affirm their own existence. A lifelong cycle of depression, mistrust of others, blaming, and violence can result. Recently a vivid example of "Don't be" came from a parent interview I conducted with a new battering client in his first individual session. A parent interview is a variation of the two-chair technique, in which you allow the client to sit in the open chair and be his parent while you question him, or let him occupy his chair and speak for the open chair as you direct your questions to the open chair. This gives the therapist an opportunity to see the client or the situation from the point of view of the internalized Parent ego state. This battering client complained of seeing his father occasionally in public settings but his father would not speak to him. In fact, his father and his family had disowned my client for many years. The client had no knowledge (or so he thought) of why his father treated him so badly. I asked him to put his father in the empty chair. The following dialogue ensued:

Therapist: Why don't you talk to your son when you see him?
Client: [speaking as his father] He is not my son.
Therapist: I don't understand what you're saying. He is your son.
Client: I did not want his mother to be pregnant.
Therapist: That is not his fault.
Client: He should not have been born.
Therapist: Lots of kids are not planned for.
Client: He is not my son.

At this point I asked the client if he needed his father's recognition to have a happy life. He said no. I suggested he say this to his father. "I do not need your recognition to live my life."

Client: [facing the open chair] I do not need your approval to live my life.
Client: [as Father] You can think whatever you want to.
Client: I will.
Client: [as Father] Whatever.

This is an example of a "Don't be" injunction, given to the client by the Child ego state of his father and still being reinforced in present time by the father's actions when he sees his adult son. The client, upon completion of his dialogue with his father, seemed relieved. He said that he understood the situation better and smiled. This was the beginning of his redecision work.

A second injunction of "Don't feel your feeling" (except for anger, as our culture permits) is a lethal combination for men who batter. If women are the modeled enemy, then it's the woman's fault that I feel this way. I take no responsibility for my emotional life. I expect her to do that for me. I'm the victim here.

Counterinjunctions also play a large part with batterers. If they received strong Parent ego state messages from their parents that are restrictive in nature, for example, Be strong, Be perfect, Please me, A woman's place is in the home, A man is the head of the family, the stage is set for interpersonal conflict. These counterinjunctions are often the strongest with men who are successful and who have not experienced a childhood of witnessing or receiving physical abuse. Again, empty chair work with the parent of the past begins the discovery process. A common dialogue is as follows:

Client: [speaking to his mother of the past in the empty chair] Did Dad make all the decisions in our family?
Client: [as Mother] Yes, he did.
Client: Did you always agree?

Client: [as Mother] Yes, after we talked it over.

Client: So he got his way.

Client: [as Mother] Yes, I guess so. But I didn't think of it that way.

Client: Did you ever disagree with Dad?

Client: [as Mother] No, I didn't.

Client: Why?

Client: [as Mother] He knew best.

Client: My wife has her own ideas about things. She doesn't like my decisions a lot. What should I do?

Client: [as Mother] I don't know what to tell you. Your father and I always agreed.

Client: Always?

Client: [as Mother] Yes, always.

This client has no experience of his parents solving a disagreement, so he keeps trying to force his decision on his wife with a conflicted result. He didn't marry his mother.

Treatment Techniques

Before treating batterers in a group, I do a two-session assessment to get a clearer picture of what is really going on at home, in addition to the initial intake presentation of the problem. Sometimes I will disqualify a batterer if he is actively alcoholic or drug addicted and will not attend AA or NA. I also disqualify men who are too volatile or psychiatrically unfit for group participation. With those who are selected I make a no-suicide, no-homicide, no-insanity contract for as long as we are working together. This means I take their problems seriously and suggests to them the urgency of putting a new show on the road.

A treatment contract for change with nonvoluntary clients is absolutely necessary. They may treat it lightly, but I take it seriously. I presume they want to change even if they are ambivalent. I want them to know that I have faith in their ability to change, that another man is interested enough in their life to expect something from them. I keep the contract in front of them every time we are together. Valid battering contracts are: I want to/will stop being violent with my partner; I want to/will stop saying cruel and hurtful things; I want to/am willing to listen more to my partner; and I want to/will not be in trouble with the law again for domestic violence.

Invalid contracts, or cons, are: I *need* to change, we *need* to communicate/talk more, I *should* stop drinking so much, I *should* control my temper. The *need* and *should* cons reflect the batterer's belief that somehow he is not responsible for his behavior. I counter these assertions with the challenge of, "You need to change, or you will change?" "You should control your temper, or you will control your temper?" I confront until I get a valid contract.

Having the batterer look at the consequences of not accomplishing his contract is important. Most batterers do not want to lose the relationship with their spouses. This possibility is one of the natural consequences of their continued abusive behavior. By keeping the loss of the relationship and the possibility of more jail time ever present the therapist has added leverage for change.

In group, two of my goals are to engage the batterer's Adult ego state in trying new behaviors and to assist the batterer to access feelings in the Child ego state when he was the victim and not the perpetrator of violence. A good example of accessing his Child's feelings is found in the following exercise. In a relaxed, comfortable group setting, I ask all participants to remember the first time they witnessed someone being physically hurt by another person (perhaps a sibling or their parents fighting); secondly, to think of a time when they were the victim of abuse or violence as a child or adult. Thirdly, I ask them to recall the scene when they last inflicted violence on someone.

Upon completion of this exercise I ask for a volunteer who is willing to share his experience with the group. Recently in group the volunteer reported a scene in which he was locked in a closet as a child as punishment after he almost hanged himself jumping out of a tree in the back yard while playing with a rope. He reported how frightened and scared he was about almost taking his life and began to sob. When I asked him how it felt to be punished he reported he thought his mother was cruel for locking him up. (This is a man who has been locked up as an adult three times for a total of 12 years.) He talked about his mother's cruelty in other situations. I had him put his mother in the chair and tell her how he felt about what had happened. He was very angry and yelled at her. I asked him to tell his mother how this early experience had affected his life to date. He said, "I have always been cruel to women just like you were cruel to me. It has affected all my relationships with women." I asked him if he would be willing to give his cruelty back to his mother because it really belonged to her. He did so tearfully and confidently dismissed her from the chair.

The room was very quiet. Some group members were so stirred up by this experience that they could not sit in their chairs. They were moving around the room pretending to be busy. Two other men were glued to their seats with tears in their eyes. One of these two said to the volunteer, "You are very brave to give up your cruelty. I could not, because that is me. That is all of me, and I would have nothing left."

The volunteer made a very important first step toward redecision from the same ego state in which the original decision was made (the Child). His violent behavior toward his partner has stopped. His cruelty is significantly modified and he is continuing to work on his goals for change.

Another method I use engages the Adult ego state of the batterer. I challenge all group members to give up defending themselves with their partners. No matter what their partner says or does they are never to defend themselves either verbally or physically. "Real men do not need to defend themselves against a woman," I say. Men who are willing to make this behavioral change report some interesting results. Initially they have an increase in anxiety when not defending themselves, then they report their wives are suspicious about what they are doing. Thirdly, they report how much better the relationship is going, and finally that they are thinking about what was said to them rather than reacting out of feelings, and that this has improved

their overall ability and confidence in themselves. They see themselves behaving as they desire to be seen.

To accomplish these changes many two-chair scenes between a
husband and wife are played out. An example of a typical two-chair
confrontation follows:

> *Client:* [facing the open chair] I work hard every day and you don't
> respect me. A woman should respect her husband.
> *Client:* [as wife] I do respect you, but I'm tired of you doing
> nothing around the house.
> *Client:* [back in his chair] I'm sick of you bitching at me.
> *Client:* [as wife] You call expressing my feelings bitching. You
> never listen to me.
> *Client:* Well, I'm listening now.
> *Client:* [as wife] You're yelling at me again.

At this juncture I usually have him stand up beside me and observe
this fight. I ask him what's going on with these two people. He says,
"It's the same old fight over and over. I hate it. She doesn't respect
me." The last statement indicates he is still in his Adapted Child ego
state. I place another chair beside his chair and ask him to sit in it.
I tell him this is a grown-up man sitting here. "What does the
grown-up man in you want to say to her?" From this chair he says to
her:

> *Client:* I don't like to fight with you.
> *Client:* [as wife] I don't like this either.
> *Client:* I yelled at you and I'm sorry.
> *Client:* [as wife] Yes, you did.
> *Client:* What is it you want me to do that I'm not doing?
> *Client:* [as wife] I want you to notice what's going on when you
> come home and give me some help with the kids.
> *Client:* You mean like change Joey's diaper or take the kids to the
> park?

Client: [as wife] Yes, it's hard to fix dinner with two kids bothering me.

Client: Okay. I can do that.

I ask him if he will do it and he says yes. So I have him change his last statement to "I will do that" and address that to her. This man knows more about being a grownup than he thinks he does. He needs to discover that he knows how. This is a method for him to access his Adult ego state and begin the process of changing the way he hears his wife's requests. Simply listening to her is a big change for this couple.

As I see it, in battering couples the relationship is the symptom of the problem, not the problem itself. Family of origin work and redecision work are necessary to make a permanent change in the batterer's behavior. Both batterer and victim partner are having the best relationship they are capable of at the beginning of treatment. They are deserving of better, but each is stuck in his own communication style. Men and women with dependency issues allow themselves to be controlled by each other's behavior.

Men who get "Don't grow up" injunctions from the Child ego state of either parent make up a large subgroup of batterers. They usually were not victims as children nor did they see their parents abuse one another. They are accustomed to getting what they want from parents and this carries over into their adult relationships with women. They are emotionally children in adult bodies. When more is expected of them in adult relationships they are incensed. They feel controlled by their female partners and resent any feedback that they are childlike or not pulling their load. The narcissistic injury of having their partners point out their shortcomings shatters their perfectionist sub-script, and a rage reaction is likely.

One evening in group, a new batterer reported that he had returned home from work, sat down and began to watch TV. His wife was angry at his inability to notice that the kids needed tending to, that the house needed to be picked up and swept, and that she needed him to be with the children while she studied for the law school entrance exam. She called him her fourth child and threatened to dissolve the marriage. He was angered by her last comment, grabbed her by the throat, and shoved her out the door. The police were called, and he was charged with family violence and sent to group. He felt justified in hitting her and thought she should be in counseling, not him.

This man grew up in a family where his bad behavior was excused and covered up. He got his first battering charge dismissed using his family's influence. He was not supporting his child from his first marriage, he worked sporadically, he wrecked his cars, and so on. Now he was married again to a woman who expected something of him and told him so regularly. She pointed out his childish behavior and resented his not stepping up to his problems. This couple fought violently before he was referred for counseling. She was a better verbal fighter but he would have the last word.

Slowly this man began to face the fact that he was not grown up emotionally. With the group support and many two-chair sessions (with his wife and parents) he began listening more and reacting less to his wife's complaints. He got a higher-paying job, worked steadily, and received promotions. He felt powerful by contributing to his family more. He was very proud of his wife's academic accomplishments. Once he stopped defending himself and began to listen he became more self-critical and was willing to accept constructive criticism from others. He self-revealed more and took responsibility for his behavior. After his required attendance he became a permanent member of the group and only recently left after a two-year sojourn. Giving up narcissism takes some time.

Men who receive "Don't grow up" injunctions as described above have a Child-contaminated Adult ego state. The Free/Adapted Child ego state is running their lives and making a great many of their everyday decisions. The treatment goal is to examine parental injunctions and early decision making, then to strengthen their Adult ego state through contract reparenting work.

Conclusion

Using redecision therapy with batterers gives the therapist some powerful tools in his therapy kit. Violence is symptomatic of deeper power and control issues manifested in relationships. Examining the primary relationships of the past is the key to unlocking and understanding present symptoms. Men and women are not born violent. This behavior is connected to early decision making as one path of responding to, or dealing with, environments and significant others. Early decisions in response to parental injunctions can be reframed or redecided in adulthood. Confronting significant others of the past and redeciding responses to current situations and relationships are the basic underpinnings of redecision therapy. It offers a theory of personality development and a methodology for changing behavior. Feelings, thinking, and behaving are all addressed in the change process. Working in a group setting further enhances the possibility for real and permanent changes. Of course, it does not cure all men who batter, but it offers real empowerment and change for the courageous, those men who want to put a new show on the road.

References

Benjamin, L. S. (1993). *Interpersonal Diagnosis and Treatment of Personality Disorders*. New York: Guilford.

Gelles, R. J. (1994). Lack of reliable research strangles effort to prevent domestic violence. *Psychotherapy Letter* 6:1–5.

Goulding, M. M., and Goulding, R. L. (1979). *Changing Lives through Redecision Therapy*. New York: Brunner/Mazel.

Pence, E., and Paymar, M. (1993). *Education Groups for Men Who Batter: The Duluth Model*. Duluth, MN: Springer.

Samenow, S. E. (1989). *Before It's Too Late*. New York: Times Books.

Speer, J. K. (1994). Unpublished study of 59 batterers.

Woolams, S., Brown, M., and Huige, K. (1976). *Transactional Analysis in Brief*, 3rd ed. Ann Arbor, MI: Huron Valley Institute.

14

Working with Children and Adolescents

James R. Allen, M.D.
Barbara Ann Allen, M.S.W., Ph.D.

By the time he was in kindergarten, it was apparent our son Michael could read, yet he was insistent he could not. Then, while being driven to school one day, he finally explained this peculiar situation.

We were older parents, he sobbed, and he was afraid we would die and leave him. He had decided that if he did not learn to read, he could stop time and keep us alive. With assurance, some facts, and a little encouragement, he made a new decision. He decided it was safe to show he really could read. All this took place in a very short period of time—on the way to school.

This story, similar to ones many parents could tell, is an example of a childhood decision and redecision. Given the world as they know it and the kind of thinking—intuitive and somewhat magical—of which they are capable, young children make the best decisions they can. It makes sense to them, and seems to have survival value at the time. Such decisions will influence the course of their lives. With support, permission, and some new information or new experience they can make new decisions.

In this chapter, we will look at some aspects of redecision work with children and adolescents.

Early Messages: Permissions and Injunctions

Children and adolescents live in a storied world of messages as to who they are, how they are to behave, and what is to become of them. Some of these messages are verbal. Others are nonverbal. Some come from one person, the most important messages from someone important for nurturance. Others come from the milieu in general.

Some of these messages can be conceptualized as taking a negative form, such as "Don't be" or "Don't grow up." We call these injunctions. Some, their opposites, can be seen as taking the form of permissions (Allen and Allen 1996).

The most common of these permissions are:

to be (both to occupy space and to live with zest)
to be aware of sensations and needs
to express needs and to get them met appropriately
to trust appropriately and to feel secure
to be aware of one's feelings (all—not just certain ones)
to be able to express one's feelings
to be oneself
to be close, yet separate
to feel happy
to be O.K.
to be one's appropriate sex and age (including to grow up and to leave)
to belong
to receive accurate feedback
to think clearly and solve problems effectively
to understand what is going on psychologically
to be sane
to be successful, however that be defined
to find or make meaning

There is also a second group of permissions that are necessary. These can be seen as freeing the child to stop overdoing the things that please grownups. To be perfect is impossible; consequently it really is a command to fail. A child needs permission not to be perfect, but to explore and learn from his mistakes. Similarly, a child needs permission not to please others, not to work harder, not to hurry up, and not to be strong at all cost. Children need to be able to decide how much of each of these is appropriate and when it is time to stop, to please themselves, to know how hard or fast is enough, and to feel.

At some point, children begin to ask four important questions: 1) "Who am I?"; 2) "What happens to people like me in this world?"; 3) "What is expected of me?"; and 4) "How do I go about getting the most love possible?" (Allen and Allen 1979). They decide this as best they can, depending on their stage of development and on information available to them, including fantasies as well as what they are told by the people who are important to them.

Case Examples

At age 9, John was already a chronic mental patient when his mother brought him for yet another hospitalization. Reportedly, he had been in and out of hospitals since he was about 4. Indeed, he had been out of institutions for only about six weeks the previous year. At one point, a doctor in another state diagnosed him as having a bipolar disorder and had given him lithium and Tegretol. However, his mother soon found him uncontrollable again—as he had been since he first "sexually abused" her by putting his hand on her vagina when he was about 3.

John was indeed oppositional and he frequently refused to follow adult requests. When confronted, he would demand to know how many children with bipolar disorder the staff had worked with previously. He was also soon accusing them of making pejorative racial slurs—something he did himself—and this was immediately seized on by his mother as evidence either of the staff's "cultural insensitivity" or as evidence of his having auditory hallucinations.

At 10, Peter was brought to the hospital by his mother who was a psychiatric nurse. She presented the symptoms and diagnoses of a wide variety of disorders: attention deficit hyperactivity disorder, major depression, conduct disorder, multiple personality disorder, and temporal-lobe epilepsy. She had attended numerous parenting classes, had mastered and tried every parenting technique known, but nothing had worked. Yet, on the unit, Peter showed only moderate oppositionality. His psychological testing and neurological workup were also unremarkable.

As we worked with these two children, it became apparent that they had several things in common. First, almost everything they did or said had been interpreted by their mothers as evidence of very serious pathology. For example, his mother apparently never considered that John might lie or try to intimidate and manipulate, only that he had auditory hallucinations. Second, the behavior of these children was interpreted out of context. It was not considered that a 3-year-old might just happen to place his hand on his mother's vagina or that he might be exploring. Rather, his behavior was interpreted as a deliberate attempt to "sexually abuse" her. Her role in not removing his hand or shifting her body was not acknowledged. Third, many other "facts" in these histories could be interpreted in a number of alternative ways. True, a psychiatrist had prescribed Tegretol and lithium for John, but his version of the story was that he had done so in a desperate attempt to find something that would help him get John out of the hospital. Each time the child was about to be discharged, he became "uncontrollable." On closer examination, it seems this occurred after every trial visit home. Rather than concluding that John was in need of medication, the data could have been interpreted as evidence of problems in his interactions with his mother or his mother's interactions with him. Fourth, although both mothers had suffered great inconvenience and expense due to their children's long-term and multiple treatments, they had evaded any treatment for themselves. Yet there was ample evidence of problems elsewhere in their lives. John's mother had worked as a receptionist in a psychologist's office. Her strong efforts to convince many of her employer's patients that their problems were all due to past sexual abuse had created such community turmoil that he was obligated to relocate. Peter's mother freely admitted that he, of all her children, was special. He was the most sensitive, and the most like her. Somehow she "knew" that the well-being of both herself and the family depended on him. It was necessary to resolve these maternal problems in order to prevent the boys' treatment becoming one more stop in their long history of treatment failures.

While both these boys can be diagnosed as having Munchausen's Disorder by Proxy (*DSM-IV* Fictitious Disorder by Proxy), they can also be seen as demonstrating, in an exaggerated way, problems common to all children: the impact of the demands, expectations, stories, and interpretations of their important grownups. Because there were no grandparents, permanent father figures, or other potentially ameliorating adults in their lives, these children's definitions of themselves and what was expected of them was derived largely from their mothers' comments and behavior. Unfortunately, both mothers had also been efficient in using and perhaps distorting the opinions and suggestions of mental health professionals. The children were programmed not to have lives, but to be psychiatric case studies—and they accepted this and used it.

When we work with adult patients, we see the effects of early decisions. In redecision therapy, under contract we encourage the patient return to early key scenes, to reexperience them in a new way, to learn something new about them, and to make new decisions. When we work with children, these decisions are often still being made or are of relatively recent origin. Sometimes, we can actually prevent pathological decisions; at other times, we facilitate early redecision. Whether we are doing actual redecision work or trying to prevent pathogenic decisions, there are four important therapeutic imperatives.

Permission

Both children and adults need permission to change, and to function well. The form the permission takes needs to be altered for different age groups' cognitive and emotional levels. There seems to be a loose hierarchy of these permissions based on the child's age, level of development, and intellectual equipment, as was outlined earlier. The earliest is permission to be and to be aware of sensations.

While all permissions seem important at all ages, some become more important at certain periods, then subside. In addition, the same permission needs to be given in different forms at different ages. For example, a very young child needs permission to be close in the sense of feeling comfortable, secure, and safe with the parenting figures and the environment, while a school-age child needs permission to feel accepted and that he belongs with peers, while an older adolescent needs to feel comfortable in a closeness with peers that has growing intimate and sexual overtones. Permission to make or find meaning for an infant may mean permission to explore gravity by dropping things from the highchair and have the parent pick them up. For an adolescent this permission may involve exploration of alternative religious or political systems.

Protection

Adults generally fear change for internal reasons based on what might have happened in the past had they made decisions other than the ones they actually made. This often takes the form of a belief that the parenting figure might abandon them or die, that they themselves might die, or that the family might disintegrate. These catastrophes are not just fantasies. Family members are often very threatened, for example, when a member talks of sexual abuse, and the family may indeed reject the whistle-blower. Then, the very fact that the patient is still alive seems to give proof that the decision, however dysfunctional in outcome, at least had survival value. Children and adolescents have all these internal prohibitions and dangers to deal with, plus the actual reactions right now of their real parents and their environment.

Shelby, age 10, was afraid of her adoptive father's reaction when she began to have her menses. She dressed in boys' clothes and was his "squirrel-hunting buddy" and his companion in a loveless marriage, while her adoptive mother spent her time with Shelby's younger sisters, two "real" (non-adoptive) and more feminine daughters, who had been born to everyone's surprise after Shelby's adoption. Shelby collected used Kotex and threatened to kill her sisters. Her parents were convinced she was psychotic, and convinced a number of mental health professionals of this, especially after it was found she had packed up her clothes and a knife and had hidden them in a tree in an abortive attempt to run away.

The parents strongly objected to any encouragement of Shelby's looking more like a girl her age and made plans to send her to "a good Christian ranch" in a distant state. However, the father soon became depressed at the thought of losing his buddy and the mother became highly agitated. She had not believed she could mother Shelby when the child had entered the family because her mother had never really mothered her. The problem of "the psychotic child" was replaced by the painful but less dramatic problems of a couple dealing with a loveless marriage, a father/husband's sense of isolation and loneliness, and a mother/wife's sense of her inability to love and nurture.

It is during times of a child's redecision that several family members, not just the patient alone, need the therapist's protection from the fears, real and fantasized, of change and its possible consequences.

Power

The therapist has several types of power. One of the more important, we believe, is the ability to help the patient and the family define—or redefine—reality. After all, they have come to the therapist because they expect some special expertise, an idea fostered by the therapist's reputation, office setting, diplomas, and other professional stage effects.

As therapists, one of our major sources of potency is our ability to shape the stories of patients and their families by the very questions we ask, what we are interested in, what we emphasize, as well as by our nonverbal behaviors and our comments. Through these, we may downplay certain facts, highlight others, and help the family make a new story.

Strength Orientation

Current United States therapeutic practice is saturated with emphasis on problems, deficits, abnormalities, and disorders. Some therapists seem to have been on a witch hunt for wounded inner children, co-dependency, and other forms of pathology. Unfortunately, such a framework limits the questions that are asked, the interpretations made, and the interventions planned.

It is also possible to practice from a perspective that validates strengths and resources. Not all children who have faced trauma and pain are incapacitated. Strengths can be forged in the fires of trauma and abuse. We can appreciate what people have learned about resilience and possibilities. This discourse of strength and resilience makes it possible for the therapist to ask other questions and make other observations, and thereby leads to different interventions.

Therapeutic Interventions
After Life Decisions Have Been Made

Redecision Therapy

Redecision therapy is based on the premise that at certain key times people make major decisions about themselves and their lives. Since they decide these important issues, they can also redecide them.

Redecision work with adults has traditionally been divided into three stages: (1) the contract, (2) the reliving of the key scene, and (3) a Child redecision. In working with children and adolescents, however, we have found it useful to incorporate Prochaska and DiClemente's paradigm of change (Prochaska et al. 1994). Modifying their work a little, we suggest seven stages in the redecision process.

1. Precontemplation
2. Contemplation
3. Preparation
4. Redecision Proper
5. Action
6. Maintenance
7. Termination

Work with children and adolescents differs from work with adults in three important aspects. First, these seven stages are less likely to be made explicit, especially with younger children. Second, the child or adolescent often is at a very different stage from the one his parents are in. The latter usually have brought the patient in for treatment and are the true "customers," at least in the beginning. Third, it is usually the parents who arrange the environmental reinforcements that are of great importance in the maintenance phase.

In looking more closely at the process, we find the following progress of events:

Precontemplation

At this stage, people—children, adolescents, or adults—are unaware of any need for change. Most children are at this point when their parents bring them in for treatment. Not infrequently, adults are brought to this stage by being in a group and hearing and seeing other group members make redecisions.

Contemplation

At this stage, patients are aware that they have a problem and are thinking about it, but have not yet made a commitment to change. It is frequently useful to help them look explicitly at the pros and cons of their behavior and its effects, as well as the pros and cons of change.

Preparation

At this point, people intend to take some specific action in the near future. For adults and adolescents this stage usually ends with a specific contract, something younger children often do not do explicitly.

Redecision Proper

This stage involves reliving a key scene and the introduction into it of some new information or feeling. It ends with a redecision made in a Child ego state.

Younger children. Depending on the age of the child and his intellectual and emotional level the techniques we use need to be somewhat different from those used with adults. Young children have less free recall, greater suggestibility, and have more trouble distinguishing reality from fantasy. They have limited verbal skills and attention span and a greater tendency to fill in gaps than older children. However, by about age 5, their suggestibility is about the same as that of adults and they can encode events just as well.

Symbolic and metaphoric redecision making. Storytelling, puppet play, and drawing are useful with the younger child. In these media, their experiences and their decisions can be reworked.

Marie, age 4, played out the story of a poor baby dinosaur who called and called for the mother dinosaur because she was hungry and frightened but the mother dinosaur never came because she was always too busy and didn't like baby girl dinosaurs anyway. As this play continued, it would become more disorganized. However, the therapist introduced a kindly old lion who taught the baby dinosaur how to find some other dinosaurs who liked babies and who could nurture them. Finally, the baby dinosaur decided she could be fed and comforted by the new dinosaur mothers.

Flo, age 4, had been in a number of foster homes after she had been sexually abused in her own home. In some of these homes she was abused again. In her play, a battered baby doll was protected by putting the "bad-touch daddies" in a toy jail where they could be locked up forever. At each session, Flo would check to make sure they were still in jail and assured herself they would be reincarcerated if they escaped, and that the baby doll could be safe.

Sometimes similar work can be done through storytelling. The therapist can take the story the child produces and suggest alternative interpretations, decisions, and endings. Sometimes, the therapist can tell a story. "I once knew a little boy who . . ." or "I once had a friend who . . ." are useful beginnings.

Redecision in real life experiences. A child may recreate a key scene in her day to day life.

Marie, a 4-year-old girl who had already been in twelve foster homes, raged for a whole weekend, tearing down drapes, over-turning furniture, and pulling out large chunks of her foster mother's hair. "I guess you'll want to get rid of this bad little girl" she screamed over and over. The foster mother held firm. Despite only a few hours sleep during 48 hours, she resolutely repeated, "You cannot leave. This is your home and your family now and you have to stay here no matter what you do." After some debate as to whether this new message was genuine, Marie made an important redecision: that she could be loved and was indeed lovable. With this, her behavior changed markedly.

Sensorimotor redecision making. The literature on redecision therapy is based primarily on work with adult patients. Although people make decisions throughout their lifetimes, the earliest that have been dealt with are generally made between 4 and 7, that is, when the child ("Little Professor") is in Piaget's stage of intuitive thinking or early concrete thinking (Piaget 1962). However, we sometimes see what seems to be a redecision made at a preverbal level, Piaget's stage of sensorimotor intelligence (Piaget 1962).

In the first year of life the child receives permission to be, to be close yet separate, to experience his own experiences, and to influence his world. It is the stage of the development of basic trust and security, mutuality, containment, and effectiveness. The child does not make verbal decisions, for the child does not yet have words. Consequently, when such nonverbal "decisions" are "redecided," the redecision is not made with words. Rather, the change seems to be at a more somatic level, what Piaget called sensorimotor.

We believe that such changes are also made in therapy with adult patients. In another paper we have elaborated some of the characteristics in terms of one type of early transference (Allen and Allen 1991). In work with children, the process may be more obvious.

Joanna, a 3-year-old, had suffered years of neglect and abuse. She stormed and raged and was unable to attach to people. She did not even differentiate them enough to learn their names. It seemed that for her everyone was the same as everyone else. She constantly looked for motivations, and generally put the most paranoid interpretation on things. "They don't really mean it" was her constant way of rejecting anything good. Because of her uncontrollable behavior—destroying furniture, threatening children and adults with harm, biting herself severely, and the like—she required frequent therapeutic holding. This seemed to provide some sort of nonverbal reassurance that we were safe, would not hurt her, and would try, however awkwardly, to comfort her, calm her, and to meet her needs. Although we talked to and with her, the main therapeutic elements seemed really to be the holding and touching, our constant caring protective presence, and our steadfast refusal to allow her to hurt us or herself. A "redecision" was never verbalized. However, Joanna did settle down and begin to relate and begin to trust.

A "Vaccination" technique. Sometimes children must live with people who have very little to give them in terms of nurturance. This may be because they themselves were never adequately nurtured, or because they suffer from mental retardation, psychosis, or chemical abuse. In these cases, when the child cannot live elsewhere, we have often found the following process useful.

The child is supported in seeing what his situation really is and what he can logically expect. Usually this is very little—or worse. These children are helped to explore where they might go for different messages, love, and affection. Perhaps it is the lady next door, perhaps a teacher. The redecision is basically "I will survive. I am entitled to get what I need." Then they need practical help and planning in how to do this—and protection.

Older children and adolescents. With older children and adolescents, redecision work can be done just as with adults.

At 16, Peter was sure he was a failure. He had no friends. He was failing at school. He remembered that he had decided he would be a failure when he was about 7. He believed this was the only way he could truly please his mother, for she regarded any success he might have as evidence of how even a child could do better than she had done in her life.

In fantasy, using two-chair work, Peter was able to experience himself back at the specific time and place where he first made this decision and, with protection and permission, he told his fantasy mother that the problem was hers and that he had deserved better.

This time, he decided that he would no longer try to please her (he had failed at this too), and that he would no longer continue to protect her—especially since he couldn't do it anyway.

After this he made many changes. He grieved for the love he couldn't get and began to accept what she could give him.

Action

At this stage, patients modify their behavior and do something new. Planning of future new behaviors and how to get reinforcement (strokes) for new behaviors is important. The adults in their lives usually have to arrange this for children and younger adolescents.

Maintenance

This is a stage where patients consolidate their gains and work to prevent relapse—again work usually done by the adults for children. The therapist and older patients need to look together at how the patient is getting well. What is helping and healing? How is the patient getting rewarded and supported in his new behaviors? It is important he not slip into the old stories about himself or life.

Termination

At this stage, new behaviors are integrated into the patient's daily life and no longer require constant attention.

Other Narrative Techniques

There are several other therapeutic interventions which appear similar to redecision therapy. They may have the same outcome, however, the therapeutic processes are quite different. Four important ones are:

Freeing suppressed narratives

We use the stories we tell of ourselves and our lives to consolidate our memories and to maintain and reaffirm our identities and our expectations. However, these stories may gradually be modified and changed, for no one story covers everything that has happened to us. We edit, subtracting and adding bits and pieces, as we retell these stories.

By raising questions about missing pieces, by highlighting some aspects and de-emphasizing others, the therapist can help the patient—child, adolescent, adult, or family—create a different story, hopefully one with more options and possibilities and better outcomes.

Myron, age 19, had always felt that he was a disappointment to his father. At least, his father never praised him. No matter how hard Myron tried, his father only found fault and made innumerable suggestions for improvement. All Myron could remember was a lifelong sense of failure and his father's disapproving frown. Then by chance he found a letter his father had written to his brother, Myron's uncle. In it his father had expressed great pride in Myron's accomplishments and successes—outlining a whole series from Myron's youngest years. It was as if Myron found, in this letter, a whole new story of his life, one of success and of pleasing his father. Myron decided his father had actually been trying to be encouraging and helpful, albeit not knowing how to do it well. More importantly, Myron began to remember events he had forgotten—times his father obviously had been proud. It was as if a hidden story about Myron's life had been set free.

Myron did this spontaneously. Sometimes, as therapists, we help patients do something similar. In so doing, it is useful to look at the times the patient behaved differently than usual, or stopped pathologic behavior. In short, we help the patient create a different story about his life. We have recently written about this process under the heading of constructivist transactional analysis (Allen and Allen 1995).

False narratives

There now is a large and growing body of literature suggesting that if children hear certain stories over and over or are asked certain kinds of leading questions over and over, they may begin to incorporate them into their life stories. In the most negative form, young children quizzed over and over about satanic cult activity or sexual abuse may begin to produce stories that support their interrogators' assumptions—a possibility against which child therapists need to guard—and that is indicative of the potential malleability of our identities and histories. In the sensationalism of these stories, however, two factors are often missed. First, the constructed story has, for the patient, the feel of reality, that is, whatever its factual basis it has "psychological truth." Second, the process can also involve the child's hearing good but not totally accurate stories about himself.

Post-traumatic stress problems

Joe, age 9, was numbed by a fire that destroyed his home and his parents. He had nightmares of burning buildings, repeatedly set fires, and had other symptoms of post-traumatic stress disorder. As a part of this picture he had a foreshortened sense of the future. He did not expect to live until he was 10. He had no plans or hopes for the future, and he could not even consider the possibility of having any.

Recent studies (Yehuda and McFarlane 1995) have suggested that there may be a physiological basis—at least in part—for some of these problems. The surge of hormones at the time of a severe stressor—especially adrenal hormones—may actually destroy part of the hippocampus, a part of the brain involved in memory. It is also often very difficult for people suffering from traumatic experiences to deal with problems resulting from the trauma because even minimal cues that remind them of it may precipitate sudden uncomfortable physiological changes that interfere with attention, problem solving, and processing the trauma. In addition, two of the very symptoms of the disorder are poor concentration and avoidance. This makes it difficult to integrate the trauma into their lives and to develop a life plan.

> Until a few weeks before the Oklahoma City bombing, Jim, age 2½, had attended the nursery where several children were blown up. Repeatedly, he built buildings of sand, labelled them "my school," and stomped down the front half. This behavior, as well as his nightmares, stopped abruptly after a group of child survivors got together and saw one another again, thanks to a special group outing at McDonalds and a Barney concert.
>
> Putting together a book of photos of their lives and their friends has proved useful in helping other child victims of the Oklahoma City bombing "get things together," and go on.

In these two instances, help was centered on getting on with one's life and making and finding membership in a community, rather than dealing with pathology.

Decision therapy

Because redecision therapy has such attractive features, some therapists try to use it with almost everyone. However, if that patient has never really made a decision, we do not believe that one can talk about a redecision. It seems better that these interventions—which may indeed be quite successful—be seen as an example of the therapist's helping the patient create a useful life story.

Older patients may feel they have themselves chosen a new script. This gives them a sense of power, direction, and control over their lives. One of the strengths of the process of redecision therapy is that it provides permission to change, a framework for making a decision, an "explanation" for later changes, and a clear "marker event." The patient is left with a sense of his or her power in having chosen a new way of being in the world. However, these patients have really made a decision, not a redecision. In any event, they may have developed a useful life story.

Interventions Primarily Before and During Decision Making

It is best, when possible, to prevent pathogenic decisions or at least to facilitate healthy decisions. To do this, a variety of techniques are possible. Sometimes, this can be done directly with the child. Sometimes, it is better done through working with their grownups or siblings. Whichever is done, it is important for children to get such permissions as: to be, to be aware of their sensations and feelings, to feel close, to belong, to be themselves and of appropriate age and sex, to be happy, to think clearly and solve problems, and to make sense of their existence. Common examples of such interventions are:

Environmental Manipulation

An oldest daughter who is expected to parent her younger siblings may be freed up to be a child of her appropriate age when the family hires an appropriately aged neighbor as a babysitter. This can be seen as counteracting the injunctions "Don't be you" and "Don't be a child."

The only son of a divorced mother may need to be told by his mother that he is all right and that he does not need to be her confidante, or "the man of the house." Then he needs to be discouraged when he attempts to assume this role. This can be seen as reducing or eliminating the injunctions "Don't be you," "Don't be a child," "Don't leave—take care of me," and "Don't belong to your peer group."

A 6-year-old child is taken back to his own bed when he crawls into bed with his mother. This undercuts any message he may receive of "Don't leave" or "Don't grow up."

Reframing/Interpretation

Children cannot steal until they understand what is theirs and what is not. They cannot lie until they understand what is real and what is fantasy. Most 2-year-olds are oppositional, as a way of expressing a growing sense of identity. However, it makes a great difference whether the grownups see this expected behavior as a necessary developmental stage or as evidence of badness or even psychopathology.

"Congenital liar," "born thief," "always uncontrollable" are important descriptions of a child that the child may take as a guidebook, but they really are interpretations and conclusions and may be quite inaccurate. Unfortunately, children often use these descriptions to define themselves and what to expect of themselves and others. Sometimes, these descriptions are given as "————but————." This often represents the differing views of two important persons. Father, for example, uses one adjective, Mother the other.

One of the functions of the child–adolescent therapist is to help parents know what are appropriate expectations for a child of a given age, and what are appropriate behaviors, of both child and parent. The therapist provides a different indexing scheme and helps both parents and child elaborate a new story.

Introduction of Other People
with Alternative Perceptions and Permissions

Some children seek out people other than their parents to give them the kind of feedback and permissions the parent does not give.

Mary was a totally unplanned birth and clearly remained unwanted. "I'd rather nurse a gin-and-tonic" was a remark much reiterated by her mother. Indeed, it appeared she kept Mary only because she did not want anyone else to have her—or the welfare supplement. However, by age 5, Mary was expert at finding other messages—from the lady next door, from the mothers of her friends, from a fantasy "real mother," and from a neighbor's very affectionate cocker spaniel.

The child is not just the hapless recipient of parental and family messages. However, this is a difficult task for the child to do alone. Sometimes, as therapists, we can aid and abet the process by actively setting up situations and introducing new people who can give different messages.

Changing Stroking Patterns

Bill, age 5, was depressed. He set himself up to be treated as bad and oppositional. His grandmother, who was raising him, gave him verbal recognition but did not touch him. When others touched him, he would shrink away, not in fear but rather in surprise, uncertain how to react and in apparent discomfort with the unfamiliar.

While being read to, he was gently encouraged to let himself be held. Later, he could allow being held and rocked. As he became more comfortable with these positive strokes, he was able to give up the provocative behavior that had brought him negative ones (slaps, hits, and the verbal abuse that is the psychological equivalent).

Touch is an important human need. If we are not accustomed to getting what is enough for us in a positive sense, we may seek negative strokes. It is hard to give these negative strokes up—and the associated behaviors that get them—until we have learned to take positive strokes, for something is better than nothing. An important aspect of therapy is to help patients learn to take positive strokes. This may be difficult for them to do because their experiences have taught them not to trust. However, it is too much to expect them to give up negative strokes until they can take positive ones (Allen and Allen 1989).

Therapy of Parents

The mothers of John and Peter had major psychological problems and needed their sons to be ill. If the children were to remain with them, their own individual treatment was of major importance.

Why would parents behave this way? Not likely out of malevolence. However, there are a number of common reasons. At some level, some parents may desperately be trying to free themselves of their problem by "giving" it to the child.

> A young mother whose husband was divorcing her brought in her 2-year-old for consultation. She said the child was seriously depressed and suicidal. On examination, the child had no symptoms of depression, but the mother herself was seriously depressed and suicidal.

Some children are caught up in multigenerational family processes and roles. One son, for example, was to take the place of a recently deceased uncle, mother's younger brother, a black sheep who had recently died and whose name he had been given. Some children are being trained to be the kind of person who excites the mother's (or father's) Child or who treats the parent in the way that parent expects to be treated. If a father expects his children to treat him badly—like King Lear—he has to start training them early to perform their roles properly. Thus, it is important to look at parental and family scripts to see where this child is to fit.

At the simplest and most direct level, the parent might require treatment himself: individual therapy (including redecision therapy), medication, marital, or family therapy. For some, parent skills training is useful. For more disorganized chaotic families an in-house therapeutic aide or a case manager may be useful.

Rapid Therapeutic Diagnosis: A Typology

It does not make sense to set a full meal before someone who needs and can use only the salad. In this age of cost containment, it no longer is possible to do therapy just because a patient is miserable. Redecision therapy is not appropriate for every child or adolescent problem. Consequently, it is important in working with children and adolescents to diagnose what the problem is rapidly, and then to make the most relevant and appropriate intervention. In this task we have found the following typology useful.

External Interferences and Deficits

A child may be getting too much or too little something, such as nurturance or limit-setting, or be may be getting something that is more appropriate for a child of another age. In these instances, the intervention of choice is environmental manipulation. Sometimes, this requires treatment of a parent or the parental relationships. Parent training, therapeutic aides in the home, social skills training, and placement all fit into this category. Diagnostic confirmation occurs if, when the environment is changed, often just slightly, the child changes.

Organic medical and neurophysiological conditions such as attention deficit problems or perceptual and motor delays will very much affect the child–environment fit (Greenspan 1989). These need specific medical and educational interventions.

By age 6 or 7, the child's problems may have become more internalized. Changing the environment alone may no longer be enough. Now the child needs more traditional therapy as well.

Interstructural Conflict (Type I Impasse)

These are conflicts between different ego states, usually between Parent and Child. The aim of treatment is to come to some type of resolution of this conflict, often to reduce the punitive nature of the Critical Parent.

Mark, age 9, poured lighter fluid on his arm and set himself ablaze. He did this to punish himself for his "bad behavior"— something his father substantiated at great length. Indeed, his father recently had quit his job and moved out of the house to punish his wife and children who, he declared, did not keep it clean enough. Mark's self-immolation was both a way of giving himself the punishment his Critical Parent said he needed and a peace offering to its origin, his actual father.

Intrastructural Conflict (Type III Impasse)

These are conflicts between different aspects of one ego state. This includes conflicts between Adapted Child and Natural Child or between a Critical Parent and Nurturant Parent.

Mark was able to describe conflict between "good Mark" and "bad Mark." It was the latter he punished by setting his arm afire. Interestingly, the separation between the two were sufficiently strong that "good Mark," he claimed, did not feel the pain. Mark was able to work this out using art therapy, drawing the "good Mark" and the "bad Mark" and developing dialogue and communication between them, and between them and his Critical Parent.

In this era of controversy about multiple personality disorder, some readers may be inclined to consider this an example of the latter condition rather than the shifting energizing of two Child ego states (Natural Child and Adapted Child). However, Mark did not meet *DSM-IV* criteria for Dissociative Personality Disorder (Multiple Personality Disorder). In any event, in treatment, using art and puppets, the split was rapidly resolved.

Script decisions (Type II Impasse)

For this type of problem, classic redecision therapy or the freeing of suppressed narratives, as already described, are the treatments of choice.

Externalized Conflict

A patient may take an internalized conflict, project it on the environment, and try to fight it there. This often appears as an external interference and is treated as such. Unfortunately, environmental manipulation alone is not a sufficient treatment for this problem. The internal conflict also must be resolved.

> Brent, age 14, called the police to inform them he had taken an overdose of pills. This was an active effort to get himself removed from his father's home. He felt he was neglected—he was—and had several times before succeeded in getting himself taken from the home, but he had always prevented extended placement in the foster home or group home he said he wanted. When he got in a new situation, he began to complain of neglect and maltreatment and set people up to treat him badly. Thus, he repeated in each new setting his experience in his father's home and made certain he would return to it.

In working with Brent, we had to deal with two issues simultaneously: the real neglect in his life and the internal conflict he projected on the environment. The latter responded to redecision therapy, using stories and drawings, around his early decision that he was unwanted and neglected and always would be. Both issues were treated with the "vaccination" process.

Conclusion

In real life, many children and adolescents present with a mixture of different kinds of problems. Each problem needs to be treated in its own right. However, this typology allows the therapist to quickly sort out what needs to be done.

Case Example

Justin, age 19, had with great difficulty gotten accepted into a junior college. His parents helped him study six or seven hours a night, but his best grade was still a C. Gradually his weight increased to 260 pounds. He had no friends. He was depressed, feeling himself worthless, rejected, and helpless. He thought seriously of suicide.

He had serious attention impairment and was highly distractible (an organic/neurophysiological problem). This responded well to stimulant medication. He also had major problems in visual spatial perception and auditory processing. Educational and occupational therapy were useful in helping him make sense of how these deficits interfered with his performance, and how he could compensate for them. For example, by wearing a ring on his right hand, he could tell which was his right hand. He tape recorded lectures so that he could review them at his leisure.

With this new information he was able to go back to early scenes in which he had decided he was stupid and worthless and always would be. He had new information and new experience and, using traditional two-chair work, he redecided he was neither stupid nor worthless.

With new Adult information he was able to interrupt his internal self-harassment (interstructural conflict: Parent–Child dialogue) that he was stupid, ugly, and incompetent. He then decided to lose weight, went on a diet, and began an exercise program.

A year later, he had lost a hundred pounds, had joined a judo team, and was able to get C's and low B's with about two hours of study a night. The weight loss was a result of exercise and diet, not stimulant use. He had begun to date, and his parents, relieved of having to spend six hours a night on his homework, had found a new interest in one another.

Children make the decisions they do because these decisions seem to have some survival value to them. If some pathogenic process is still going on and needs to be remediated but no decision has been made, the situation can be remediated through environmental manipulation. Once a decision is made, however, people begin to interact in the world in a way that reinforces their basic decisions, tending to ignore information that seems discrepant. Thus they confirm over and over the basic decision. Not infrequently, they elaborate internal dialogue that supports the decision.

In the adult, brief redecision therapy can go rapidly to the heart of the entire psychological problem, if the problem is based on an early decision. Indeed, redecision therapy often seems much like cutting down a tree by sawing the main trunk, rather than picking off small branches and leaves one by one. With children, however, we often can prevent the tree from growing in the first place.

References

Allen, J. R., and Allen, B. A. (1979). Discipline: a transactional-analytic view. In *Six Approaches to Discipline and Child Rearing*, ed. D. Dorr, pp. 99–149. New York: Brunner/Mazel.

———— (1989a). Ego states, self, and script. *Transactional Analysis Journal* 19(1):4–13.

———— (1989b). Stroking: biological underpinnings and direct observations. *Transactional Analysis Journal* 19(1):26–30.

———— (1991). Concepts of transference: a critique, a typology, an alternative hypothesis, and some proposals. *Transactional Analysis Journal* 21(2):77–91.

———— (1995). Narrative theory, redecision therapy, and postmodernism. *Transactional Analysis Journal* 25(4):327–334.

Allen, J. R., et. al. (1996). The role of permission: two decades later. *Transactional Analysis Journal* 26(3):196–205.

Goulding, R., and Goulding, M. (1976). Injunctions, decisions, and redecisions. *Transactional Analysis Journal* 6(11):41–48.

Greenspan, S. (1989). *The Development of the Ego*. Madison, CT: International Universities Press.

Piaget, J. (1962). The stages of intellectual development of the child. In *Childhood Psychopathology*, ed. S. Harrison and J. McDermott, pp. 157–166. New York: International Universities Press.

Prochaska, J. O., Norcross, J. C., and DiClemente, C. C. (1994). *Changing for Good*. New York: William Morrow.

Yehuda, R., and McFarlane, A. C. (1995). Conflict between current knowledge about PTSD and its original conceptual basis. *American Journal of Psychiatry* 152:1705–1713.

15

Redecision Stories from within an HMO with a Special Emphasis in Chemical Dependency

Gail Ardman, M.S.S.W.

Whenever I am in the company of therapists in private practice and the unmentionable is mentioned, that is, managed care, I hold my head high, as I am one of the "traitors" employed by an HMO, and I believe that I provide good mental health care for my clients. There was a time when I would not mention working for an HMO for fear of being derided by my colleagues. The mission of our Mental Health Department at Kaiser Foundation Health Plan is "to deliver high quality mental health care utilizing a model of 'short term' [quotes mine] treatment with a regional staff committed to providing timely, appropriate, safe and cost-effective services, thereby promoting the optimal health and functioning of each member and mental health professional." In other words, we give a bigger bang for the clients' buck, or at least as big a bang.

Within the parameters of my employment requirements, I have the freedom to utilize whatever model of treatment I choose, and monitor and review my own client outcomes. I find utilizing redecision therapy as the primary therapy intervention with my clients enables me to fulfill my employment contract as well as my client and therapist contract. Redecision therapy is contract oriented, client empowering, and, if need be, can easily be explained and quantified for any accountability my company may require. I am a generalist, and redecision therapy works with the majority of clients I treat. My practice includes clients who have been abused, are chemically dependent, terminally ill, grieving, depressed, anxious, experiencing problems in their marriages, their families, and work. I find using redecision therapy with individuals, couples, families, and groups facilitates client change.

After assessing clients to see that they meet the criteria for treatment by me, I begin to introduce them to redecision therapy. I may first do a genogram to see scripts and games that are going on currently and generationally in the family. This is helpful for me to imprint the client's story in my mind and helpful for the client to begin to see script connections and possible events that occurred when early decisions were made. In this initial interview I begin to introduce clients to accurate and responsible language usage that will be monitored during treatment: correcting and explaining the difference between "can't" and "won't" statements, and replacing "makes me feel" with "feel" and vague words such as "it" with the specific noun or phrase being described. I begin interrupting clients when they talk about how others victimize them and instead direct them to ask themselves what they would like to change about themselves to make their lives better. Sometime in this initial session, or in the second session, I introduce them to the model of redecision therapy and begin to educate them to the implications of their early life and how these decisions are continuing to impact their lives in a way that is no longer working and is creating pain for them. I usually recommend clients begin readings for consciousness raising about assertiveness, dysfunctional family systems, chemical dependency, and support groups.

Often clients in crisis get what they need in one therapy session.

Others may be so fragile that one session is all they can tolerate. Clients who want treatment, but are reluctant to make changes, I put into groups. In group, because of contagion, resistance breaks down more quickly and clients begin to be willing to make contracts to work. Clients find out right away that when they come in to see me it is their time and their agenda. My first question to them is, "What do you want to change about yourself today?" or "What do you want different?" If clients come in to see me individually with no particular agenda and have nothing they want to change or explore about themselves, I ask them if we have completed our therapy contract at this point in time. I do not hold on to clients, but let them know they can come back during crisis or for maintenance checks at any time in the course of their membership in our HMO.

Susie is a 27-year-old divorced female, diagnosed with major depression by one of our staff psychiatrists, placed on Prozac, and referred to counseling. Her depression began following a breakup with her boyfriend of three months. Susie is the youngest of three children whose parents and siblings are professional people. She presents as a beautiful woman who is very thoughtful before she responds to any question, quiet as if waiting to be spoken to, almost like a mannequin. She is very reticent to respond in any spontaneous way, and is very concise in giving any personal information. Susie maintains a pleasant demeanor no matter how emotional the issue being discussed. She presents like a Barbie Doll who speaks. When asked what she would like to change about herself in the first interview, Susie said she wanted to be able to "express her feelings, make decisions, and stop avoiding conflict." She sees herself as "isolated and lost" in the family. Currently in relationships men break up with Susie after two or three months for being "too clingy." Because of her difficulty expressing herself one-on-one, I felt she might do better in a mixed group I was forming. In group, Susie was quiet for the first three sessions but extremely attentive to the work of others. In the fourth group session Susie asked to work on being able to express her anger.

Therapist: How do you want to be able to express your anger?

Susie: I've always suppressed my anger, thinking others are always right and know what I should be doing, especially my mother. I must do everything my mother wants and be the perfect little girl. But I get so angry with her. She's critical of everything about me: clothes, friends, career goals, everything. I always wanted her approval and never got it.

Therapist: Can you remember an incident between you and your mother when you were angry with her as a kid, and kept it to yourself?

Susie: Yes, I do. I may not know a lot of things, but I have a really good sense of direction and never get lost when I'm driving.

Therapist: Be that kid.

Susie: My mother is driving the car and is not sure whether to go left or right at the stop sign. My brother is in the front seat, telling my mother which way to go. It's the wrong way. I tell them both that it's the wrong way to go. Neither one pays any attention to me and my brother tells my mother again to turn down the wrong street. They totally ignore me. I decided they could just get lost if they wouldn't listen to me. In fact, I would never offer them my opinion again since no one ever listened to me anyway.

Therapist: There your mother and brother are [indicating empty chair]. Tell them how angry you are about being ignored by them.

Susie: [talking to the chair] I'm really mad that both of you won't listen to me when I know where to go and you don't.

Therapist: What are they saying?

Susie: They're continuing to ignore me.

Therapist: Tell them so they can hear you.

Susie: [talking louder] Listen to me, you two! I know where to go and you don't.

Therapist: Are they listening yet?

Susie: My brother is being sarcastic and Mama still isn't listening.

Therapist: Tell them if they don't listen to you, you are going to stay angry with them forever and never offer to help again if they are lost.

Susie: I'm so angry at your ignoring me, never listening, and treating me like I'm a little girl that I'm going to be mad and quiet forever. [long pause] I don't think I want to do that anymore.

Therapist: What would you do instead?

Susie: Tell them that even if they don't listen to me, I can listen to me and find other people who will listen and accept that I might know something and be right.

Therapist: Tell them that.

Susie: Mama, I'm sorry you never wanted to hear me because I really was telling it right. I am not going to feel bad anymore because you won't hear me. I'll find people who will listen and pay attention to me because what I have to say counts.

Therapist: How will you know when you really stop being angry at your mother for not listening?

Susie: When I begin to tell other people how I feel and see if they react without discounting me.

Therapist: What if they continue to discount you?

Susie: Then I'll let them know if they want to have a relationship with me, they better pay attention and hear me because I have a right to be heard and am going to be heard.

Three sessions later, Susie stopped me before the session convened and told me she was feeling much better and had gotten what she needed from the group. She asked to attend that session and thank the group for their help. One year later she is off Prozac and continues to function well, according to the psychiatrist who was following her medication. This brief intervention with medication and redecision therapy was enough to alleviate symptoms that brought Susie into our offices in the first place. This was a good beginning for her. This was a Type 2 impasse. She was confronting the parental injunctions, "Don't know what you know," "Don't be," "Don't feel," perhaps even, "Don't exist."

Harry, an individual client I have been seeing on and off for two and a half years, is a 45-year-old male working in a governmental agency. Within the past ten years, he has stopped using alcohol and stopped battering women. Harry originally wanted to deal with his rage toward his supervisor at work. Harry said he felt like a "pressure cooker." He reported fantasies at the time of cutting people up at work, even his only friend. He had a fear that he might lose control and bring an ax to work and do it. His father had died the year before, as had his favorite aunt. His mother had died when he was 22 years old. He grew up in Tennessee in a strict Christian fundamentalist home, and was the second son of a physically and emotionally abusive father. He used to think of himself as trying to be a "good little soldier." His brother was the favored child. One of his major issues was his fear of abandonment. By the end of his first year of therapy he connected with a CODA group, which became more and more important to him. During the course of therapy he revealed abusing Ativan, and stopped using soon after this disclosure. After the first year of treatment, Harry was more comfortable at work and even applied for a supervisory position. In the second year he saw me fifteen times and in the past eight months I have seen him three times. The last time he came in for therapy, his presenting complaint was still missing his father, whose death had occurred three years past.

Therapist: Are you ready to let your father go and say goodbye to him?

Harry: No. [starts to cry]

Therapist: Will you put your father in the chair and talk to him?

Harry: Daddy, I keep missing you so and we just started really talking when you died.

Therapist: Tell him you want to stop missing him.

Harry: I keep wanting you here to talk to. I don't think I can stand letting you go. This is how I always wanted us to be and it was too short a time.

Therapist: What is your father doing?

Harry: He is smiling at me and shaking his head.

Therapist: Tell your father how grateful you are that you finally could relate to him after all the years of abuse.

Harry: Daddy, you were so mean to me and I never could understand, but you wanted me to be tough so I could take care of myself.

Therapist: What is your father doing?

Harry: He has tears in his eyes.

Therapist: Would you be your father?

Harry: [slowly gets up and goes to the other chair] Son, you're going to be all right without me. I'm sorry I was so hard on you. I never meant to hurt you. I love you.

Therapist: Do you have anything else to say to your son?

Harry: Son, it's O.K. to let me go, you're going to do just fine.

Therapist: Will you come back to your chair?

Harry: [cries while returning to his chair] I don't want to let you go but I know now I will be all right and I don't need to keep you anymore. [stops crying]

Therapist: What are you experiencing now?

Harry: I feel lighter. I really wanted my father to be more than he was, but I see him as more human now.

Therapist: Would you say goodbye to your father and let him be at peace?

Harry: Goodbye, Dad, I'm going to be all right. [sitting straighter in his chair and no longer crying]

Therapist: O.K., is anything left unfinished with your father?

Harry: No. I'm done.

Goodbyes are often a big part of my practice at Kaiser. For many clients that is the only time they may ever feel it is O.K. to see a therapist. Grief is a universal issue and clients do not see themselves as crazy because they are grieving.

Chemically dependent (CD) client populations are among the most difficult populations to treat in therapy. I am not always sure I have a client. Prochaska and colleagues (1992) recognized that the processes of change included "precontemplation, contemplation, preparation, action, and maintenance." Their study showed that patients with addictive behaviors who seek psychotherapy will recycle several times through the stages before achieving long-term maintenance. For the most part, people who first come to treatment are the "contemplators" and have a great deal of catch-up work to do, as they are far from the "action" stage and feelings of autonomy. Most of my CD clients are there because of a "dirty" urinalysis, a threat of drug testing by an employer, an employee assistance program has intervened on the employee's behalf, a spouse or family member is threatening to remove financial or emotional support of the CD client, the client is awaiting DWI charges or court-ordered chemical dependency treatment, a referral by a doctor who has uncovered alcohol or drug abuse, or a referral by a psychiatrist who has evaluated the patient for depression and uncovered substance abuse. These clients are often there not because they want to quit abusing some substance, but to fulfill a contract with a third party of which I may not be aware. This often sets the stage for the therapist to allow herself to feel manipulated, conned, or victimized by the client's own denial system and pain. This can interfere with making clear contracts for redecision therapy. It is important for therapists to have good boundaries when working with the CD population. Among my CD colleagues it is often said, "No good deed goes unpunished." I quickly found out what that means with the CD population. When you are "conned" into enabling a chemically dependent client by giving them extra time, a lunch hour appointment, running interference for them with an EAP counselor or their boss, not confronting the excuse as to why they missed that extra effort appointment you gave them at your expense, or a typewritten letter they must have today for their court date today, you are a participant in the game of "No good deed goes unpunished." The therapist is the one who allows herself to be punished. CD therapists call this behavior by a therapist *enabling*. The therapist must clarify for herself what her boundaries are for treating a client's alcoholism or drug use. In our chemical dependency program, the burden of responsibility for sobriety rests with the client. Once the client is sober, relapse prevention becomes the goal and a treatment contract can be established. My personal requirements are abstinence. Relapse may occur, but I will not treat them if they do not have abstinence as their goal. The clients understand from the beginning that they have a life-threatening illness and only they can make the choice to live. If clients agree to this contract, I encourage them to go to a twelve-step group, get a temporary or permanent sponsor, attend Kaiser's Relapse Prevention Group, and continue seeing me individually. After three to six months of continuous sobriety, I offer them one of my redecision groups. I find placing CD clients in redecision groups allows them to contract for change around issues often affecting their continuing sobriety. Most clients find redecision work reinforces their twelve-step programs. Twelve-step programs are not antithetical to redecision therapy; one seems to enhance the other. Often placing sober CD clients in redecision groups uncovers other alcohol and drug abusers who have been in denial.

Another way that the chemically addicted client can con the therapist is to lie about how much mind-altering substance they may be using. Abstinence from mind-altering chemicals is a requirement in a sexual abuse group I do with a co-therapist. It became apparent that a client did not disclose to us the extent of her alcohol usage after the group began. In fact, her alcohol abuse was exacerbated by the stress of confronting sexual abuse issues in the group. It was not long before she became aware that she had to face her alcohol dependency before she could begin her recovery from the trauma of childhood sexual abuse.

Eva, a 38-year-old, emotionally guarded, chemical dependency client is a client I continue to softly confront about her behaviors. Eva was referred for chemical dependency counseling by her company's Employee Assistance Program (EAP) after being reported by her supervisor and co-workers for threatening other employees, high absenteeism, and a bad attitude at work. Her resistance is typical of many EAP referrals. She had an arrest history of DWI. She stopped drinking when she was 25 years old and then began "conning" doctors into giving her pain medication, developing a preference for codeine as her drug of choice. After three visits over a four-week period, I acquired the necessary intake information requested by the Texas Commission on Drug and Alcohol Abuse in order to fulfill Kaiser's licensing requirements. The client at this time was compliant with attending Narcotics Anonymous meetings about four times a week and had gotten a sponsor. The client was compliant but otherwise not invested in her therapy sessions, showing little affect and expecting me to do the work. She would come to sessions, often with somatic complaints, such as headaches, toothaches, or flu onset. She would often be interrupted by her beeper going off, and otherwise kept herself distracted. I often felt I had no person that I could really connect with, although I did believe she was maintaining sobriety. Some of her behaviors may be attributed to the long-term use of narcotics and the process of detoxifying. Most of our sessions were spent with me getting basic information for CD intake and her expressing physical complaints. This was hardly an atmosphere for change. On the client's fourth visit, she walked into my office with what I would call her sardonic attitude, and began to relate how she went out Friday and got drunk and didn't know how she got home. When asked if she had spoken about this with her sponsor or members of her NA group, her response was, "You've got to be kidding. I don't want to hear any flak." When asked about the specific trigger for drinking, she said. "I don't have a clue, and I've been wondering why." Eva told me some friends had invited her to go out clubbing earlier that day but she had refused. She was going to pick up her 14-year-old daughter who had been visiting with Eva's mother in Oklahoma for two weeks (she didn't go). She stated that about 7:00 P.M. she decided to go to some clubs and then head for Oklahoma. The last thing she remembered is drinking in a bar until her husband, who works late nights, awakened her in her own bed at 7:00 A.M. the next morning. He was angry about her car being parked in the yard and the front door being left open all night. The client said it was really "scary" to not know why she went clubbing, and to have no memory of what she drank, who she drank with, what she did, or how she got home. Eva and I then had a discussion about cross-addiction.

Therapist: Is there anything you want to change about you?

Eva: Yes, I want to improve my attitude about how I feel about other people.

Therapist: How do you feel about other people?

Eva: They owe me.

Therapist: So it isn't that you want to change how you feel about other people so much as you want to change feeling that other people owe you.

Eva: Yeah.

Therapist: What's your first memory of others owing you?

Eva: When Charles was killed in a car crash. [Charles, Eva's first husband, was killed in a motor vehicle accident when he and the client were 23 years old.]

Therapist: Were you angry about his death?

Eva: Yeah, with God, but I got over that and He and I are O.K. It was my ex-mother-in-law who was the beneficiary of all my husband's insurance, as he never got around to changing beneficiaries. You know we thought we had forever. She told me I had only been married to him for five months, but she had been his mom forever. But I sued her and I got the money. Then I never let her see her granddaughter until two years ago, when I told my mother she could arrange a visit when Charlene was in Oklahoma. I guess my mother still takes her over there.

Therapist: Would you put that part of yourself, the one with the attitude, in the chair over there and tell me about her?

Eva: She is really pissed at everyone and doesn't trust no one.

Therapist: No one?

Eva: Yeah, except she trusts her mother.

Therapist: Now will you go into the chair and be her? [client does this reluctantly]

Eva: Hey, am I one of those split persons?

Therapist: No, but you do have some conflicts inside you that I think you might like to know about. Like, is this the part of yourself that relapsed?

Eva: Yeah, I just don't give a shit over here. [begins to show some feelings and lets down her guard for the first time]

Therapist: Do you trust her? [pointing to the chair she just left]

Eva: Naw, she can't stop me from doing anything I want to do.

Therapist: What do you want from her?

Eva: She might try talking nicer to me.

Therapist: Move back into the other chair. What do you think she wants from you?

Eva: I guess I haven't been very nice myself. I sure don't keep her out of trouble.

Therapist: Will you tell her that you will take better care of her and pay attention to her anger, pain, and discomfort?

Eva: I'm going to pay attention to you and notice what you think about and do. Maybe find out what you're going to do next and talk you out of it or get help, like my sponsor. I could have been killed Friday night.

The client is back where she started. Perhaps she has some insight into how her part in not knowing keeps her from taking responsibility for what happens to her. This is a Type 3 impasse, with the dialogue between the Adapted Child and Free Child. It is important for clients to be awake before they can change. Eva was making a beginning at awakening.

Dave is an alcoholic, a 46-year-old man referred to me by a psychiatrist. He had come in for depression, and the psychiatrist refused to treat him with antidepressants until he got sober. It is difficult to differentiate a diagnosis of depression versus an alcohol-related mood disorder until the client is drug and alcohol free. Dave was drinking two six-packs of beer a night and more on weekends. He presented to me as wanting to quit alcohol because of the physical affects it had begun to have on him. He suffered from high blood pressure and his short-term memory was impaired. Dave, a sales-man, had moved his family down to Texas from Illinois ten years ago. After being here three years, he went into business for himself. Under the stress of owning his own business, he began drinking daily. He asked his primary physician to give him Antabuse when he knew his drinking was out of control. In the summer months, when he knew he wanted to continue drinking, he would stop the Antabuse. Dave had been drinking since he was 18 years old and knew from the beginning that alcohol gave him courage with women and allowed him to be more sociable with friends. According to him, his life growing up had been "fine," his marriage of 25 years was "good," and his family was "very close." He had some business setbacks in the past two years and because of these setbacks he had to reduce his living standards drastically.

He went to one AA meeting and decided he did not want to hear any sad stories and refused to attend any others. As far as he was concerned, people should "shut the door on things that are upsetting." This was all the information that I gathered in the first session. In the second session, I began asking questions from the psychosocial form, a questionnaire required for fulfilling the state CD requirements. I was asking questions about his mother and filling in the genogram on the form when Dave burst into tears and said he was angry with his mother. At that point I stopped the questionnaire and began exploring what caused the behavioral outburst. (As my supervisor, John Gladfelter, always says, "I must follow them, because I am their leader.") Dave said he remembers his mother was always depressed when he was a little child. She would pass out in church (they always sat in the front pew) and his father would pick her up and carry her out. After these church episodes, his mother would be in bed for two weeks. Dave said his parents were abstinent from alcohol but his mother had all kinds of pills in the medicine cabinet. He admitted being "so ashamed" when she did this, and thought secretly she was "faking it." He began crying again while relating the following story. He was 6 years old and his mother was in her sickbed and he was playing in her room while workmen were helping his father do some remodeling downstairs. One of the men who was working on their home walked into his mother's bedroom and began kissing her while Dave was sitting on the floor playing by her bed. His mother began to scream and he didn't know what to do. Dave said he felt "frozen to the spot." Finally his father entered the room and grabbed the man and kicked him out. Dave was sobbing by this time and began berating himself for not protecting his mother. It was at this point that I had him put his parents in the chair.

Therapist: Tell your parents how ashamed you are of yourself for not protecting your mother.

Dave: Mother, I am so sorry I didn't protect you from that man. I have always felt so ashamed of myself, I couldn't even hear songs that would have the word "kiss" in them.

Therapist: What are you experiencing now?

Dave: I am so ashamed. I am so chicken. I'll always be a scared little chicken.

Therapist: What are your parents doing?

Dave: Mother is looking down and Dad is giving me a dirty look, like how could I possibly tell this?

Therapist: Tell your parents that you will feel ashamed forever unless they let you off the hook for not defending your mother's honor.

Dave: Dad, I am so ashamed I couldn't stop that man from kissing Mother and until you forgive me I will feel bad about this forever.

Therapist: What is your father saying?

Dave: Both of them are saying, "It's O.K., son, you're just a boy. How can you expect to stop a grown man?"

Therapist: Do you believe them? Do you believe little kids can't stop grown men?

Dave: Yes, I believe them.

Therapist: What are you experiencing now?

Dave: Some relief. It's really silly. God, I've carried that memory for a long time. Wow, I have no idea why I remembered that.

Therapist: How do you feel about that 6-year-old kid who didn't stop that man?

Dave: I guess I've condemned him for a long time and even felt ashamed and scared like him.

Therapist: Will you let him off the hook? Can a 6-year-old child know what is expected of him in grown-up situations, if grownups don't tell him?

Dave: No. You're right. [becomes angry]

Therapist: Tell them.

Dave: I've felt bad enough about this. Why didn't you tell me what to do, Mother? I would have done anything you told me. I didn't know if I was supposed to stop him, get Dad, or not say anything. In fact, I felt ashamed of you for letting it happen at all, Mother. Why didn't you say something when he walked into the room? In fact, why the silence every time we passed that man's house? Who's shame is it? I'm tired of this.

Therapist: What are you experiencing now?

Dave: [smiling] I'm not sure, but I sure feel better.

The client continued to see me and tried another AA group where he felt more comfortable. Most of his issues continue to be about shame and rigid rules he has placed on himself. Marital and vocational issues emerged in time. My first encounter with Dave removed the block that stopped him from proceeding. What he did was a Type 1 impasse. His parental counterinjunction was "Be brave and courageous, and always take care of women." This was a big order for a small kid.

General client population cons, like CD cons, come in all sorts of guises from daily phone calls, threats, or letters to supervisors, calling member services to complain, lawsuits, seductive behaviors, stand-up rages, and walking out of the office slamming doors so hard pictures fall off the walls. My experience and training in redecision therapy has helped me set better boundaries with my clients. Contractual boundaries clarify for me and the client what I can and will do and what they can or won't do in my office. This allows both of us to feel safe. I set rules for the groups that I do and when clients are noncompliant with the rules, they are firing me. I allow anger but they may

not throw anything, break anything, or touch or hit anyone, including the therapist. The best tool I have found for setting limits with
clients puts the choice for stopping the behavior with the client. With
this tool they can decide anytime when they want to stop work with
me.

A male narcissistic client of mine, who had come into treatment to
deal with his uncontrollable rages with his ex-girlfriend, on occasion
would stand up and rage at me and then sit down and be fully
composed. Soon after his first rage against me, I had him put his
anger in the chair and describe it, then become the anger and have a
dialogue with himself, which he did, discovering how his anger no
longer continued to serve him. I finally told him that the next time he
raged at me I would consider him firing me. He agreed to the
contract and never raged at me again throughout his treatment. This
tool works effectively in couple therapy also. You may see the couple
only one time, but you have effectively modeled for an abused spouse
how to begin setting a boundary of care for herself. Once I start
contracting for what is acceptable behavior in my office, and clients
understand their choices, we can talk about how they see my role in
their relationship.

Many times the couple wants to use the therapist as a rescuer. This
is especially true when I see a couple with one partner who is chemically addicted. I have had wives call telling me I had to make their
spouses stop drinking, threatening me that it was my job. Sometimes
it would be more subtle. One spouse called asking if her husband
was at his appointment as she had locked her car and left her keys in
the ignition and needed him to come home after the appointment to
pick up their children at school. Another spouse called to make sure
the deposit got to the bank. All these elaborate stories just to see if
their spouses made the appointment, indicative of the nonalcoholic
spouse's psychic pain. One wife of a schizophrenic/alcoholic asked
me to guarantee that he wouldn't drink if she came back home to live
with him. It is always with regret that I have to inform the spouse that
I am as helpless as she is to stop the addictive behavior unless the
addicted spouse wants to stop and is asking for my help in quitting. I

encourage them to get into Al-Anon, Nar-Anon, CODA or the support group of their choice. If they are in crisis themselves, I encourage them to get into treatment with a mental health professional.

I find practicing redecision therapy inside an HMO is an ethical way I can fulfill my contractual responsibilities to my clients and to my employer. I am respectful of Kaiser's guidelines for the Mental Health Department. My employer does not purport to be all things to all clients. If clients want to be in total charge of their treatment with no restrictions other than what occurs between them and their therapists, then they have a right to find private practitioners and pay for it. The private practitioner is alive and well. To my clients I offer brief therapy by utilizing the redecision therapy model, but it is never "fast therapy." Redecision therapy meets clients where they are and provides a catalyst for change no matter where the milieu and what the problem. I trust clients to grow at their own pace.

References

Goulding, M. M., and Goulding, R. L. (1979). *Changing Lives through Redecision Therapy*. New York: Brunner/Mazel.

Mental Health Department (1994). Texas Region: Kaiser Permanente Mission Statement. Dallas, TX.

Prochaska, J. O., DiClemente, C. C., and Norcross, J. C. (1992). In search of how people change: applications to addictive behaviors. *American Psychologist* 47(9):1102–1114.

Steiner, C. (1971). *Games Alcoholics Play*. New York: Ballantine.

III

Training

16

The Application of the Redecision Therapy Model to Experiential Group Supervision

Michael Andronico, Ph.D.
Barbara Dazzo, M.S.W., Ph.D.

The redecision therapy model (Goulding and Goulding 1979) is an effective and efficient model of psychotherapy. In addition to its usefulness as a therapeutic intervention, the authors have adapted this approach to an experiential supervision model (Andronico and Dazzo 1991). This model takes place in a group setting that provides many important supportive, educational, and therapeutic aspects.

The Model

The basic assumption in a redecision model is that people are stuck or fixated at points of unresolved conflict that occurred during their childhood. The work is aimed at identifying the present-day triggering mechanisms or stimuli for regression that lead the individual back to the point of the original unresolved conflict. This regression is usually beyond the individual's awareness and stimulates responses that are often inappropriate and ineffective for the present situation. Through therapeutic intervention, usually gestalt empty chair work, a real or symbolic scene of unresolved conflict emerges. The decision that was made at that time in response to this conflict is then discovered and clarified. At this point therapeutic interventions such as the use of imagery, role play, and hypnotic suggestion are utilized to help the client make a more realistic, updated, and appropriate decision or redecision. This redecision is then anchored through an associational process that helps to remind the client to practice and maintain the redecision and the good feelings associated with it (Goulding and Goulding 1979).

The Value of the Model for Supervision

The value of this model for supervision is manyfold. Because it is a model that was originally designed for a 20-minute session, it is a valuable model for teaching the identification of relevant psychological issues and the rapid interventions into these issues. Many supervisees, especially beginning professionals, have difficulty deciding where and when to intervene therapeutically. Their anxieties concerning timing and fear of mistakes often delay their interventions, resulting in poor timing and missed opportunities. This model provides both encouragement and a rationale for early evaluation of the client's experience at the moment of observation. By having a model that legitimizes appropriate early interventions, supervisees learn to become less hesitant about making interventions early as long as they are based on the process of the client. This is particularly relevant to those supervisees who may have a theoretical orientation that encourages more extensive exploration before intervening. Even though this is a rapid approach, if it is done following the client's process without interpretation it does not lead to premature interventions. This expectation of rapid intervention helps supervisees, particularly those of other orientations, to more clearly differentiate between their hesitation being attributed to their own theoretical orientation or to their own anxieties. It is therefore helpful in supervising professionals who are not trained in redecision therapy.

By seeing and experiencing the effectiveness of following or tracking the client's process, the supervisee soon learns to have more confidence in following unconscious processes even though the results at the time may not be obvious to them. This confidence helps therapists to allay their anxieties during this tracking and prevents premature or ill-timed interventions and interpretations.

Dealing With Nonverbal Behavior

Because this model approaches both verbal and nonverbal productions of the client, it is valuable in helping supervisees to focus on all of the ways in which clients express their feelings, particularly their unresolved conflicts. Most psychotherapies are verbally oriented. Although therapists will note exaggerated gestures and posture, and even interpret them at times, they usually limit this knowledge to observation, without further pursuit. This model teaches the value of conceptualizing nonverbal expressions as important symbols and indicators of the client's process that can be worked with in the same way as verbalizations. For example, in much the same way that a therapist would note but not intervene around certain verbalizations but would intervene extensively around others, this redecision model teaches the importance of intervening around nonverbal expressions that are repetitive, exaggerated, or indicative of regressive states. An example of such exaggerated gesture would be a client who is sitting with a clenched fist during a silence. In a strictly verbal orientation the clinician might point out that the client's fist is clenched or ask what the client is experiencing at that time.

In this model one might ask the client to either put a voice to the fist or role play the fist and might even encourage the client to have a dialogue between the clenched fist and the unclenched fist. The value of this is that role playing body parts and inanimate objects is usually beyond the experience of most adults but not children. This tends to encourage clients to stay at the regressed younger age. In addition, there are no norms for right or wrong as to what body parts or inanimate objects can say to each other. This allows clients to circumvent their usual verbal defenses. Behaviors that are indicative of regressed states are immature wording, whining and other vocal variations, uncoordinated gestures, postures, or movements, all of which are more typical of younger children than adults (Andronico 1985). This focusing on nonverbal expressions and the utilization of these expressions provides the supervisees with a widely expanded scope of awareness in approaching their clients.

Applying this redecision model to an experiential group supervision setting gives supervisees an additional opportunity to explore and observe a variety of therapeutic interventions in the safety of the group. This is done by the supervisor facilitating the work of members of the group. At other times this is done by having a supervisee take the supervisor role with another supervisee and working with him on his countertransferential issues as well as issues in his work environment. This enables supervisees to both practice interventions and experience the interventions of their colleagues, and to observe a variety of differing intervention styles that they can question and discuss. Further, it stimulates more learning and expansion of their own repertoire of interventions and allows for a wider, more informed theoretical foundation. This process of exploring and learning sheds further light on the supervisees' own struggles as well as helping supervisees to more clearly separate their issues from those of their clients.

Differentiating Between Supervision, Therapy, and Training

In supervision as in therapy the recognition and adherence to boundaries is a critical issue. Content is the essential difference between using the redecision therapy model as a training model and as a supervision model. In the therapy model the client, of course, is free to bring up any issues that he wishes to change. In the training model any trainee role playing himself is in the client role and therefore can also select any content that he wishes to change. In contrast, in supervision the supervisee is restricted to choosing only those issues which are directly related to problems or "stuck points" he is having with one or more clients.

The first boundary that is dealt with is differentiating between a lack of knowledge and an emotional issue of the supervisee. The former is easily handled through group exchange of knowledge and issues of experience. For example, Dave came to one of the early group sessions and said he was feeling uncomfortable in his new job working with court-referred teenage boys and girls. He had been accustomed to working in a group with depressed teenagers at a local family service agency. He needed to structure and enforce group boundaries around tardiness, expressions of hostility, and carrying weapons to group sessions. Even though he was inclined toward appropriate limit setting, his prior experience of encouraging depressed teenagers to express themselves as a vehicle for change resulted in ambivalent feelings toward imposing rules. A group discussion bringing to the fore the difference in the needs and goals of these different populations of teenagers ensued. Dave was then able to better understand the dynamics of this population and put this understanding into action. The fact that he could do this without needing any further work is an indication that his issue was more one of ignorance and some lack of confidence, and not a deep-seated emotional issue.

Emotional issues are more complex and involve working with the supervisee's emotional experience. These issues can be as minor as a lack of confidence because the supervisee, unlike the last example, is knowledgeable but hesitant and insecure about implementing this knowledge. In these cases support and encouragement from the group through discussion of the issue is usually sufficient to help the supervisee. The deeper emotional issues require more in-depth work. This in-depth emotional work more closely approximates the redecision training and therapy model. In this case the problem is presented by the supervisee, and when she is asked what she wants to change, the answer takes the form of a specific feeling state that she wants to attain or change in reference to the client. For example, a supervisee might say, "What I want to change is not knowing what to say when Jack says, 'I'm feeling depressed' and I don't know what to do." At this point the supervisor helps the supervisee to clarify her contract by helping her arrive at a statement such as, "What I want to change are my feelings of helplessness when Jack expresses his hopeless feelings of depression." Here the supervisor explores the supervisee's feelings toward her client through the use of the gestalt empty chair technique. Using conventional redecision methods the supervisor places the supervisee in the empty chair. The supervisee often arrives at a childhood decision that is either similar to the client's or is directly related to her work with the client. For example, one supervisee, Tom, expressed feeling frustrated in his work with a client because he thought that the client was not progressing quickly enough. Tom stated that he was further frustrated by his difficulties in appropriately confronting his client. At this point Tom entered into a dialogue with his absent client. Using the gestalt empty chair approach, Tom was able to express his feelings more directly because the client was not actually there. In the dialogue Tom took the role of his client. At one point, while role playing his client, Tom experienced a sudden burst of feelings and saw his father in the therapist's chair. The feelings continued and intensified as the role playing switched from a dialogue between Tom and his client to a dialogue between Tom and Tom's father. Tom expressed strong feelings of sadness and anger towards his father, who he felt had always demanded too much from him and was never satisfied by Tom's achievements. This was typified by his father's dissatisfaction with Tom's interest in the piano and lack of interest in playing athletics. His father frequently referred to Tom as the "nonperformer." At one point in this dialogue, Tom came up with another memory. It was a scene where Tom and his father would occasionally visit a friend of Tom's father and his son, and the four of them would spend an afternoon playing touch football. Tom often felt embarrassed and humiliated at his lack of athletic prowess. He remembered the laughter of the others at his mistakes, especially his father's laughter. In the course of this dialogue, Tom was wiggling his fingers, and through the redecision work discovered his decision to "try harder" to gain his father's approval, while feeling he would never succeed. He then made a redecision that he was indeed a "performer," an almost virtuoso pianist. He expressed these feelings to his father saying, "I'm a great performer and I do it in my own way, not your damn way." He experienced feeling successful while saying this to his father. Tom anchored this delightful discovery with the wiggling of his fingers, telling himself, "This is my touchdown; you can have yours," and claimed he would do this whenever he felt inadequate and not "performing" well enough. In the following discussion, Tom further anchored his work by saying to his client that "It's O.K. for you to 'perform' in your way, you don't have to 'perform' in my way."

The Use of the Group Setting for Supervision

There are many advantages of a group setting to this supervisory model. Most supervisees tend to feel self-conscious and inadequate during supervision. These feelings are manifested in a variety of defensive mechanisms. Just as in group therapy, where the presence and support of peers helps to reduce anxieties, the group supervision format provides a reassuring supportive environment. This helps each supervisee to reduce his or her insecurities and fears of being discovered as inadequate. The initial piece of work in the group is particularly helpful in this process. The first encounter of the supervisory group leader's work with the first volunteer supervisee sets the tone of safety for the work to be done. The supervisor's attitude toward the supervisee and his or her work is crucial. This attitude is one of demonstrating behaviors that are expected to be emulated by the supervisees. The supervisor must patiently follow the supervisee's emotional process with a minimum of leading and direction and without negative judgment. An empathic approach toward the supervisee's processing of his or her work is a further demonstration to the rest of the group of an accepting positive response to the one who has worked. This manner of relating to someone who has demonstrated his or her vulnerability substantially increases the feelings of safety in the group. It also tends to encourage other group members to come forth and present their own problems with their own clients. This reduces the feelings of isolation and inferiority on the part of other supervisees.

Another advantage of this from a learning point of view is that it gives the supervisees an opportunity to play and learn multiple roles. It is necessary to have several people to fulfill these roles. After a few demonstrations by the supervisor, a supervisee is encouraged to take the supervisor's role while another supervisee enacts the problem between himself and his client. A third role is taken by another supervisee, who observes the nonverbal behavior of both the above supervisees. A fourth supervisee observes the verbal communication of the interaction for language usage and expressive style. The remaining participants become involved by selecting one of the above positions of observation. In supervisory groups, as in other groups where the focus is on one member, there is a tendency for the other members to be less involved and therefore may tend toward lack of interest or boredom even though they are observing. The advantage of this group model is that the entire group tends to be involved in each supervisee's presentation and the discussion that follows. In this way the entire group reaps the benefit of a more comprehensive view of what has actually taken place and the learning becomes more multifaceted.

Dealing with Shame, Humiliation, and Competition

Shame and humiliation are always potentially present in group settings. This is particularly true in supervisory groups where people are fearful of being judged by their peers as well as their supervisors. The supervisor's praising of a supervisee for risk taking in his or her presentation and empathizing with his or her emotional responses substantially reduces this fear of being shamed. The initial demonstration of the safety of the group environment must be maintained by the supervisor during the discussion and subsequent supervisory sessions as a proof that the first demonstration session was indicative of the ongoing group atmosphere. On those occasions when the supervisee, despite this supportive atmosphere experiences shame, the other supervisees' empathic responses and sharing of their own experiences help to ameliorate the intensity of these feelings and reduce the feelings of shame.

Competitive feelings are always present in a supervisory group, particularly in the beginning. The supervisor can help to reduce these feelings by stressing positive cooperation and minimizing negative criticisms and judgments. In co-leadership, which will be discussed later, the supervisors do not engage in competition with each other or the group.

In a single-leader model the leader would not compete with any of the supervisees in the group. This is particularly important during the discussion period of the work that has been done. Supervisors begin the feedback with positive and supportive statements, such as "I liked your moving right in and saying . . ." or "I liked the way you spotted that arm movement and. . . ." Suggestions for improvement are also communicated in positive terms, such as "When you responded to Joe's leg kicking that was a good nonverbal observation. Perhaps the next time Joe does that you might ask him how it feels rather than asking him if he feels like kicking anybody. You're probably right that he does feel like kicking somebody but it's more effective if it comes from him and there's always the slight chance that it might be something else."

Once the supervisee, either through observation or demonstration, has experienced the vulnerabilities of presenting and then has experienced or observed supportive and empathic responses from the rest of the group, he is less likely to express his competitiveness in hostile feedback to other group members. This is indicative of how quickly group members pick up the norms of the group as reflected by the group leader's attitudes and value system.

Co-Leadership in Supervision

The presence of two leaders allows for a wider scope of interventive strategies. At times one or the other will work with a supervisee and other times both will work with a supervisee simultaneously. By supervisees' observing each supervisor's similarities and the way that the supervisors accept each other's differences without criticism, they learn to accept differences in their own approaches and styles of intervention.

The most effective therapists are those that are comfortable with themselves and with their own therapy approaches. Supervisees soon learn that clients give varying clues that can successfully be followed in a variety of ways, not just in one way, and almost any of those ways, when completely pursued, can lead to the core of their conflict.

The dynamics of co-leadership present an obvious parental model. As in all groups, participants (supervisees) tend to respond to the group in ways similar to the ways they responded to their families of origin. Co-leaders then tend to be viewed as parental figures, regardless of their gender. These feelings of vulnerability, competition, and shame and humiliation further contribute to a regressive atmosphere. This in turn stimulates and intensifies the feelings associated with the unresolved childhood conflicts and fears of the supervisee. Given the supportive atmosphere of the group setting, the presence of two leaders offers more of an opportunity for safety. This is especially true for those supervisees in conflict with one, but not both, leader's style and/or personality.

These stylistic conflicts or transferential feelings can occur from the beginning of the group meetings but are seldom expressed until the comfort and safety of the group have been established. At these times the presence of a co-leader helps to bring out the supervisee's questions or conflicting feelings about how one of the supervisors has responded to a supervisee. The "noninvolved" supervisor has the opportunity to help the supervisee deal with these issues by supporting a dialogue between the supervisee and the involved supervisor.

In a situation where there are theoretical differences this often results in the clarification of the supervisee's understanding of his or her own orientation and perhaps even the supervisor's orientation. This can become a role model for dealing with professional differences, and contributes to furthering the safety of the group, since both supervisors have openly dealt with the disagreement without insinuations or other pejoratives being directed at the supervisee. The role of both supervisors is crucial here. The "noninvolved" supervisor's stance needs to be one of nonjudgmental support of both the other supervisor and the supervisee. This is done by helping to clarify each of the two positions and pointing out similarities and differences between the two. The "involved" supervisor's stance needs to be one of nondefensive willingness to see where the supervisee and he or she agree and where they disagree, in an open attitude of willingness to learn. This, of course, can be difficult at times, especially when the supervisor's position is not on firm theoretical ground and could be easily challenged. In this case especially, it is important for the supervisor to feel comfortable in helping to point out the validity of the theoretical challenge, and to also graciously accept the same valid challenge. When this is done well, the supportive atmosphere of the group increases substantially.

In the situation where there appears to be an emotional reaction to one of the supervisors by a supervisee, similar to a transferential reaction in therapy, the co-leadership model is also helpful. Here again, the nonverbal supervisor plays a key role by stepping in and facilitating the expression of the supervisee's feelings towards the involved supervisor. Much like the clarification of the theoretical position mentioned above, this noninvolved supervisor establishes a safe environment for the supervisee to express and explore his or her transferential feelings towards the involved supervisor. Extending this analogy further, the involved supervisor does not get involved with the supervisee at this time but allows the other supervisor to deal with the situation and responds according to the other supervisor's suggestions. For example, at one point during a supervision group, a supervisee expressed difficulty in dealing with a highly critical male client who consistently rejected and criticized the supervisee's therapy interventions. One of the supervisors suggested that the supervisee put her client in the empty chair and have a dialogue with him. When the supervisee did so, the supervisor then made another suggestion and the supervisee exploded, saying, "You're just like my damned father. Nothing I do is good enough!" The "uninvolved" supervisor then intervened and encouraged the supervisee to have a dialogue with her father.

An important piece of redecision work then followed in which the supervisee was able to redecide that she would be a competent therapist despite her father's criticism. The "uninvolved" supervisor then asked the supervisee to say the same to the "involved" supervisor, who smiled approvingly and then said, "In the future, please tell me when you think I am critical." Completing the supervisory piece, the noninvolved supervisor then suggested that the supervisee finish the role play with her client, which the supervisee did in the usual manner.

Since most countertransferential issues are related to the supervisee's own unresolved conflicts, which are very often rooted in childhood issues, the group setting, for the reasons mentioned above, tends to stimulate these issues more than individual supervision. Also as mentioned above, the role modeling of the leaders' open but respectful disagreements further demonstrates the safety of the group around differences. This increased safety stimulates supervisees to openly question and disagree with peers as well as the leaders during discussion.

Helping Supervisees with Their Own Theory of Change

With the opportunity to give and receive a wider range of feedback covering the supervisee's verbal and nonverbal interactions and behaviors, the group setting permits participants to gather useful information about where they are consistent with their theoretical orientation and where they are in conflict. Through this method of feedback, participants are given more of an opportunity to better integrate their personalities with their approaches, and make more conscious choices around their interventions. In this manner supervisees are likely to become more congruent with what they perceive they do and what they really do. For example, a supervisee who professed a theoretical orientation that included no self-disclosure reported being in conflict working with a depressed mother. In an emotionally moving role play, she found herself empathizing and telling the depressed client how she could fully understand her depression because of her own experience when her child was born. This led to an effective resolution of her impasse with her client. During her work she expressed discomfort about revealing her experience because it was in conflict with her stated position of not disclosing personal experiences to her clients. During the ensuing discussion she was able to reduce her conflict around self-disclosure by modifying her position. Her exploration of what she believed and had found to be effective through her own experience was confirmed by the experience of others in the group. Through this discussion she was then able to differentiate between when it is most effective to share and empathize and when it is counterproductive to the client's therapy. This was a first step for her in modifying her theoretical approach by integrating her education with her own experience and thinking.

Conclusion

The redecision therapy model is an efficient and effective model that lends itself readily to a supervisory model. The rapid interventions necessary in a 20-minute (or slightly more) session, including work with nonverbal behavior in an expanded manner, make this model particularly appealing for supervision. The value of a group setting further enhances this model by helping supervisees reduce their anxieties and, in turn, their defensiveness, build their confidence, and feel less vulnerable. The group setting also helps reduce feelings of shame, humiliation, and competitiveness through the development of group cohesiveness. It also helps supervisees develop more empathy for clients, as well as affording an opportunity to learn more about psychodynamics and psychotherapy. In addition, this model within a group setting stimulates family dynamics and creates an opportunity to explore and reduce personal issues as they affect the supervisee's work with clients.

References

Andronico, M. (1985). The chronological elevator: a redecision model for both the TA and the non-TA therapist. In *Redecision Therapy: Expanded Perspectives*, ed. L. B. Kadis, pp. 60–64. Watsonville, CA: Western Institute for Group and Family Therapy.

Andronico, M., and Dazzo, B. (1991). Experiental group supervision. *New Jersey Psychologist* 41(2):11–14.

Goulding, M., and Goulding, R. (1979). *Changing Lives through Redecision Therapy*. New York: Brunner/Mazel.

17

Training
Redecision Therapists

John Gladfelter, Ph.D.

Benefits to the Clinician

Redecision therapy is a treatment modality that is completely congruent with the current trends in managed care, short-term therapy, and use of limited economic resources. It allows both clients and the therapist the maximum freedom of choice and responsibility for the treatment process. The flexibility of this approach enables clients to work at as deep a level as they choose and extend their therapy boundaries to suit their personal needs. At the same time, the treatment boundaries of a group provide the safety and protection necessary to facilitate the change experience. The sharing of the responsibility for change enables the therapist to work within the time constraints available to the client and empowers clients to range as widely and as deeply as they choose. Clients have an awareness of change processes as they occur, and can validate for themselves the progress of their treatment. The redecision therapy approach is transparent to the user and consumer; clients are aware of the processes of the experience and can easily manage them to their liking. In the treatment process, clients are well aware of their control over the process and can continuously lead the therapy in the direction that seems to their benefit. At the same time, the therapist can recognize the particular dimension and stage of the treatment and can document that treatment in plain language. Such language enables clients to have an experience of hope and expectation that is essential for the continuation of the treatment experience. When clients can understand that their treatment is in their hands, that they have the power to change aspects of themselves, and that they are an able resource in the therapy, their level of hope and anticipation increases and further energizes the change process.

Information is a valuable part of the redecision approach. It is important that clients be given as much information as they can effectively use about themselves. Clients can be encouraged to read about redecision therapy, transactional analysis, and psychotherapy in general if they choose. Simultaneously, the therapist must access as much information from clients as is possible. The therapist must discover what clients want to be different about themselves and enable the treatment to that end. Clients need to know what advantages and limits there are to that information exchange and what might be expected from any further exchanges. The therapist benefits from the clarity of the treatment structure and the sharing of responsibility for the change process. Being able to accurately describe the process of treatment and the change process occurring within the lives of clients makes much of the accountability in paperwork quite easy. The therapist can provide to referring resources an account of the treatment process without significantly violating the limits of confidentiality. There is also the satisfaction that clients are taking a significant role in their own change processes and can be aware of their choices about their lives. Redecision therapy places clients in the center of the treatment process as full partners in whatever is to happen and engages clients in becoming aware of and budgeting their personal resources as much as they choose.

Although the most efficacious process for this treatment technique is in a group, the method is quite effective in traditional one-to-one therapy, couples therapy, and family therapy. With minor adjustments in the process, the therapist can enable the client to work in the type of relationship that addresses his or her discomfort or distress. A further advantage of redecision therapy for the therapist is the opportunity to use any of the techniques of treatment previously learned, in the theoretical structure of this approach. Therapists trained in gestalt therapy, cognitive-behavioral therapies, and rational-emotive therapy will find these approaches readily adaptable to this therapy. The conceptual framework enables the therapist with minimal learning opportunities to adapt all of his or her previous experience to redecision therapy. This treatment approach enables the most diverse application of treatment approaches to the most diverse populations. The use of treatment contracts provides protection for both clients and therapist. Because of the treatment techniques and the group atmosphere, the clients may use the language and culture they grew up with as a resource for their treatment.

Beginning the Learning Process

The theoretical foundation of redecision therapy is in transactional analysis. There are, however, important differences. After a student has acquired a general foundation in TA, they will have a reading list of the books written by Mary and Bob Goulding (1986) on redecision therapy that use basic TA as a departure point. These resources are easy to read and have a common-sense quality about them that will make identifying the fundamental concepts effortless. Most therapists, when reading the material at first, may think that the ideas are simplistic. This is because most of the ideas are rich in interpersonal context and have their roots in an oral tradition. Experiential training quickly dispels the question of simplicity. Eric Berne (1961, 1966) chose to disseminate his transactional approach through the oral teaching of a course that he called TA 101. It was a two-day opportunity for therapists to discuss with a teacher the full meaning of what are phenomenological realities. Redecision therapy follows in that tradition and, along with readings, the meanings of the concepts are developed through the interchange between a student and mentor. The idea is more than the word, and therapists who attempt to learn and practice redecision therapy only through reading will fall significantly short of applying this method effectively.

The Training Process

Redecision therapy training is based on an experiential mode of work. This training approach was developed by Bob and Mary Goulding and refined over more than a decade of training therapists. A modified marathon is the training envelope, usually involving several full days of experience and up to as much as a week or a month. Trainees work in a full-day time structure with occasional events in the evening, and remain together as a group for the training period. Theory and practice are interwoven throughout the experience. Each trainee has an opportunity to work as a therapist, as a patient, and as a supervisor. In the experiential portion of the training workshop one student elects to be a patient, another elects to be a therapist, and a third elects to be a supervisor. The trainer then invites the student working as supervisor to make a supervisory contract with the student therapist. That contract involves observing whatever aspects of the resulting therapy process the student therapist would like, and feedback as to therapeutic options, observation of ego states, effectiveness of the therapy, and other aspects of the treatment process. Upon completion of the therapeutic work between patient and therapist, the student supervisor provides feedback as contracted for. Following the supervisory process, the trainer provides feedback to the student supervisor and discusses from a redecision therapy point of view the treatment ramifications of the work.

The Role of Supervision in Redecision Training

Supervision is an essential part of redecision therapy training. The basic ideas of the approach are integrated with TA theory so that supervision becomes the hands-on experiential modality for learning. Contractual supervision, like contractual therapy, enables learning therapists to discover their strengths and to grow from the experience of working with people. For therapists new to redecision therapy, learning to contract for supervision is an important way to maintain responsibility for their own growth as therapists and to gain positive emotional support for the process. Positive strokes are an important part of the supervisory process. The training therapists learn to ask for positive strokes for their work and learn to give themselves positive strokes for what they do. The redecision trainer and student are careful to decline to give negative or conditional strokes. Supervision in the all-day group is a built-in process. Supervision on a weekly basis is more difficult to obtain and will require the therapist to often use the outside resources of other trainers and teachers of redecision therapy when available. One aspect that can be a concern to trainers is the potential for harmful dual relationships. This is managed carefully by attending to any transferential relationships that might emerge in the training process.

Redecision therapy is not a transferential approach to therapy and any emergence of transference is confronted directly and minimized as much as possible. Early in the training process, the trainer reduces the interpersonal interactions of the training group and confronts and limits the amount of group interaction. There is ample opportunity for group discussion but it is kept trainer-centered by the trainer. Student therapists in this training do not role play as clients and will often address personal material that can be painful and distressing. The trainer is always in the position of handling any crises that occur and working through whatever problems might arise.

Qualifications for Training in Redecision Therapy

Experiential opportunities for learning psychotherapy are the foundation for learning redecision therapy. The experience of working with students who are clients will enable beginning therapists to decide if this is the career for them and will enable them to experience the process of working with people in confusion, distress, psychological pain, and interpersonal conflict. Beginners can begin training in their graduate work whether they have had previous training in therapy or not. This treatment approach, in fact, can be an excellent starting point for learning about psychotherapy and the process of working with people. Although there are few opportunities in traditional training centers for learning redecision therapy, students can often, on their own, use personal resources to find week-long training, weekend training, or group psychotherapy conferences and institutes to experience the process of redecision therapy and the beginning skills.

The humanistic and phenomenological basis for transactional analysis and redecision therapy make explanation of human experience and behavior easily understood. Students who have been to a TA 101 course are often positively surprised and excited by their awareness and knowledge of much interpersonal process. Knowledge of ego states, transactions, games, and scripts provides a vista of people in the real world that becomes a springboard for the processes that enable people to change.

Trainers in Redecision Therapy

Many of the current trainers in redecision therapy are teaching members of the International Transactional Analysis Association and have had extensive training and experience in redecision therapy. They are usually senior clinicians in their particular professions and are usually licensed practitioners. They will usually have a certificate attesting to their being Level II Transactional Analysts and often certificates indicating that they have had further training in redecision therapy. There is a growing number of licensed professionals, however, who have trained extensively in redecision therapy and have chosen not to become teaching members of ITAA. They can show documentation of training in redecision therapy from those trainers who have extensive credentials in redecision therapy. A check with their trainers is in order if there is any doubt as to their qualifications and training.

Qualified Training in Redecision Therapy

Qualifications to do redecision therapy depend more on experience, range of training, professional credentials, and personal therapy than on specific written or oral exams. Trainers are the best people to ask about readiness to do redecision therapy. Therapists who already have extensive training may find the process relatively short. People who are beginning their training in therapy will need to have a solid background in their particular professions before they can consider themselves ready to do therapy. Although there are various judgments made as to readiness to do redecision therapy, the trainer is usually the only person who has first-hand knowledge of what the student does and his or her abilities to do it in a safe and prudent fashion. It is good to train with several people before one can consider oneself adequately trained. Having a sound background in professional ethics and licensing rules and regulations is always required for responsible practice.

Credentials to do Redecision Therapy Training

The current state of the redecision therapy field is that there are no credentials for this approach. The only credential available for therapists in this modality would be either clinical or clinical teaching member status in ITAA. Both of these credentials require extensive examinations, both written and oral, and a training contract established before training begins. This credential has been available for many years but has fallen out of favor because of the many other credentials and exams professionals must take before they practice. This does not mean that levels of proficiency are not important. In training programs, trainers regularly evaluate many of the characteristics of treatment that are inherent and rateable in the process of training. It may be a matter of choice on the part of any student to request this sort of rating, although most trainers do this as a matter of course. It is also worthwhile for people who are in training in redecision therapy to join the ITAA, and receive the monthly newsletter and the quarterly journal. *The Transactional Analysis Journal.* Students will find many articles in current and prior issues of the journal that will address many theoretical issues and many innovative practices and ideas.

Obtaining Training in Redecision Therapy

Training is available from many of the authors of the chapters in this book. Some trainers have ongoing programs available, while other trainers may be available for supervision and introductory workshops. If a graduate student or a therapist wants training in redecision therapy, the surest way to find it is to ask the many authors of this book. Many may not have training currently available but will develop such a program on request. At first look, it would seem to be difficult to get training. Determined students usually find trainers and many excellent opportunities to learn more about redecision therapy. Annual conferences of the International Transactional Analysis Association, The American Group Psychotherapy Association, and other regional group therapy organizations regularly offer workshops in this modality. These meetings offer the opportunity to meet trainers, discuss with them particular needs, and evaluate training opportunities. It is difficult to describe at any given time what is available for training. Most well-balanced and structured programs will require a couple of years of ongoing work. Although redecision therapy is a readily understandable method, learning to be skilled with it takes time, as with any substantive therapy training programs.

The Future of Redecision Therapy

The development of redecision therapy was a fortuitous process growing out of the experiences of two senior clinicians, Mary and Bob Goulding, who had trained with two of the pioneers in psychotherapy, Eric Berne and Fritz Perls. Their own learning experiences brought them to the realization through experience that a blend of transactional analysis and gestalt therapy was an important breakthrough in facilitating the change process in therapy. Their subsequent work as trainers at Mt. Madonna, their training center in Watsonville, California, brought therapists from the United States and the rest of the world to learn from them. Their work and the subsequent continuation of the work by Mary Goulding is a boon to the growth of redecision therapy throughout the world. Group therapy conferences over the last two decades have introduced many therapists to this approach, and recent conferences of both the International Transactional Analysis Association and the American Group Psychotherapy Association have featured the work of the Gouldings in this approach. The creative work of Bob and Mary is paying off in rich dividends in the benefits to a broad range of clients in diverse settings in both short-term and long-term therapeutic experiences. Many of the techniques developed by them have been scientifically studied and are continuing to be studied in many settings. A number of senior clinicians around the world who trained with Bob and Mary have contributed to the development of redecision therapy. Many of them have also participated in national and international conferences where they have presented workshops and training. The true beneficiaries of the Gouldings' work are the many clients who have changed and will continue to gain from economical short- and long-term group therapy.

References

Berne, E. (1961). *Transactional Analysis in Psychotherapy.* New York: Grove.

———— (1966). *Principles of Group Treatment.* New York: Oxford.

Gladfelter, J. (1984). Enjoying every minute. In *Transactional Analysis After Eric Berne,* ed. G. Barnes, pp. 394–424. New York: Harper's College Press.

———— (1992). Redecision therapy. *International Journal of Group Psychotherapy* 42:319–334.

Goulding, M. M., and Goulding, R. L. (1986). *Changing Lives through Redecision Therapy.* New York: Grove.

Goulding, R. (1989). Teaching transactional analysis and redecision therapy. Special issue: variations on teaching and supervising group therapy. *Journal of Independent Social Work* 3(4):71–86.

18

Underlying Values in Redecision Therapy

Moon Kerson, Ph.D.
Marti Kranzberg, Ph.D.

The aspect of redecision therapy that has had the most profound impact on us personally and professionally is its continued, unerring respect for personal autonomy. The Gouldings have been staunch in their promotion of the value of life and of the importance of individuals taking responsibility for the choices they make about feelings, thoughts, and actions.

Grounded in existential philosophy, the concept of autonomy encompasses freedom, choice, and accountability. Our freedom to choose among alternatives, and our consequent responsibility for the impact of these choices, is fundamental. These beliefs about autonomy create the foundation for redecision therapists to think about how people change.

Awareness is central to recognizing our autonomy. Developing the awareness that we are continuously making choices allows us to take charge of our lives and create meaning in each moment. We are able to feel peaceful on a crowded freeway. We can appreciate the awesome beauty of a sunset. We can allow ourselves to fully experience the unfathomable loss of someone we have loved. We are accountable for choices whether we make them with or without awareness. With awareness, however, we have the power to change how we feel, think, and behave.

The Gouldings appreciated the complexity of the change process and recognized that choice-making involves more than a cognitive process. Simply resolving to change does not work, as anyone who has made a New Year's resolution knows. Decisions often have a strong affective component that must be addressed for us to be able to make real and enduring changes. The unique potency of their model comes from its ability to address both affect and cognition.

One important way for a client to effect change is through the re-experiencing of a childhood scene. During this process talking *about* the past is discouraged. Instead, scenes are reenacted in the present and allow the client to become aware of what she feels and thinks about herself, other people, or the world. Once she identifies her decision and its significance in her life, she may redecide to think, feel, or act differently.

The individual is seen as continually making decisions about herself and the world based on her experiences and how she makes sense of them. Early decisions are necessarily limited because they were made by children whose developmental limitations restricted their intellectual and emotional capacities. They also lacked the range of options that are available to them later in life. Since children are dependent on adults for their very existence, early decisions are survival-oriented. These decisions are adaptive to the context in which they were made and limited by the child's perspective. The redecision therapist acknowledges the relevance and creativity of these early decisions.

However, these decisions that made so much sense in the past may become a problem in the present. When a client feels stuck in bad feelings, he is experiencing his adult world as he did as a child, thereby limiting himself. As an adult, he has a range of skills, abilities, and choices that he did not have as a child. Reexperiencing the early scene affords the client the opportunity to reexperience and identify the early decisions. With this new awareness he has the option of changing how he feels about himself, the other person, and life.

Because promoting specific change is central to this theory, contracting is the focal point of redecision therapy. The most important contract that the client makes is to close his escape hatches. With this contract, the client is accountable for his commitment to his own life. Once the client makes this contract, the redecision therapist continues to be vigilant in observing whether the client has reopened his escape hatches. If so, the therapist confronts this abdication of responsibility. This attention to escape hatches provides an important ethical safeguard for the therapist and the client.

Implicit in the contracting process is the firmly held belief that the power to change lies within the client. Contract making underscores the importance of the client claiming her power to be in charge of her own life. Therefore, contracting is focused on what the client wants to change about herself and not on how she wants someone else to change. The Gouldings' maxim, "the power is in the patient," highlights the essential value of this empowerment process.

The Gouldings' profound respect for the client includes attunement to communication that reflects autonomy and accountability rather than victimization and blame. The therapist challenges the client to change passive language. "Can't" is confronted as "won't." "He made me angry" is countered with "I felt angry." In making a contract, a client is encouraged to decide what she "will" do rather than what she "wants" to do.

Mary and Bob Goulding's emphasis on responsibility challenges us to remove ourselves from the cloak of victimization. Regardless of our childhood experiences in our families and our world, we are each accountable for how we lead our lives as adults. We no longer have to feel inadequate because we could never please our fathers. We do not have to feel ugly because we were teased by classmates. Although these were significant events in our lives, they do not have to define beliefs about ourselves or the world because we have the power to change their significance.

The focus on choice making and responsibility also helps redecision therapists to avoid discounting ourselves or our clients. Since we respect the client's ability to make choices and thereby shape her own life, we do not rescue, give advice, or presume to know what is best for her. We are less likely then to feel victimized and frustrated when clients don't change in the ways we think they "should." We are less prone to be critical of them for "resisting" our interventions and having the audacity to do their therapy in their own way and at their own pace!

In redecision therapy, the decision not to change is honored as a valid choice. Rather than being labeled as resistance, this is seen as a way for the client to protect himself. The client may maintain an early decision until he wants to experience himself in new ways, or he may choose not to change. In either case, he will have gained awareness of his early decision.

Like the notion of resistance, the concept of the unconscious is conspicuously absent from the Gouldings' model. The concept of awareness precludes the notion of unconsciousness. People are either aware or unaware of their thoughts, feelings, actions, and the decisions they make. Any of these that are out of awareness are accessible through early scenes. In this way we have access to what has traditionally been viewed as "unconscious material."

Redecision therapy demonstrates further originality in its method of addressing the concept of transference. Transferential material is never addressed through interpretation, self-disclosure, or dyadic exchange. Instead, the feelings that the client is experiencing with the therapist are traced to an early scene. The client may then discover the origins of the feelings and begin to understand how the early decision is contaminating his present interactions.

While the concept of early decisions is explicit in its respect for the autonomy of the individual, there is also a tacit appreciation of the primacy of connection to other people and their impact on our lives. Decisions are never made in isolation. They are created out of our experiences with other people. Although the Gouldings never directly addressed this interpersonal aspect of redecision therapy, implicit is the belief that we cannot truly be present with another person when we are operating out of a restrictive early decision. If we respond to a woman as if she were the critical mother of our childhood, our interactions with her are forever tainted. Until we identify and change these early decisions, it is difficult to interact with others without distorting our present experiences. Once we have cleared away the debris of the past, we are free to fully engage with others in the present moment.

The belief in autonomy, then, is not antithetical to a focus on interpersonal relationships. It is instead the bedrock on which clear interactions must rest. Because redecision therapists emphasize individual work in a group setting, and because they don't emphasize interactions between group members, they are sometimes accused of disregarding the importance of interpersonal relationships. However, by refusing to allow scapegoating or advice giving, and by requiring each client to take responsibility for her own thinking, feeling, and acting, redecision therapists teach group members to interact without blame or distortion.

The unifying principle of autonomy in redecision therapy informs beliefs about how people change, delineates the power of the client, defines the role of therapist, and determines the course of therapy. The chapters in this book identify the myriad of ways in which this is manifested in theory, practice, and training. The indefatigable respect for human beings inherent in the redecision model provides the foundation for this effective, empowering, and humanizing therapy that clinicians of every persuasion may use in working with a wide range of clients in a variety of settings.

Index